The Rock of Truth

OR

Spiritualism,
The Coming World Religion

BY

J. ARTHUR FINDLAY

Author of

On the Edge of the Etheric

Truth, whether in or out of fashion, is the measure of
Knowledge. Whatever is beside that, however authorised
by consent, is nothing but ignorance or something worse.
Locke.

.

PHILADELPHIA

DAVID McKAY COMPANY

WASHINGTON SQUARE

———

1933

Printing Statement:

Due to the very old age and scarcity of this book,
many of the pages may be hard to read due to the
blurring of the original text, possible missing pages,
missing text and other issues beyond our control.

Because this is such an important and rare work, we
believe it is best to reproduce this book regardless of
its original condition.

Thank you for your understanding.

CONTENTS.

PART I.

PART II.

1st	Impression,	August 1933.
2nd	Impression,	August 1933.
3rd	Impression,	August 1933.
4th	Impression,	August 1933.
5th	Impression,	August 1933.
6th	Impression,	September 1933.
7th	Impression,	September 1933.
8th	Impression,	September 1933.
9th	Impression,	September 1933.
10th	Impression,	September 1933.
11th	Impression,	September 1933.

FOREWORD.

THIS book is a continuation of *On the Edge of the Etheric,* as the arguments commenced in that book are continued in this one. The two books together make one complete whole, the first being an introduction to the subject; this, the second, being its amplification into a philosophy or religion for mankind.

Spiritualism is the only religion mankind needs, as it gives a scientific explanation of the reasons for man's existence here on earth and the proof positive of his continued existence after death. Spiritualism explains life here and hereafter. It explains this world and the Etheric World to which we pass at death. It does not fall back on ancient tradition, it does not rest on faith; all that it asserts can be proved and vouched for here and now. Everyone can prove what it asserts for himself or herself, under conditions to satisfy the most exacting critics.

Spiritualism is the coming religion of mankind. It is the basis of all the religions of the past, which have been corrupted through the ignorance of the times in which they were born and through which they passed.

Incorrectly as the founders of the great religions of the past have been recorded owing to the lack of the means we now have of recording our observations, it may be possible in some instances to discern through the extraneous matter which has gathered around their teachings that they were guided by super-mundane intelligences working through some psychic power, with which they were specially gifted.

As they were unique in their day and generation, much of what they said was misunderstood, misinterpreted and confused, both by their contemporaries and those who handed down their teachings by word of mouth from generation to generation. How much of their teachings which have survived can be accepted as reliable, it is difficult to say, but fortunately we need not go back to ancient tradition, as we have to-day in our midst many who have this same psychic power, through which we can get into contact with the great intelligences of the Etheric World, who are able and willing to guide us throughout our earthly existence.

Those great teachers of the past, of whose doings and sayings we have such a feeble record, were undoubtedly the fore-runners of the gospel of Spiritualism, many of the principles of which they taught to an ignorant multitude. Unfortunately their message was passed on in a form which cannot now be accepted or appreciated by intelligent and thoughtful people.

As the result of the development of psychic gifts in recent times we are acquiring a greater and better understanding of our place in the Universe, our origin and our destiny. The great teachers of the past doubtless attempted to make this understood but failed, by reason of the ignorance of their times. In consequence of the growth of knowledge and the great achievements of science, we are now able to understand better the meaning of the great truths which are coming through to us from the advanced minds in the Etheric World, and these are being correctly recorded. For nearly a century the fundamental principles of Spiritualism have been repeated time and again through Mediums in every part of the world.

It is the purpose of this book to help to make this knowledge, possessed by but a few, known throughout the whole world, as only from this knowledge, and the teachings of which we have been the recipients, can we rise to higher levels, attain increased happiness, and gain a real understanding of the reason for our existence here, and our destiny hereafter.

J. ARTHUR FINDLAY.

Stansted Hall, Essex.
16th May 1933.

AUTHOR'S NOTE.

THE first four chapters of Part I of this book contain statements against each of which I should have liked to quote my authority.

This I found impossible to do and at the same time keep the book within a reasonable length.

However, the reader is assured that there is good authority behind each statement made. Moreover, these four chapters have been carefully read over, checked, and passed by one of our greatest authorities on the various world religions in general, and Christianity in particular.

J.A.F.

PART I.

CHAPTER I.

THE TRUTH.

WHAT is the truth? has ever been the cry of mankind, but always in the past the answer seems to have eluded him. Only since we became intelligent enough to adopt precise methods of investigation has it been possible to say with greater certainty what the truth really is. To the ancients it seemed to be the truth that the sun circled round the earth, but we with our greater knowledge now know that this apparent motion is caused by the rotation of the earth on its own axis. We may accept it as a scientific fact that this is really what occurs, just as we can accept the fact that water always finds its own level. Truth to-day is therefore very different from truth as understood by the ancients, and the truth as it appears to us to-day may, and probably will, mean something far different to the generations yet unborn.

Truth is but a gradual unfolding of some grand panorama, and though we see now more than those who preceded us, yet it is still but a glimpse of the whole and no more.

Truth is eternal and unchangeable. We who are finite and subject to change can only grasp it little by little. Truth is always the same, but as we change and advance mentally we can grasp it better. Until we are fully developed mentally, truth will not be fully comprehended, but as we develop, it slowly becomes clearer.   Often we in ignorance mistake for truth what is error, and the history of man is the history of error gradually giving place to truth.

The following remarks, made by a well-known man, shortly before his passing on, make my meaning clear.   " My life is ended, I have now written the last page.   I have put my hand to the last word, my book of life is finished."   Life, if we take his words literally, is but a narrow vale between two bleak eternities, one short span between the cradle and the grave.   That remark no doubt represented the truth to him, but it does not represent the truth to a Spiritualist, as he knows that this life on earth is only the starting point of our conscious existence, and that our life continues in the Etheric World, to which we shall all pass at death.

In the past the future life was a question of faith, not a question of knowledge, and in this slough of ignorance atheism and agnosticism flourished.   To Spiritualists death is not a wall but a door ; it is not the end but the beginning of an endless day ; it is not the closing of wings for ever, but the opening of pinions to fly.

Life and death to the orthodox are very different from life and death to Spiritualists, but the former have never had the wonderful opportunity we have been privileged to enjoy of getting into touch with those we knew on earth who, as we now know, continue to live in the Etheric World, about and around this physical world of ours.   One of the fundamental doctrines of Christianity teaches that the dead are consigned to the grave until the great Resurrection Day, when they will rise again in their physical bodies.* No wonder it was considered that the end of life would come at death !

The fact of death was accepted as it appeared. The appearance of death was taken as a reality, but much of what we accept in life as true is directly the opposite of what is really the fact. Appearances are deceptive, and nothing is more deceptive in its appearance than death. When, therefore, we attend a funeral and hear from the lips of ignorance the orthodox funeral service, and we come away with the thought in our minds that never again shall we see our friend, never again shall we clasp his hand or hear his voice, we are the victims of another of nature's illusions. Appearances are so different from reality. Spiritualists have often spoken to friends, who have just passed into the Etheric World, at exactly the same time as their funeral was taking place, and have discussed this event with them, which lets us understand that as far as they are concerned, what happened to their physical bodies did not concern them any longer, and that the orthodox view of the body sleeping till some future Resurrection day is false and a delusion.

Before the year 1543, everything was taken as it appeared to be. There then existed a great mental calm which was broken by the great German astronomer Copernicus. In that year he announced his belief in the rotation of the planets round the sun.

---

* This statement may be disputed by some, but nevertheless it is true. According to Cruden, one of the greatest authorities on the Christian Faith and whose *Concordance* is in nearly every clergyman's study:—" The belief in the general resurrection of the dead, which will come to pass at the end of the world, and which will be followed by an immortality, either of happiness or misery, is a principal article of the Christian Religion, and is very expressly taught both in the Old and New Testaments."

This apparently absurd idea was, however, accepted by another, the astronomer Kepler, one of the founders of modern astronomy, who propounded what are now known as his three laws. His contemporary, Galileo, asked the priests of his time to look through his telescope and see for themselves that what Copernicus said was true, but they would not do so. The telescope, they said, was the invention of the Devil, as what it showed was contrary to Holy Scripture. Galileo was made to recant under threat of imprisonment and torture.

During the same period Leonardo da Vinci, that brilliant all-round man of science, engineer, anatomist, botanist, geologist, sculptor, painter, architect, and musician, also gave his great mind to help in breaking down the arrogance and ignorance of his times. During the same period, noted for its pioneers of modern science, Giordano Bruno, one of the most genial of men, suffered death at the stake in Rome after seven years' imprisonment. He was tried, convicted, and imprisoned in a dungeon. He was offered his liberty if he would accept the scriptures as God-inspired, but he refused. After seven years' imprisonment he was taken to the place of execution, draped in a robe on which were painted devils. He was chained to the stake and around his body were piled faggots. The priests then lit them to the glory of God and in the name of Jesus Christ, and thus perished one of the noblest and grandest men who ever trod this earth. He was the first martyr to science, who met his death without thought of reward or punishment, his only crime being that he helped to lay the foundations of our modern Science of

Astronomy. He has rightly been called the Morning Star of the Renaissance, as he never varied in his opinions, which neither imprisonment nor torture could induce him to modify.

From that time onwards things were easier for those who put knowledge before faith, but still Newton and Darwin and many others had to suffer much from the jeers and diatribes of the ignorant. From every pulpit in Christendom Darwin was denounced, and the greater the ignorance of the parson the more devout a Christian he was considered to be. In 1859 Darwin published his great work entitled *Origin of Species*, showing that man, instead of having fallen from a high state, was the outcome of a slow but continuous evolution from a lower to a higher state.

Eighty-five years ago there occurred mysterious rappings in the presence of two girls of the name of Fox in the little town of Hydesville in New York State, U.S.A. The Fox family consisted of John David Fox, the father, who was a farmer, his wife, and two daughters, Margaretta aged fifteen and Catherine aged twelve. In this quiet little place, on 31st March 1848, noises occurred in their house, into which they had just removed, that could not be accounted for, and they disturbed the entire family. The girls were naturally looked on as being the cause of these noises, and every effort was made to discover how they occurred. Mrs. Fox thought that if the raps were caused by some intelligence it would be able to answer questions, so she said, "count ten," and ten raps occurred. She then asked how many children she had and received the correct reply.

Gradually it became apparent that there was an intelligence working behind the raps. From this it was easy to get intelligent answers by means of the alphabet. The communicator stated that he had been murdered in that house and buried in the cellar. He gave the name of the previous tenant called Bell as the murderer. All this was found out later to be true though unknown to the Fox family at the time.

This is how Modern Spiritualism began, and arising from this simple occurrence we are now receiving the most profound teaching from those who inhabit the Etheric World. Very many thousands have received comfort and consolation through the converse they have had with those they loved, and who have passed on to this world of finer matter, but only a comparatively small proportion of the human race realise that inter-communication between the two worlds has been opened up, and only a still smaller number of persons have been privileged to receive instruction and guidance from those higher minds.

Just as we are deceived in respect to the sun, so are we deceived when we regard space as being empty. Those of us who have been in close touch with the Etheric World know that what seems to be empty space is but finer substance interpenetrating this physical world, and that the universe consists of substance, or, to be correct, etheric vibrations. We all know that the sky is not a dome, that the earth goes round the sun, that the earth is not flat and that it revolves on its own axis ; but few know that the physical body is not the real body, and that we have an etheric duplicate which holds the physical body together ; further, that this etheric body is the real body, and, governed by mind, it continues to exist after death, leaving the physical body behind it. Only Spiritualists know that the Physical World is only a very small part of the real world, that the Etheric World is much the greater part of the real world, and that the Physical Universe is but a fraction of the real Universe. Only when we die shall we begin to gain experience of the greater Universe, and then the physical to us will cease to be of account.

Everything, as I say, is different from what it appears to be to us physical creatures. It may be asked, why is it that only now we are discovering these great truths of reality? The answer is simple. We are the product of ages of ignorance, and some of the most barbaric ignorance is to be found in what many people of this country still call the Word of God, commonly known as the Bible. This book is in places the product of savages. It approves and encourages the most barbaric cruelties. In it, in the book of Leviticus, there is a text, "Thou shalt not suffer a witch to live," and this text for five hundred years ruled Europe. Peter of Aragon in 1197 was the first ruler in Europe to promulgate the law that heretics or those who differed from the teachings of the Church should suffer death. From that date till the end of the 18th century, when the last witch was burned in Belgium, European history teems with one record after another of slaughter.

All who had the character to think for themselves and use the great gift of reason were treated as enemies of the Church and tortured and slain. In Geneva the Protestants there burned five hundred witches at the stake within three months. In the diocese of Como in Northern Italy one thousand were burned in one year, and in Germany it is calculated that over one hundred thousand suffered this fate, the last being burned in 1739, but the persecution continued in Switzerland till 1780, and in Belgium till a later date. In England alone in two hundred years, 30,000 so-called witches were burned to death, and these witches are what we to-day call Mediums. Witch burning also took place in what is now called the United States, founded by the Puritan Fathers, who could not get liberty in England to worship as they pleased. Such was the bigotry of those days, that whenever the sufferers obtained power, they in turn made others suffer. This text "Thou shalt not suffer a witch to live," was the cause of unimaginable misery and cruelty, and as mediumship is a hereditary gift, Mediums were almost extinguished. Thus we entered an age of gross materialism which culminated in the Great War of 1914.

In the year 1576, Bessie Dunlop of Lyne, in Ayrshire, was burnt as a witch because in her presence voices were heard which claimed to be those of people who had passed into the beyond. In other words, she was a Direct Voice Medium, of whom we have a number in our midst to-day, one of the most developed being Sloan, to whom much reference is made in my book *On the Edge of the Etheric*. Many instances similar to the above could be given.

From 1712, when the burning of witches ceased in England, mediumship has developed and is expanding at an increasing ratio everywhere. At its present rate of progress, in consequence of what is

revealed through mediumship, this, the most enlightened country in the world, will accept generally
the principles of Spiritualism within the next twenty
years or so.

This book will attempt to tell the truth as the
author sees it, as nothing is greater, nothing is of
more importance than to find truth amid the darkness
and errors of life. This book will make a candid
examination of the beliefs of the past and the present.
It will attempt to make clear the past and present
errors of humanity, and show how they can be
avoided in the future. It will not be a popular book
to many and will be attributed to the devil by some.
This, however, will be history just repeating itself,
as everyone who has propounded something new or
told the unpalatable truth has been linked with the
devil, and if the orthodox are right, this mythical
individual has been responsible for all the knowledge
we possess to-day. On the other hand an earthquake, an eruption or a tornado is termed an act of
God. The orthodox, with the aid of the devil and
the Bible, have fought a losing battle throughout the
centuries of Christendom. They have been driven
from one defence to another, and now that Spiritualists can give proof positive of a life to come, they
fight it tooth and nail, ignoring the fact that Spiritualism is now giving knowledge in place of hope, and
facts instead of meaningless words.

Throughout the ages, by countless efforts, man
slowly developed a brain, changed four legs into two
legs and two arms, and two feet into two hands. Into
the darkness of his brain has penetrated some glim-
mering of reason. Through remembering his
mistakes, he has advanced just in proportion as

he has put his reason first and faith second. Through countless ages he has groped, struggled, stumbled, and climbed towards the light.   In the name of education mistakes have been given him for instruction instead of facts.   In the name of religion he has been given ignorant speculations as a divine revelation.   With love he has been taught hatred, and as well as forgiveness he has been taught revenge.   But for the past hundred years Europe has been slowly entering a new age of thought.   Almost unnoticed, the intellectual world has changed, and books could be written of what was once considered essential to man's salvation, and now is considered of no importance whatever.   For sixteen centuries free speech and free thought in Europe were considered an insult to God.   To express an honest opinion was considered a crime against the Almighty.

To-day, however, we are living in changed times.   The orthodox are now looked on by most as the ignorant, and the people who think for themselves are now respected and honoured.   The religion which will attract the intellectual, the honest and good, must rest on a foundation of established facts, not on tradition, not on faith, not on a so-called Holy Book or Holy Church.   The religion of the future will make men free, will make them honest, will make them kind, and will make them good.   The religion of the future, through uniting our knowledge of this world with our knowledge of the next, by abolishing sects, and dethroning false gods, will stop war, and bring humanity into one great family.   Only Spiritualism can do this.   It is the religion of the future because it rests on truth scientifically established.

CHAPTER II.

THE OLD RELIGIONS.

RELIGION and politics are the two principal factors which govern our lives. The one deals with the future and the other with the present. We are thinking creatures, and besides the present we give thought to the future. Besides our bodily comforts we at times think of what is to happen to us when the hour strikes for us to enter a new environment. Our surroundings here and what they are to be hereafter occupy our thoughts almost entirely throughout our earthly life. Just as right thinking in politics and economics means comfort on earth, so right thinking as regards religion gives us an enlarged and correct view respecting our future.

A profound change is coming over the thoughts of all thinking people at the present time. It has been slow in coming, but all important changes in the world's history, which have become permanent, have been slow in appealing to the reason of mankind. The effects of evolution are permanent, but the effects of revolution seldom are. Nature makes all her changes slowly, but surely. This new orientation of belief will, when absorbed, completely alter our outlook on life from every point of view. Already its influence is changing our religious outlook. Science also is moving towards a new plane of thought. From a social point of view this changing outlook is just beginning to be felt, but medically, as will be explained later, its effect is hardly yet realised.

This change of outlook will give to mankind an entirely new idea of his origin and destiny. It is

B

disclosing a new world, and in so doing is revealing in truer light the mistakes and failures of the past.

Into the frozen North man has gone. He has conquered the ice, the snow and the bitter cold. Into the jungles of the tropics he has found his way, and he has explored the Seven Seas ; he has chartered their depths, he knows every hidden rock. But there is another world to be explored, and this will engage his energies and his thoughts in the years to come, because into that world we shall all pass at death. The more we know about it the more anxious we shall be to learn how best we can fit ourselves to enable us to enter it, not in ignorance as did our ancestors, but so adequately equipped mentally that we shall be able to accept our new environment calmly and naturally.

It is the purpose of this book to give to its readers the very valuable information I have received from those who have spoken to me from the Etheric World about and around us. Over a period of five years I have spoken on numerous occasions for hours at a time with those whom the world called dead. Hundreds have spoken in their own voices, many of which have been recognised, and they have told me things which at first I found extremely difficult to understand or appreciate. Only as I came to understand better the laws governing the Universe was I able to comprehend what was told me by those who once lived here on earth.

Those who read this book, who disbelieve in the possibility of communication between the two worlds, those who consider that what goes under the name of Spiritualism is either humbug or fraud, had better lay down this book at once, as it is not for them. If they are anxious to learn and know something of the inter-communication which is daily and hourly increasing between the two worlds, then there are many books, full of evidence on the subject, and many opportunities to acquire experience of communication, should the wish for it exist. My daily post brings me a budget of letters from people anxious to find out for themselves the truth of the claims of Spiritualism and asking how this can be done. I would recommend anyone to go to one of the recognised Societies or Spiritualist Churches advertised in the weekly Spiritualist press, as there they will find proved and tried Mediums who can be trusted. The leading Spiritualist newspapers run by people of repute and great experience in this subject are

    Quarterly : *Psychic Science ;*

    Monthlies : *Psychic Gazette, The Spiritualist, Survival ;*

    Weeklies : *Psychic News, Light, The Two Worlds, The Greater World ;*

which can be obtained through any newsagent.

The earlier chapters of this book give a rapid survey of the principal religions of the world, what we might term the old religions, and the later chapters give more detailed attention to the new religion. As the old is the ancestor of the new, so were ancient religions the forerunners of the new religion. The religious instinct in man is based on inherent belief that this world does not constitute the sum of all his interests and activities. The feeling has generally existed in a vague way that the cemetery is not the end of life. To-day, with our greater knowledge, we can understand better the reason for the instinct that life on this earth is only one stage in our career.

We know now that men and women are possessed of an Etheric Body which is an exact duplicate of the Physical Body. We know that this etheric body is governed by Mind, and that through the etheric body Mind controls the physical body.

During one of my many talks with those who have passed on I asked particulars about our etheric body and this was the answer given in a clear, distinct voice, quite apart from the Medium, and taken down in shorthand.

"I have a body which is a duplicate of what I had on earth, the same hands, arms, legs, and feet, and they move in the same way as yours do. This etheric body I had on earth interpenetrated the physical body. The etheric is the real body and an exact duplicate of our earth body. At death we just emerge from our flesh covering and continue our life in the Etheric World, functioning by means of the etheric body just as we functioned on earth in the physical body. This etheric body is just as substantial to us now as the physical body was to us when we lived on earth. We have the same sensations. When we touch an object we can feel it, when we look at something we can see it. Though our bodies are not material, yet they have form, feature, and expression. We move from place to place as you do, but much more quickly than you can. You bring your mind over here with you. You leave your physical brain on earth. Our mind here acts on our etheric brain and through it on our etheric body, just as your physical brain acts on your physical body."

As to the reality of the world in which they live,

the following is the answer I received in reply to my enquiry.

" Our world is not material but it is real for all that. It is tangible, composed of substance in a much higher state of vibration than the matter which makes up your world. We live in a real, tangible world, though the atoms composing it differ from the atoms which make your world. All in the same plane can see and touch the same things. If we look at a field it is a field to all who look at it. Everything is real to us. We can sit down together and enjoy each other's company just as you can on earth. We have books, and we can read them. We have the same feelings as you have. We can have a long walk in the country and meet a friend whom we have not seen for a long time. We all smell the same aroma of our flowers as you do. We gather the flowers as you do. All is tangible, but in a higher degree of beauty than anything on earth."

Nothing could be clearer or more definite than that. The next world is a very real world to its inhabitants.

We now know that this Universe is made up of substance, and what we sense, namely physical substance, is only etheric vibrations. In other words, the Universe is made up of a gigantic scale of vibrations, which goes under the name of substance. Now there is a physical substance which we can see and handle, but there is also etheric substance, no less real, which in our physical bodies we are unable to sense. Our physical bodies are a trinity, made up of mind, etheric substance and physical substance, but owing to our having this etheric body, and owing to the fact that the physical body is but a cloak or a covering, it can be understood how throughout the

ages mankind has had always a vague instinct, which
enabled him to look on the physical world as a state
of preparation for the world to come, and that there
was intelligence governing the world.

This being so, religion throughout history and
before history has been one of the most powerful
influences in moulding the characters and shaping the
destinies of humanity.   Those who have made a
study of religious history consider that the original
religion must have been a kind of indistinct naturism,
an adoration of the natural phenomena.   As primitive man cannot have had much consciousness of his
superiority over the animals, he could not conceive
this instinct within him other than in some way related to nature.   Hence to the savage the sun, the
the moon and the stars, thunder and lightning were
his superiors to which he gave the name God.   He
was a child of nature, he lived in the woods and nature
he worshipped.   Doubtless the first religion was Sun
worship.   Could anything be more natural, seeing
that the Sun gives us light, warmth, comfort, and
growth.   For our food and raiment we must thank
the Sun.   Darkness is death.   Light is life.   The
Sun is born in the morning and dies at night.   Sun
worship ultimately developed into a complicated
system but it is the basis of all world religions.

Then to outstanding men, after death, or to Gods
were attributed the activities and powers of the Sun.
Apollo was the Sun who conquered the serpent of
night.   Krishna was the Sun.   The Ganges at his
birth thrilled from its source to the sea, and all living
things burst into life. Hercules was a sun God, and so
were Bacchus, Mithra, Hermes, Adonis, Zoroaster,

Samson, Perseus, Osiris, Horus, Rameses, and Jesus Christ. Cyrus was considered the son of a God and his mother a virgin. Adonis after death rose again the next day and ascended into Heaven. Julius Cæsar was believed to be the son of Apollo and his mother a virgin. Jesus had a virgin for a mother, he died like the Sun at night, and like the Sun rose in the morning, and so on. To give them all would be wearisome. They were depicted with the Sun behind their heads, which is the origin of the halo ; many lived as men and were deified after death, as all the great were in those days of ignorance. Deification meant that to them were attributed the powers of the Sun.

All the Gods of the past had Gods for their fathers and virgins for their mothers. Their births were all announced by the position of the stars. At birth celestial music was heard and voices declared that blessing had come on earth. At the birth of Buddha the celestial choir sang, "This day is born for the good of men Buddha, and to dispel the darkness of ignorance, to give joy and peace to the world," just as it sang something similar at the birth of Jesus. Tyrants sought to kill all the Gods when they were young. The story of Buddha's birth and what followed is similar to the story of Jesus.

Just as at their birth all was gladness, so at their death all was darkness and gloom. At the death of Prometheus the earth shook and the whole frame of Nature became convulsed, the rocks were rent, the graves opened, and the dead came out of them "when the Saviour gave up the ghost." He then rose from the dead and ascended into Heaven.

These Gods were born at the time of the year now called December, at the date the days commence to lengthen, and were worshipped by wise men. They all met with violent deaths and rose again from the dead. This is the story of the Sun; it dies in a red or fierce sky into blackness to rise again, and round this natural event have been woven similar stories of all the Gods of the past. Likewise the belief in the second coming of Christ can be traced to the same source, namely, the return the next day of the sun after its setting the previous night. The belief in a virgin birth arose from the sun rising out of what seemed a flat earth, born from a single parent. This idea further developed, and Mother Earth was supposed to be fertilised by the rain and heat from Heaven and thus produce offspring. This contact of Heaven with Earth came to be applied to the various Vegetation Gods in that to them were ascribed virgin births. Later it came to be ascribed to god-men, and this belief is to be found in almost every part of the world.

All religions have as a basis of the stories about their Gods the same thread running through them—miraculous birth, light coming to the world, then the descent into the darkness of the grave to rise again, and the giving of life to the world. Just as they were born when winter was turning into spring, so after death they rose from the dead just when spring was turning into summer.

The different seasons of the year had a story about the Sun, which came to be woven into the life of each great teacher after his death, and Jesus was no exception. The story of the Sun at midsummer, for instance, was that he was the feeder of the earth's multitudes from a few loaves and fishes, symbolising a bountiful harvest from a comparatively small quantity of seed, the loaves representing the seed and the fishes the rain. Like the Sun the god-man rose steadily in strength and power, and just as steadily his power waned. Throughout this waxing and waning appropriate stories were recorded more or less similar for each god-man. There was a story about the Sun for every month in the year, which became interwoven with the lives of the great teachers of the past, Jesus included. In all, the number of god-men known to history comes to thirty-four ; of these seventeen were crucified saviours, and round the lives of all these saviours runs a story similar to that told about Jesus.

Much labour has been expended by men of eminence tracing out the connection between all the world's religions and the rites connected with Sun worship. The more diligent the search the clearer it becomes that all theological affirmations, symbols and rites originated in the apparent annual and daily journey of the sun through the sky. Day was the symbol of good, and night of evil. Each day of the week was dedicated to a planet or a star, which were considered to be gods. The months of the year were dedicated to the moon. Periods of years, centuries, and ages were mapped out for incidents in the lives of the solar deities.

For thousands of years the ancients pursued their astronomical studies, during which they elaborated their various systems of solar worship. They mapped out an imaginary zone in the heavens within which lie the paths of the sun, moon and the principal planets.   It was divided into twelve signs and marked by twelve constellations called the Zodiac.   There was a feast to celebrate the entrance of the sun into each sign, and the ancients regarded the various heavenly bodies as visible expressions of divine intelligence.   The twelve constellations were considered as the sun's body-guard, which number was given to the human sun-god as the number of his disciples.   Every 600 years a Messiah or world saviour was expected, whose history on earth after death was made to correspond to the legends attributed to the sun.   When an outstanding man arose about that time he was deified after death, and round his life was wound these stories, as was done with Jesus.   Jesus is the last sun-god, as solar worship and modern astronomy do not go together.   Mahomet followed Jesus 600 years later, but by his time intelligence had advanced sufficiently to enable his followers to regard him only as a prophet from God and not God Himself.

The heavens above, to the ancients, were a stage divided into various scenes of astronomical time.   The heavenly bodies were the actors, and their movements were their performance during each act in a grand heavenly drama, which lasted into eternity, and were witnessed by the inhabitants of this globe, who were the audience, and the earth the auditorium.

Theology with all its rites and mysteries is astronomy as it appeared to those of long ago, and ecclesiasticism is the play composed of myths and legends wound round real or imaginary lives to whom were attributed all that was attributed to the sun.

Hence on to the lives of the great and noble were draped those mythical stories, most of which are familiar to us from the writings in the Gospels.

After death these men, as I say, were deified to become sun-gods. The god-man was generally a moral teacher. He was given a virgin as his mother whose name was Maria or something similar. Our translation of the word is Mary, and the month we call May probably derives its name from this virgin mother. The word means the sea from which sprang all life. This god-man was born in a stable or something similar, this being the story associated with the sun in the sign "Capricornus."

The Saviour-God's birth was foretold by a dream. He was born of a virgin mother in consequence of her contact with a God. He was visited by wise men, guided to his birthplace by a star, who had read of his birth in the heavens ; and also by shepherds. Angels were with him at his birth. He was of royal descent. He was preceded by a kinsman who prepared the way for his teaching. A tyrant sought to kill him and murdered many innocent children of similar age in his attempt, but the young child and his parents escaped to another country. He astonished the wise men of his time by his learning at an early age, and he was tempted by the devil on a mountain. Miracles were numerous. He was transfigured, cured lepers, turned water into wine, and healed the sick. Ointment was poured on him by a woman and he washed the feet of the outcasts. He had a triumphal procession riding on an ass. He incurred the anger of the people and had a farewell supper with his disciples, who numbered

twelve.   Then came the betrayal, the agony and
fear, the trial, the crown of thorns, the scourging,
and crucifixion.   At the God's death the earth shook
as the result of a great earthquake, and the dead rose
from the graves.   He descended into Hades, rose
again, was first met by sorrowing women, and
ascended into Heaven to resume his part with the
other two gods making up the Trinity, and some day
it was believed he would return to judge the earth
and receive his followers into glory.   These looked
on him as the Saviour of all believers, he having taken
the punishment for their sins.

Such is the story, with just a variation in the
number of these details, of the sixteen crucified
saviour-gods known to history previous to the birth
of Jesus.   For details regarding each I would refer the
reader to the book entitled *The World's Sixteen
Crucified Saviours*, by Graves, that painstaking and
careful American authority on ancient religion.   I
would also suggest a careful study of *Christianity and
Mythology*, by the Rt. Hon. John M. Robertson,
P.C., late Parliamentary Secretary to the Board of
Trade, and one of our greatest authorities on pre-
Christian religions.   In this book he takes every
incident in the life of Jesus as reported in the gospels,
and shows how each one is paralleled in previous
religions.   Every statement he makes he supports
by making reference to other well-known authorities
on the subject.   Robertson I knew personally ; he
was a man for whom I had the greatest respect ; his
honesty, his accuracy, his care for detail, his caution
and his fairness were always apparent, and these
qualities were duly acknowledged by the press at the
time of his death in January of this year.

The legends surrounding Krishna, the god of the Hindus, are in many important respects similar to what I have just written. He became incarnate, so we are told, 575 years before the birth of Jesus, and the place to which he was taken when a tyrant king sought to kill him is exactly the same place, namely Mathura, which in one of the early gospels, not included in the canon, was given as the place to which Joseph and Mary took Jesus. His sayings and claims are similar to those of Jesus, and students of his life find 346 striking analogies between his sayings and doings and those of Jesus. Images of ancient Indian gods have been found, and on each there is a figure of a man nailed to a cross, with feet placed one over the other, pierced, the hands pierced, and also the side, and round their heads is wound a band which may represent a crown of thorns.

Mithra, another saviour-god, had attributed to him much the same as Krishna and Jesus. He was worshipped in Persia 400 years before the birth of Jesus. Osiris, the great Egyptian deity, had similar miraculous events attributed to him, and these legends go back thousands of years. In the ancient *Egyptian Book of the Dead* one named Petra was the door-keeper of Heaven. In China similar legends exist as are found in India, Persia, Babylonia and Egypt and as came to surround Jesus. Many other examples could be given, such as the legends surrounding the lives of Pythagoras, Prometheus, Apollonius, and many others, but it would just end in repetition, as all that is attributed to Jesus was attributed to the god-men who lived long before the Christian era.

The Jewish records in the original Hebrew contain two different words to represent the Creator, though in the Bible translation both words are translated God. The first God mentioned in the first chapter of Genesis is Elohim and later on another called Yahveh, translated Jehovah, who was one of the gods who made up the Elohim Godhead. Both words may be of Egyptian origin. The former, some authorities believe, is a plural word embracing several gods, so that the translation of the creation could read " In the beginning the Gods created the heaven and the earth." Elohim occurs more than 2,000 times in the Old Testament and in each case could have been translated " The Gods." This, however, is open to argument, and within Biblical times it has been accepted as representing one God only.

The modes of Egyptian worship were not unlike those instituted by Moses. The Ark of the Covenant of the Hebrews was copied from Egypt, and so also was the Passover, which was a copy of an Egyptian feast. It is thought that the rite of circumcision came from Egypt, and likewise the order of the Jewish priesthood, with its ornaments and dress, which were exact copies of Egyptian models. The Jewish fast days, their celebrations and musical instruments, also came from Egypt.

Both Egypt and Babylon contributed largely to the religion of the Jews, whose scriptures are based on Cabala or secret doctrines handed down through the priesthood. Biblical prophecies are based mostly on astronomy. The ten commandments as we now know them are to be found in the ancient sacred books of China, which are much older than the Bible. The Bible is a storehouse of some of the wisdom, folly, and cruelty of the ancients, drawn from all the countries surrounding Judea and from as far away as India and China. Volumes could not contain the noble truths and gracious sentiment, combined with ignorance and cruelty, to be found in the scriptures of the Hindus, Egyptians, Persians and Babylonians. All ancient sacred books contain good and bad, wisdom and folly, and are the product of the times in which they were written.

The Devil figures in all religions in one form or another. The one Christianity copied came from Paganism, and to it he was known as Pan the mountain Goat-God, with horns, hoofs and tail. He was God of the mountains, and the legend of Jesus being taken up a high mountain to be tempted by the Devil is just the story borrowed from the Pagans of Pan taking Jupiter to a mountain-top and offering him the surrounding country.

All the forms, symbols and ceremonies of Christianity are borrowed from sources further back, and can be traced to forms and ceremonies connected with primitive worship. The Hindus, Egyptians, Greeks and Romans used holy water. Baptism is an ancient ceremony, infant baptism coming from the Romans, as did the confessing of sins to the priest. The rite of the Eucharist or Holy Communion came also from the pagans. They had their eucharistic feasts after the harvest when the wheat and the wine had been gathered, and gave thanks to Ceres the Goddess of the fields and Bacchus the God of the vine, saying, " This is the flesh of the

Goddess,'' when eating cakes made from the wheat, and " This is the blood of our God," when drinking the wine.   This was the outcome of a more primitive ceremony, when the body of the victim sacrificed was eaten, and the blood drunk.   This victim was in some cases human, in others an animal, and the partakers of this celebration considered, just as Christians do to-day, that the victim received the punishment of their sins.

A design similar to the cross has been used as the symbol of life for thousands of years and is found on the graves of inhabitants of Italy long before the time of the Etruscans.   In South America on the ruined temples thousands of years old, the cross is found and on it a bleeding victim.   In Egypt the cross was a symbol of life for thousands of years, and in an ancient sculpture on the wall of the temple at Luxor the annunciation to the Virgin Mother is depicted, the Egyptian Holy Spirit being shown as holding a cross before the face of the Virgin Mother.   In consequence of this she is shown in the next scene as having given birth to a god-child, and being surrounded by figures in adoration.   The cross was the symbol of love and sacrifice in Greece and likewise in India and Tibet.   The origin of the cross as a symbol of life came doubtless from the ancient fire worship, the fire-god being always represented by two crossed sticks.   To the ancients fire represented life, and we can assume that the two crossed sticks became the symbol of life, because fire was produced through the friction caused by their being rubbed together.

The Trinity is not exclusively a Christian belief, In Egypt the Father, Son, and Holy Ghost were

Osiris, Isis, and Horus, and were worshipped thousands of years ago. Mithra was the second person in the Persian Trinity. Brahma, Vishnu and Siva made up the Trinity of the old religion of India. What Christians call the fall of man and the atonement are much older than Christianity. The atonement was incorporated into Christianity long after Christ's death and was introduced with reference to Christ. The sixteen pre-Christian crucified saviour-gods were all supposed to have died for the sins of the world, the belief being general amongst the ancients that only through the suffering and death of a god-man could salvation and immortality be secured after death. It was at least a century after the birth of Jesus that the virgin birth was thought of. There is no mention of it in the Epistles, the earliest of Christian writings ; in fact his paternal ancestry to David is given in Matthew, and Jesus himself declared he was not God. The gospels explicitly say that Joseph was his father, and it is clear that the original writers thought so. Besides this the word translated "virgin" in the original Hebrew (Isaiah, 7-14) means "a young married woman."

All religion, as I say, can be traced back to Sun worship. All natural phenomena were worshipped, and gave birth to the ceremonials and beliefs which came later.*

---

* Some of the standard works on this subject are Frazer's *Golden Bough* ; Grant Allen's *Evolution of the Idea of God* ; Robertson's *Pagan Christs*, and *Christianity and Mythology* ; Dupuis' *L'Origin de tous les Cultes* ; and Bryant's *Eastern Antiquities*. A comprehensive review of Eastern religions will be found in *Asiatic Researches*, a monumental work of 16 volumes, revised and added to by several authorities, especially by Sir William Jones, one of the most learned of Oriental scholars, and past president of the Asiatic Society. Refer also to Child's *Progress of Religious Ideas* ; to Higgins' *Anacalypsis*, and to Gerald Massey's *The Beginnings* and *Ancient Egypt*.

C

From this primitive naturism it will be noticed sprang anthropomorphic polytheism, which was an advance on the more primitive naturism, as man now conceived his superiors in the form of himself rather than that of inanimate matter. His gods were like man, only greater and wiser. Idolatry naturally followed and he carved his gods into graven images. Then came the adoration of one God and one God only, the tribal god Jehovah with all man's passions and weakness, or Brahma with four heads and four arms. Lastly come the most advanced religions of all, conceiving God as the father of the human race, protecting and guiding his children.

The earliest religions, many of which exist at the present day, are what might be termed nature religions. To this class belong the religions of the most primitive people. Many of those religions existing to-day are but depraved remnants of what they once were. Excluding these, the world's religions can be divided into two groups. One we might term anthropomorphic and the other ethical. In the former group can be placed the ancient basic religions of India ; the religion of Judea, Media, Persia, Babylonia and Assyria ; those of Phœnicia and Armenia and the Celtic, Germanic, Hellenic and Greco-Roman religions.

On the other hand, the world's ethical religions are found in China as Taoism and Confucianism : in India as Brahmanism ; in Burmah, Japan, Tibet, China, Siam, Ceylon and elsewhere as Buddhism ; in Persia as Mazdaism, commonly called Zoroastrianism. The other two great and outstanding ethical religions are known under the names of Islam and Christianity.

Those who have followed the discoveries and researches of Professor Max Müller, who did so much to raise the study of comparative religion to the rank of a science, can only come to the conclusion that religion is the result of a slow growth, that underlying all religions one finds a similar root, and that this root is man's instinctive belief that there is a hereafter, and that there is some power in the Universe guiding and controlling his destiny. From this root has sprung the tree from which branches have shot out in every direction, and be he Christian or Jew, Buddhist or Mohammedan, man's beliefs can be traced back to this one origin.

Just as languages are the result of the geographical distribution of races, so also are religions, and in the earlier times religion and language generally went together. Owing to this isolation each race thought its own religion and its own political system was the best. Just as each race thought that other nations were its inferiors, so it thought that those who held different religious beliefs were wrong, and consequently were under the displeasure of its God or Gods. No one can read the history of the Jewish race as recorded in the Bible without realising how closely nationalism and religion were associated. The children of Abraham considered that they and they only worshipped the one and only true God.

Religions differ in their beginning just as they differ in their teachings. On the one hand we have religions which are the product of the wisdom of many and are the unconscious growth of years, and on the other hand religions proceeding from an individual founder, who as the leading representative of a better insight of his time, makes a stand against the formalities and ignorance of his day, recalling his followers to a new faith and hope, to which he himself gives shape and form.   Under this heading comes Christianity, Mohammedanism, Zoroastrianism, Buddhism and Taoism.   Here we have five religions with individuals as founders who preached a universal religion for the whole human race.   These religions have been the most permanent and embracing of the world's religions as far as history records.   On the other hand, if the founders of the five great religions of the world were themselves responsible for their origin, there has undoubtedly been growth and accretion to their teachings.   They gave the initial tenets and their followers have supplied their own interpretations, so that even these individualistic religions must be considered as the work of numerous minds.

The comparative study of religion proves that though each religion revered its founder often to the extent even of Deification, yet the doctrines of each were never shaped by the founders but by the followers who came after.   The founders only laid the foundation of the new religion, not because they intended to form one, but because they introduced new and pregnant principles, which they revealed to the world by their teachings and their lives.

Neither Buddhism, Mohammedanism nor Christianity were national religions, their founders preaching a doctrine to embrace the whole human race. Strangely enough, the founders of Christianity and Buddhism were rejected by the people to whom they belonged by birth, and Mohammedanism owes its position to-day largely to the high position to which it was raised, not in Arabia, but in Persia.

Besides these organised religions, mankind has been helped and guided by philosophical teachers such as Pythagoras, Socrates, Plato and Aristotle in Greece. To come to more modern times, the philosophic teachings of Kant, Hume, Locke, and Herbert Spencer, to mention only some of the outstanding names which occur to one, have helped many in their enquiries into the mysteries which surround us. These individuals have moulded intellectual thought, whereas orthodox religions have appealed to the ignorant masses.

Each religion of the past has been insistent on the fact that it is of divine origin, that its teachings must be observed by its followers, and that its records were sacred and divinely inspired. Incidentally, everyone who did not accept its teachings was condemned, but those who were its true followers would be saved in the life to come. If we, therefore, had been born in Turkey we should have been the followers of Mohammed and believed in the inspiration of the Koran ; that Mohammed visited Heaven and talked with the angel Gabriel. If, being born in Turkey, we had denied these beliefs and held the opinion that Christianity was the true faith, we should have been branded as infidels and, in the old days, put to death. We should have been told that the best and wisest had always believed in the Koran, that the Koran was the best of books, and that to it and to it alone Turkey owed her greatness. We should have been told that millions had died, gladdened and helped by the passages from the Koran, and the mourners had been comforted by the thought of the departed partaking of the joys and delights of Heaven. '' There is but one God and Mohammed is his Prophet," would have been instilled into us as the truth, and we in our simplicity and ignorance should have looked on all those who held other religious beliefs as pitiable creatures and fit only for destruction.   Had we been born in India we should have been given the old records to read and told that they were true and sacred.   Had we been born in China we should have been told that to worship our ancestors was the only worship pleasing in the sight of God.

In like manner, where Christianity prevailed, its adherents were taught by the Church that it was the only true religion, and through it only could the portals of Heaven be entered.   All religions have this belief in common, namely that there is only one way to Heaven, that the only right way is that which is defined by a particular revelation, and that all other ways are of the Devil.   This is as true to-day as it was yesterday, and, in all probability, similar beliefs were held before history was ever recorded.

Into the dim and misty past we peer through ages of history to the time before history began.   In that far-off past we can only imagine the religions of man born from the subconscious instinct in him, which made him different from the beasts.   In this vast cemetery most of the world's religions lie, dead and forgotten.   Olympus is silent, Venus is now but a graven image.   No longer does Jehovah speak to his chosen people.   Mount Sinai's thunders have ceased.   Many of the sacred temples of India are in ruin.   The ancient religions of Peru and Mexico are forgotten.   The sacred Nile no longer harbours the wandering Isis searching for the dead Osiris.   Memnon is no more. From the wild North we never hear the mighty Thor dashing the mountains to pieces, and with him has gone Odin, the giver of life and death. The Druids no longer dominate this fair land of ours, which once was theirs, and with them have gone all the gods brought here with Cæsar's conquering legions, whose names are now borne by the planets of our solar system.

Religions like nations have their periods of birth, growth and decay. What is orthodox in one age is rejected in contempt by the next. Gods, like their creators, have passed away like those who created them. Those worshipped to-day will receive no reverence to-morrow. Mithra in Persia, Zeus in Greece, Isis and Osiris in Egypt, and Jove in Rome have all been dethroned and others have been put in their place. What has happened in the past will happen in the future. The Christian religion will be no exception. Already Jehovah has lost the place he once held; his cruel laws are no longer obeyed. Many of the extravagant claims once made for Jesus by his zealous devotees have now been abandoned, and to-day amongst enlightened Christians his simple, unselfish life, his teachings of the fatherhood of God and the brotherhood of man, are put forward with emphasis. Amongst the more enlightened clergy these aspects of his life are stressed to the disregard of others.

Many have now come to a realisation of the fact that man must be his own saviour; that not the death of another can save him from his own misdeeds. As a man soweth so shall he reap. Man is his own saviour, and the most intelligent have now ceased to consider themselves miserable wretches, believing that another has taken their punishment. Far nobler is it to enter the next world, without a mortgage hanging like a millstone around one's neck, and have the satisfaction of knowing that the place one occupies has been reached by one's own effort, and not through the suffering and the death of one who lived nearly two thousand years before we were born.   Such a belief makes men and women intolerant and selfish, and is quite contrary to the teachings of Jesus, as will be seen in Chapter IV.

CHAPTER III.

THE CHRISTIAN RELIGION.

ITS ORIGIN.

The Christian religion, it is generally believed, owes its origin to Jesus of Nazareth who, according to tradition, suffered on a cross at Calvary, near Jerusalem, having been sentenced to death by Pontius Pilate, who was governor of Judea from **26** to **36** A.D. This belief has had a profound influence on world history. The tradition of the birth, life and death of Jesus is recorded in what is termed the New Testament, the record being in the form of four biographies written at different dates. The authors are unknown but they go under the names of four men associated with early Christianity. No original document of the gospels has survived, and no record exists of such documents ever having been seen.

Some authorities hold the view that the origin of Christianity can be traced back to the year 100 B.C., to one called Jesus Barabbas, who was handed over to the people at the time of the Passover as a sacrifice. Against this it must be remembered that Irenæus, the early Church Father, stated that when he was a boy he met Polycarp, and that Polycarp spoke of his intercourse with John and others who had seen and heard the Lord. This is a chain of evidence going back from Irenæus, through Polycarp and John, to Jesus and is well worth remembering.

Without doubt the central figure of Christianity is shrouded in uncertainty, the reason being, as Gibbon says, that ''The scanty and suspicious

materials of ecclesiastical history seldom enable us
to dispel the dark cloud that hangs over the first age
of the Church." However, for the purpose of this
book, what is natural is assumed to have happened,
as during the last half of the first century on to the
year 120 there appeared a dozen independent documents, based solely on tradition, but all alike testifying
to a certain Jesus, a Jew of Galilee, who was considered by a small section of his countrymen as the
Messiah.

In consequence of this tradition, what are known
as epistles or letters were written, and to these at a
later date names were given. These are also included in what is called the New Testament. The
books of the New Testament are not historical documents, no one knows who wrote them, nobody has
reported ever having seen the original documents, and
nobody knows when they were written. Various
estimates have been made as to the dates of their
origin, but nothing is known for certain.

One thing, however, is certain, that a profound
mental change occurred in Palestine nineteen hundred
years ago, and an acorn which was sown those many
years ago has to-day spread into an oak tree of great
magnitude. What did Jesus really teach is the great
question. We know what the Church says he
taught, but the great difficulty is to know what he
really did teach, as there is every reason to doubt
that what the Church says he taught he ever taught
at all.

Before, however, I touch on this question and
examine the origin of the records purporting to contain his teaching, let us consider what is now known

regarding Christianity from sources apart from the New Testament.

As to the origin of Christianity, St. Augustine wrote as follows :—" For the thing itself which is now called the Christian religion was known to the ancients, and was not wanting at any time from the beginning of the human race until the time that Christ came in the flesh, from whence the true religion that had existed previously began to be called Christian, and this in our day is the Christian religion, not as having been wanting in former times but as having in later times received the name."

St. Augustine was one of the early Christian fathers, born in **354** A.D., and his remarks will be better understood by the time this section of the chapter is read. This opinion of St. Augustine was also the opinion of Eusebius, the father of ecclesiastical history, born in Palestine in **265** A.D., who says " Those ancient Therapeutæ were Christians and their writings were our gospels and epistles," and "the religion published by Jesus Christ to all nations is neither new nor strange," expressing the view that what is called Christianity was borrowed from the Therapeutæ or Essenes— a view held also by other outstanding men of the early Christian Church. These Therapeutæ were known under the name of Essenes or healers, and they had their origin in Egypt. It was there that the Essenes principally dwelt for over two hundred years before the birth of Jesus. Their centre was Alexandria, the world's theological university, where the wisdom of the time was centred in those days, and where there was the greatest library of the

ancient world.   These Essenes were taught the art
of healing at the University of Alexandria which had
a special medical school, and along with this art of
healing certain mystical rites were observed.   Their
belief in the immortality of the soul came from the
influence of Greek philosophy.   The Essenes were
established in Alexandria several hundred years
before the birth of Jesus, and were also the cus-
todians of the teaching followed for hundreds of years
before the birth of Jesus, which came to be incorporated in the New Testament at a much later date.
Alexandria should be looked on as the birthplace of
Christianity, as there centred all the knowledge of
the world's various religions, out of which developed
what we to-day call Christianity.

According to Philo, the great Jewish historian,
who lived at the time of Jesus, the Essenes were
philosophers and ascetics as well as healers.   They
divested themselves of all worldly goods and thus
relieved themselves of all worldly cares.   Their outlook on life can be summed up in the words, ''sell
all that thou hast and give to the poor,'' and ''lay
not up treasures on Earth, but rather in Heaven
where moth and rust do not corrupt.''   The teachings
of Jesus and the teachings of the Essenes are remarkably similar, and the similarity of many of the
sayings found in the gospels to those of the Essenes
is striking.   The teachings of Jesus with regard to
this world and the next can be traced to Essene
sources.   What is known as the Sermon on the
Mount can be traced to the same sources ; in fact the
sermon is just a stringing together of quotations from
the Psalms, Proverbs, and other Jewish literature,

all of which were well known to this sect.   As a community they were equal as far as worldly goods were concerned, and none exercised authority over the other, all rendering mutual service to the community.   The Essenes strove to live lives of purity and holiness, sacrificing this world's pleasures for the happiness of the world to come.   They lived a monastic life, which may account for nothing being known of Jesus till the years of his ministry.

At the time of the birth of Jesus the Jewish race was divided into Pharisees, Sadducees, and Essenes, and most Jews belonged to one or the other of these sects.   Jesus constantly rebuked the Scribes and the Pharisees, but never the Essenes, the reason probably being that he was one of them.   The Essenes taught what to-day we call Psychic healing, and so did Jesus.   This art he taught his disciples, but it was lost to the Christian Church which, preferring dogmas and creeds, has left their Master's teaching to others.

Professor Ginsburg, LL.D., the well known Hebrew scholar, who in 1870 was appointed one of the first members of the committee for the revision of the English Version of the Old Testament, contributed a comprehensive article on the relationship of Essenism to Christianity in *Kitto's Cyclopedia of Biblical Literature.*   Therein he shows that what Jesus is reported to have taught, the Essenes taught before him.   The article is too long to quote, and I only refer to it in case some may be sufficiently interested to wish to study this question more deeply than it can be dealt with here.   *The Encyclopedia Britannica,* under "The Essenes," also gives a detailed account of this sect, and there are various other authorities on the subject. Gibbon was of the opinion that early Christianity, before it became surrounded by the myths, legends, doctrines, and ceremonials of other religions, was just a new name given to the teachings of Essenism.

Whence came this holy brotherhood? They can be traced first from Judea to Egypt and from Egypt to India. In other words the Essenes were in all probability the Western offshoot of the followers of Buddha. That Spiritually Enlightened One, Prince Siddhartha Gautama, commonly known as Buddha, was probably the source whence sprang the teachings of the Essenes.

The origin of many of the ethical teachings of Christianity, therefore, do not date from 1,900 years ago, but from 560 B.C., when Buddha was born. He died 480 B.C. Doubtless the teachings of Buddha can be traced back to an even earlier date, and there is little doubt that he was greatly influenced in what he taught by the teachings of Brahmanic philosophy in which he had been nurtured. According to tradition, Buddha the Enlightened was not born perfect; neither was Jesus. As Buddha obtained the name Buddha the Enlightened, so Jesus received the name Christ, the Anointed. Both grew to perfection and to wisdom through suffering. Both had miraculous birth attributed to them. To both at their birth came wise men with rich gifts. Both were hailed at birth as the Saviours of the World, by an aged saint, who used similar words, the only difference being that Buddha was born in the garden of a tavern under a tree and Jesus was born in a stable.

Just as there is a correspondence as regards the environment and associations surrounding the births, lives and teaching of these great religious teachers, so also there is a corresponding degradation of their teachings to be traced after their deaths. What Constantine did for Christianity at the Council of Nicaea in the year 325 A.D. King Asoka did for Buddhism. Both these potentates consolidated the simple teaching of these great men into creeds and dogmas. In both cases the words of the master were collected into a body of doctrines fixed and definite. Just as after the death of Jesus differences of opinion sprang up amongst his followers, so after the death of Buddha differences occurred amongst his followers, and Councils and Conferences followed for the purpose of trying to bring all the followers into harmony. Again, just as numerous gospels, reporting what Jesus said and did, were written, similarly numerous gospels were written narrating what Buddha did and said. These are known to-day under the name of Buddhist Suttas. As amongst early Christians there were Gnostics and Arians, so were there similar sects who took different views with regard to Buddha. Some called him divine and others took the view that he was human like themselves, just as Gnostics and Arians held the view that Jesus was human and not God, or part of God. The early Church father, Saint Clement of Alexandria, in the third century stated that the enlightened or perfect Christian is a Gnostic.

As Constantine made Christianity through adopting it as a state religion, so also Asoka, adopting it as a state religion, made Buddhism, the only difference being that Asoka was a great and wise ruler and Constantine an unscrupulous rascal and murderer.   He murdered his own wife, son, and nephew.   Both religions on entering under state control began to entertain worldly aspirations.   Then orthodoxy was born.   Some four centuries after Buddha's death, about the year 88 B.C., the canon was compiled just as was the Christian canon in the fourth century of our era.   In the year 397 A.D. at the Council of Carthage it was decided what writings should be considered suitable for the canon and what were to be rejected.   It was then that the New Testament, more or less as we know it to-day, came into being.   It was written on papyrus without points, and without commas.   Before that there were no authorised gospels or epistles, and in consequence there was much diversity of opinion.   The means adopted by the Council to decide what books were to be included in the New Testament were so un-worthy of an important assemblage that they are unbelievable in the present time.   Much discussion centred on which of the numerous gospels were to be included, the two most influential men, Augustine and Jerome, failing to agree.   The opinions of Augustine and Jerome carried great weight, but to-day could only be ridiculed by intelligent people.

The foregoing, however, refers to the adoption of the New Testament by the Church officially. Irenaeus, another Church father, at the end of the second century expressed his opinion that there should be only four gospels and not more, as there were four winds and there were four corners of the earth. By his time it was considered that only the four gospels, the Acts, the thirteen epistles of St. Paul, the first epistle of St. John, and the Revelation of St. John were authoritative. It was not, however, until the year **397**, as I said, that what was called the canon was adopted officially, and from that date the crystallising process set in, and orthodox Christianity became firmly established.

As in the case of Buddhism, so also in the case of Christianity, after an interval of hundreds of years the fundamentals of the religion were in a state of flux, of doubt, and the subject of constant debate. The virgin birth and all the other miraculous happenings which in course of time had gathered round these two came to be focussed and centred in written documents authorised by the Church, under the protection of the State. Many of the teachings of Buddha and Christ are similar in character, for instance the stories of the Prodigal Son, the Loaves and the Fishes, and the admonition as to the plucking out of the right eye if it gives offence, to mention only a few. Other incidents of a similar nature are common to both records, such as the story of Peter walking on the sea, and the woman at the well.* The Jewish Talmud contains parables which recall those of the Marriage Feast, the Labourers in the Vineyard, and the Pearl of Great Price.

What Christians call the Last Supper originated in an Essene custom observed when taking leave of a brother about to depart on a journey, and this simple story is now surrounded by rites, ceremonies and beliefs taken from Mithraism. It has been changed

---

* Max Müller in *Science of Religion* remarks " Some of the Buddhist legends and parables sound as if taken from the New Testament, though we know that many of them existed before the beginning of the Christian era."

D

into a mystical rite by the Christian Church.   We
can thus trace the origin of many of the teachings
attributed to Jesus through Essenism, and so back
to the teachings of Gautama Buddha.   Many other
Christian beliefs are common to both religions, such
as justification by faith and purgatory, to mention only
two.   The Buddhists have their Madonna and Child ;
their priests, until recently, were celibates, and they
have masses for the souls of the dead.   The resemblance between the two religions is so obvious that
early Catholic missionaries thought that the Buddhists
had copied their religion from Christianity.   It will
now be interesting to consider more closely the origin
and development of Christianity itself.

We are told in the Acts of the Apostles that
Christians received their name at Antioch, and
that Saul of Tarsus, as the result of his con-
version, was principally responsible after the death
of Jesus for gathering together the scattered band of
the Nazarene's followers, into whom he instilled some
of his great enthusiasm for the cause.   The origin
of the name Christian was the fact that oil was
used in anointing Kings and Priests, and Jesus was
ultimately given the additional name of Christ, the
Anointed One, and finally it resolved into Jesus the
Christ or Jesus Christ.   Prior to this, however, Saul,
now called Paul, had retired to Arabia to be imbued
doubtless with the teachings of the older religions,
and he returned to join the disciples full of
the idea that Jesus was the longed-for Messiah
awaited by the Jews.

The earliest trace we have of an account of the
life of Jesus describes him only in human terms.   The

reconstructed Quelle document, a Greek translation of an earlier Aramaic document, which is quite as early as the early part of Mark, and is the furthest back we can get, makes no reference to the miraculous. The birth, death and resurrection legends are not referred to, only his teaching. This then is the best evidence we have of the real Jesus, a teacher and reformer, and but for the idea evolved in the mind of Paul that he was the Messiah he would never have been regarded as anything else.

Other Jewish Messiahs have come and gone, but only those who study Jewish history know anything of them. Paul, however, decided that Jesus was to be made known to the Jews first and then to the Gentiles, and to gain converts amongst the latter his mental evolution proceeded. First of all he regarded Jesus as the Messiah of the Jews ; then the idea developed that he was the world's crucified saviour. This is noticeable as only when Paul comes into contact with the Pagans does he preach the crucified and risen saviour, which, based on their mythology of crucified saviour gods, they could understand, whereas a Jewish Messiah would mean nothing to them. The purport of his teachings, as witnessed by letters attributed to him, is that "as in Adam all die, so in Christ shall all be made alive."

The writings attributed to Paul are considered of earlier date than the gospels, and to all who have studied the ancient religion of Egypt it becomes clearly noticeable how much the writer was influenced by the beliefs surrounding Osiris. The 15th Chapter of 1st Corinthians on the arguments for the resurrection might have been written by a worshipper of

Osiris, as all the arguments therein had been current for thousands of years in the land of the Nile. It is just the old argument, but in this case the god is Jesus instead of Osiris.

Here we have the foundation of what is now termed the Christian faith, which was added to bit by bit as it absorbed something from each of the old religions. What we know to-day as the Christian beliefs did not owe their origin to Jesus, but in embryo to St. Paul, and his enthusiasm for the idea that Jesus was the longed-for Messiah of the Jews, and the Saviour of the human race. But St. Paul's views carried weight only amongst a certain section. Other leaders came on the scene who had entirely different conceptions as to the meaning of the mission of Jesus, and these opinions varied wherever Christians assembled.

According to that great Biblical authority, the Reverend Dr. Davidson, it was not till one hundred and seventy years from the birth of Jesus that the collection of Christian documents assumed any form, and only from that time onwards were some considered of more authority than others. They were uncritically taken from tradition and gradually elevated to the rank of Divine Documents, and Dr. Davidson describes those early fathers who were responsible for their choice as "credulous and blundering, passionate and one-sided."

Ultimately, as previously said, these documents were formed into a canon at the Council of Carthage in 397 A.D. To the early Christians the Old Testament was the only book which was considered inspired, and the text often quoted, that all Scripture is given by the inspiration of God, referred to the Jewish Book of the Law, and had no reference to the New Testament, which when this was written did not exist, and was not even thought of. The early Church fathers did not consider the books now contained in the New Testament as sacred documents and clothed with divine authority. To them the Old Testament was the Word of God, and only after the lapse of about two hundred years did certain writings rise in the estimation of Christians, and become considered as equal in value to those of the Old Testament.

We know that the people of Syria in the time of Jesus spoke the Aramaic language, but the earliest documents recording his deeds and sayings are known to have been written in Greek. Nothing was written in Aramaic, and no one knows when or how the Greek history of those occurrences was recorded. We know, however, that three hundred years after the events recorded something resembling our present New Testament was collated into what is now called the Latin Vulgate, a translation from the Greek documents into Latin.

The New Testament was brought together into one book at the close of the fourth century, and the two testaments were brought together into one book in the sixth century. This book differed considerably from our present Bible, which came into being as late as 1611. Prior to this, numerous conferences were held to decide which books were inspired and which were not, and finality was reached only in the seventeenth century. Before this date right back through the Christian era nearly every book now forming part of the Bible was at one time or another looked on by the Christian Church as spurious and not divinely inspired.

Were the Divines at Westminster inspired to decide which books were inspired, and if so, why were the priests composing the numerous previous Councils not also inspired? How is it that Christians had to wait till the 17th century before it could be decided what was true and what was not?

When all this is carefully considered, how foolish it seems to wrangle over texts as if they were God inspired! Did we fully realise this, how differences dividing various sects would dissolve! Had our ancestors never heard the word "inspiration," how much better it would have been for humanity! Many millions of lives would have been saved, and the Church would have come through the last nineteen hundred years with clean hands, innocent of bloodshed.

The New Testament as we know it to-day consists of books whose origin is unknown, and whose authors are unknown. They were chosen uncritically by ignorant men, steeped in superstition. What was merely tradition became elevated to the rank of sacred documents, word by word inspired by God, and Christians were exhorted to follow every divine mistake and pious contradiction. The earliest copies of any of the books now comprising the New Testament known to exist belong to the middle of the fourth century, but they are only copies, and no one knows whether they are in any way like the original documents or not.

The Arians, a sect of the early Christians which maintained that God and Jesus were not the same, and that Jesus was subordinate to God, nearly won the day at the Council of Nicaea in **325** A.D., that most decisive event in the history of the Christian Church. 'Arius, the leader, was an Alexandrian Presbyter of the Church. At that great Council, after months of arguing, the anti-divines first carried the day, and then the pro-divines, until ultimately it was decided by a narrow majority that Jesus was the Son of God and the second member of the Trinity.

To decide this great question there assembled at Nicaea 2,048 ignorant and superstitious Christian priests, and also representatives of Paganism. Numerous resolutions were presented to Constantine, who presided, but he burned them all without reading them, "lest the contentions of the priests should become known to anyone."* Out of this puerile assembly grew the Nicene creed which officially added Jesus to the Pantheon of Incarnate crucified god-men, thus increasing their number to seventeen.† The creed received royal assent, and a royal command was issued that everyone must believe it, and that Christianity thus defined was to be the state religion of Rome for the future. The bishops who opposed it were cast out as heretics, and those who had been on the winning side were promoted and given places of

---

* The history of the Council of Nicaea is given in *The History of the Christian Church*, by Canon Robertson, and in *The History of the Eastern Church*, by Dean Stanley.

† The following are the 16 crucified saviour-gods believed by their followers to have lived, and died for the sins of the world, together with their countries of origin and approximate dates:—Thulis (Egypt), 1700 B.C.; Crite (Babylon), 1200 B.C.; Atys (Phrygia), 1170 B.C.; Thammuz (Syria), 1160 B.C.; Hesus (Europe), 834 B.C.; Indra (Thibet), 725 B.C.; Bali (Asia), 725 B.C.; Iao (Nepaul), 622 B.C.; Alcestos (Euripides), 600 B.C.; Sakia (India), 600 B.C.; Quexalcote (Mexico), 587 B.C.; Wittoba (Travancore), 552 B.C.; Krishna Jeseus (India), 550 B.C.; Prometheus (Greece), 547 B.C.; Quirinus (Rome), 506 B.C.; Mithra (Persia), 400 B.C. The word "crucified" must be taken in a wider sense than usual, as several were "hanged on a tree" as St. Paul said happened to Jesus.

authority under the holy name of " orthodox." Then
persecution began, and Christianity entered on its
record of bloodshed.

Nicaea was the grave of Christianity as understood by its founder, and from 325 until the present
time it has been a religion containing many of the
superstitions of previous religions, as what was
believed to have happened to previous saviour-gods
was made to centre round Jesus.

To understand correctly how Christianity evolved
out of the simple teachings of the Nazarene, one
must keep in mind that, before Nicaea, Christianity,
was only a sect amongst numerous other sects, with no
particular standing.   When, however, the power of
Rome came behind it the position immediately altered,
and as it had been decreed that Christianity was to
be the State religion of the future, then those who
controlled its destinies were determined that it would
not be inferior to rival sects and cults of its time.
Consequently its teachings and ritual had to be up to
the level of prevailing religions, and the more the
miraculous was emphasised the more likely was the
new religion to be accepted by the ignorant masses.
Thus we find that the Nicene Creed was substantially
altered long after the Council of Nicaea, at some place
unknown, at an unknown date, by some person or
persons unknown, when the miraculous was further
stressed, and on this unauthorised creed rests the
beliefs of the Christian Church to-day.   There is no
need for touching on the Apostles' Creed, as its origin
is unknown.   It has grown out of obscurity, and
cannot be traced in its present form to an earlier
date than the middle of the 8th century.   All

that is known for certain is that the Apostles knew nothing of it, but it was given that name by the Church so as to increase its authority.   The origin of the Athanasian Creed is likewise unknown, and like the Apostles' Creed it was given the name of this leading churchman to increase its prestige, but he was certainly not the author of it, as it was not brought to light for hundreds of years after his death.*   All that need be said of it is that it has caused untold misery for centuries, and it is a document that every decent-minded Christian should be utterly ashamed to repeat as so many do on their special feast days.

The coming of Christianity under State control preserved it as a religion and as an organisation, and this event was the death knell of all other Roman cults and sects.   Had Constantine decided to uphold Mithraism instead of Christianity as the State religion, the latter would have been obliterated instead of Mithraism.   The Emperor Julian, who followed Constantine, went back to Mithraism, but his short reign of less than two years, from 361 to 363, could not change what the strong mind of Constantine had decreed.   Besides this, his defeat and death in battle in Persia, the home of Mithraism, was used by the Christians as an argument against the old and in favour of the new, and was looked on as an omen that Christianity had divine approval.   Had Julian been successful and had a long reign, the entire religious history of Europe would have been different.

Under Jovian, the Emperor who followed, the substitution of Christianity for Mithraism made further headway, and we now find Divine Sonship,

---

* For confirmation of all I say about the Christian Creeds refer to *Encyclopedia Britannica* under *Creeds*.

the Virgin Birth, the Cross, Resurrection, Salvation, Baptism, the Trinity, and the Eucharist, generally accepted as the basis of Christianity. Christianity from now onwards contained these features, which can be traced back to all the religions of the East, but especially to Mithraism, which should be looked on as the parent of the forms, ceremonials, rites, and creeds of Christianity. Christianity absorbed Mithraism and all it stood for, and thus its chief rival in the Roman Empire disappeared.

Mithraism,* the name given to the religion followed by those who worshipped the Sun God Mithra, came to Europe from Persia. From Persia it spread through Europe, including Great Britain. In point of universality it was the most wide-spread religion in the western world in the early centuries of the Christian era. It made its appeal both to freemen and bondmen, and its monumental remains are scattered about in all the countries of Europe, which then included the civilised world.

What, then, were the beliefs of this religion? These go back to a period long before the Christian era. Its followers worshipped the god Mithra, the Deity of Light and Truth created by, yet co-equal with, the Supreme Deity. They believed in the Trinity, the Father, the Son and the Holy Ghost, Mithra being the Son. Mithra was styled '' the most beloved by men,'' and to him were assigned very lofty ideals; he was also the Lamb slain for the sins of the world. They kept Sunday,

---

* Mithraism is considered at great length, and all the authorities referred to, in J. M. Robertson's standard work *Pagan Christs.* Refer also to '' Mithras '' in *Encyclopedia Britannica*, and Chapters 15 and 16 of Gibbon's *Decline and Fall of the Roman Empire*, and *Les Mysteres de Mithra*, by Franz Cumont, *Mithraism and Christianity*, by Patterson, *Mithraism*, by Stuart Jones.

the first day of the week, as their day of worship, and Mithra was its Lord, and Sunday was known as '' The Lord's Day.'' Their chief festivals were what we now call Christmas and Easter. Mithra was born at Christmas and died at Easter. At Easter the formalities representing the death of the Deity were gone through, and what is now called Lent was observed.

What is now termed the Eucharist or the Lord's Supper, or the Holy Communion, was observed, the bread being eaten and the wine drunk in memory of Mithra. Baptism was practised, and a sign believed to be that of the Cross was made on the forehead of the baptised. Mithra was the Logos, the Incarnate Word, and was sacrificed for sin. He was considered the Mediator and Saviour of all believers, conferring on them eternal life in Heaven in return for their belief. The human soul, they believed, had been separated from God, and through this sacrifice attained re-union. Mithra is represented as the Lamb slain for the sins of the world.*

Only after successive pontifical decrees were the people as a whole made to accept Jesus as the World's Saviour instead of Mithra. Mithra was born in a cave, just as in the early Christian writings Jesus is reported as being born in a cave. Shepherds came to adore him and offer him gifts, his mother was a virgin, he was buried in a rock tomb, and when they looked for his body it could not be found. Mithra after death passed into Hades and rose again from the dead, and his followers believed that on the last day a general resurrection of the dead would take place and he would then judge the world.

* Unfortunately no Mithraic documents have survived, and what is known of Mithraism is derived from its monuments and the writings of the early Christian fathers.

In view of this long series of signal parallels between Mithraism and Christianity, what other view can an intelligent individual take than that the doctrines, dogmas and ceremonials of Mithraism were added to the simple teachings of Jesus, when it is known that Mithraism is the older religion of the two? It first became known to the Romans in 70 B.C., but it was an established religion in Persia more than 400 years before Christ. These two religions lived side by side for three centuries until Christianity instead of Mithraism became officially recognised by the State. Christianity, the new State religion, absorbed its rival and they became united under one name, Christianity. There is nothing mysterious about it, all is natural, and all that happened was the dropping of the god Mithra and the substituting of a new god Jesus.

Thus, it is not surprising to find that the older religion supplied the Christians with not only many of their doctrines, symbols, and rites, but their priests with the form of their vestments, and the Vatican Mount, the site of Mithraic worship, with the site for the principal Church of Christendom, in which rests St. Peter's chair, of probable Mithraic origin, and round its dome is graven a Mithraic legend. From Mithraism Christians probably copied the placing of their Churches facing the East, the direction of the rising sun, and also the numerous forms of terminology such as "The Good Shepherd," "The King of Glory," "The Light of the World," "The Lamb of God," "Lord and Father," and "Lord of all."

By 377 we find Christianity sufficiently strong to suppress by force its former rival. In that year

Mithraic worship was suppressed both in Rome and Alexandria. Still it was a formidable opponent, and only slowly did the people forsake the old and adopt the new. Though it was the old wine, yet it was being given to them in a new bottle. Even the Emperor at this date found he had to proceed warily against this esteemed Pagan religion. Once begun, however, the persecution continued, and from being the persecuted, Christians from now onwards became the persecutors, until they finally obliterated as a separate religion that which had contributed to their forms, ceremonies, and beliefs.

It was not, however, till the year 527 that it was decided when Jesus was born, and various monks equipped with astrological learning were called in to decide this important point. Ultimately the Emperor decided that 25th December, the date of the birth of Mithra, be accepted as the date of the birth of Jesus. Up to the year 680 no thought had been given to the symbol of Jesus crucified on the cross. Prior to that date veneration was accorded to the Mithraic symbolic lamb, but from that date onwards it was ordained that in place of the lamb the figure of a man attached to a cross should be substituted.

Our greatest authorities on comparative religion concur with Augustine and Eusebius in their belief that what is called Christianity was borrowed from contemporary or ancient religions, and that it is just a new name for much older beliefs. Robertson in his book *Christianity and Mythology* remarks as follows :—" Christianity we find to be wholly manufactured from pre-existent material within historic

times "*   Sir James Frazer, O.M., F.R.S., the
greatest living authority, remarks in the *Golden
Bough*, that monumental work of eight volumes, as
follows :—" In respect both of doctrines and of rites
the cult of Mithra appears to have presented many
points of resemblance to Christianity.   Taken all
together the coincidences of the Christian with the
Heathen festivals are too close and too numerous to
be accidental.   They mark the compromise which
the Church in its hour of triumph was compelled to
make with its vanquished and yet still dangerous
rivals."

In the past all who studied Christianity in a
logical and rational way were looked on by Christians
as subverters of the truth.   It is therefore interesting
to notice the change which is taking place amongst
enlightened Christians, who are being forced by the
evidence to face the truth.   Canon Streeter, in his
book *The Buddha and the Christ*, published last
year, quotes in support of his argument the following
saying of Newman :—" A great portion of what is
generally received as Christian truth is in its rudi-
ments, or separate parts, to be found in heathen
philosophies and religions."

---

* Mr. Robertson and those who think with him, such as Dr. Drews
and Professor W. B. Smith, consider that because of the numerous legends and myths surrounding the person of Jesus, he
was a purely mythical character, and never lived on earth.
This seems to me to be overstepping the bounds of reason, as
for every effect there must always be a cause. Myths can gather
round an individual and teaching be attributed to him, but we
cannot imagine this happening to one who never lived.
Mr. F. C. Conybeare, in *The Historical Christ*, which I have
read since writing this book, puts in a few words what I have
attempted to do throughout these pages: " The critical method
tries to disengage in the traditions of Jesus the true from the
false, fact from myth, and to show how in the pagan society
(which, as it were, lifted Jesus up out of his Jewish cradle), these
myths inevitably gathered round his figure as mists thicken round
a mountain crest."

I find also in *Mythic Christs and the True*, by the Rev. W. St. Clair Tisdall, M.A., D.D., that only in three instances does he consider that there is no parallel between Mithraism and Christianity. In all the other numerous instances he admits a parallel. The exceptions he takes refer to the belief of the Mithraists that Mithra was born of a virgin, that he was buried in a rock tomb and rose from the dead. In making these exceptions he omits to consider some of the most conclusive evidence in their favour ; but this is by the way, as everything else he fully admits.

As to the story of the virgin birth, death, and resurrection of Jesus, the Christian story was doubtless taken from one of the numerous legends of deified men current at the time, and it would be incorrect to claim that these Christian incidents were solely taken from Mithraism. The evidence is all in favour of their origin being found elsewhere.

According to Mackey's *Lexicon of Freemasonry*, freemasons taught the doctrines of the crucifixion, atonement, and resurrection long before the Christian era. St. Justin, one of the early Christian fathers, argued in favour of the virgin birth, the crucifixion, resurrection and ascension of Jesus, because Christians claimed no more than the pagans did for their saviours.

Many who have studied the question believe that the origin of the crucifixion of saviour god-men at Easter came from the crossing by the sun over the equinoctial line at the commencement of Spring, as, with its increased heat, vegetation flourished and the people were saved from starvation. The chief pagan festivals were held at what we now call Christmas and Easter, the first when the sun enters the winter solstice and the days begin to lengthen, and the other when it reaches the plane of the equator and the days are of equal length.   The god-man was believed to have been born on the day the sun commences to return to give heat and life to the earth, just as it was believed that he died, rose again, and ascended into Heaven, which was symbolical of the death of winter, the return of life with spring, and the ascent of the sun into the heavens, which culminates at midsummer.

With regard to the virgin birth legend, this was attributed to so many outstanding men and gods that it was just as common to attribute a miraculous birth to a great man in those days as it was in the Christian era for a king to claim that he ruled by divine right, which claim was the rudiment of the belief in a supernatural birth.   To attribute to an outstanding man a supernatural birth was the greatest honour those who followed him could think of bestowing on his memory.   As those great ones had supernatural births conferred on them, likewise they had attributed to them in many instances supernatural deaths ; and so we find, as Mr. Vivian Phelips says in *The Churches and Modern Thought*, that "of all the old world legends the death and resurrection of a virgin-born, or in some way divinely-born, Saviour was the most widespread."

As to the death and resurrection of Jesus, I think that there is no difficulty in discovering that the story originated in Babylon, and that it is just a copy, with elaborations, of the story of the trial, death and resurrection of the god Bel, to which has been added the details of the death, and what accompanied it, related of the god Prometheus.

The account of the death of the Greek God Prometheus, more than 500 years before Christ, records how he descended to earth for the sake of elevating humanity, and after a short time on earth he was tried and sentenced to death. He was chained to a rock on Mount Caucasus, and through his death the gates of Heaven were opened to all believers. Seneca, the great Roman historian, and other writers, record this story. At the death of Prometheus the earth shook and the whole frame of Nature became convulsed, the rocks were rent, the graves opened, and the dead came out of them "when the Saviour gave up the ghost." He then rose from the dead and ascended into Heaven. The story of this god is similar to that recorded of Jesus, and "it is doubtful whether there is to be found in the whole range of Greek literature deeper pathos than that of the divine woe of the god Prometheus crucified on the Scythian Crags for his love to mortals," says *The New American Cyclopedia*. Ovid, the Roman poet, put in verse the story of the Saviour God Esculapius, whose virgin birth, life and death follow much on the same lines as the story of Jesus.

The sacrifice of a saviour-god was quite a common belief in ancient religions and took similar forms, all for the purpose of appeasing a Deity. At the time of the birth and growth of the Christian religion, the form in vogue attributed to the god-man the desire to take the world's sins and thus redeem humanity. He became the sacrifice in place of humanity, and thus appeased the Almighty. The

E

legend of the death of Prometheus is just one of many, and the account of the death of the Babylonian god Bel, known to the Jews as Baal, is just another. The Egyptian god Osiris and the Greek god Dionysos were believed to have had experiences similar to those told about Jesus.   Dionysos was termed "The only Begotten," "The Born Again," and "The Saviour," but they all received epithets similar to those later bestowed on Jesus.

From the translation of a tablet discovered in Babylonia it is evident that their god Bel was believed to have had experiences similar to those at a later date attributed to Jesus.   This tablet of Babylonian origin, produced hundreds of years before the Christian era (some believe 2,000 years), giving the record of the Babylonian Passion Drama, when placed alongside of the chief events recorded in the Christian Drama, is remarkably similar, so much so that I shall now record what it reveals, and give alongside the corresponding events of the Christian Story.

BABYLONIAN LEGEND.	CHRISTIAN LEGEND.
Bel is taken prisoner.	Jesus is taken prisoner.
Bel is tried in the Hall of Justice.	Jesus is tried in the Hall of Pilate.
Bel is smitten.	Jesus is scourged.
Bel is led away to the Mount.	Jesus is led away to Golgotha.
With Bel are taken two malefactors, one of whom is released.	With Jesus two malefactors are led away; another, Barabbas, is released.
After Bel has gone to the Mount the City breaks out into tumult.	At the death of Jesus the veil of the Temple is rent: from the graves come forth the dead, and enter the City.
Bel's clothes are carried away.	Jesus's robe is divided among the soldiers.

Bel goes down into the Mount and disappears from life.	Jesus from the grave goes down into the realm of the dead.
A weeping woman seeks him at the gate of burial.	Mary Magdalene came weeping to the tomb to seek Jesus.
Bel is brought back to life.	Jesus rises from the grave alive.

As this discovery is of comparatively recent date, and has consequently received little publicity, I called on the Curator of the Babylonian section of the British Museum to obtain confirmation of the existence of this tablet and its correct translation. I was told that the particulars I have given can be correctly considered as "a list of parallel instances (which was drawn up by the late Professor Zimmern) found both in the story of the god Bel and of the Christ. Zimmern deduced the incidents of the story of Bel from ritual texts which seem to describe a primitive kind of religious play." This confirmation as I have given it was received by me in writing and I have it now beside me as I write.

Each event recorded on the tablet is believed to have been the name given to each act of the drama, and it is not unreasonable to believe that this Babylonian programme was the basis round which the gospel writers wound the story about Jesus, each as we know differing as to details, but similar throughout. These Passion Dramas were quite common in the East prior to the Christian era, and the one favoured by the Jews, some authorities think, had as the suffering god-man one called Jesus Barabbas, Barabbas meaning "The Son of the Father."

A careful study of the gospel legends of the great Christian drama had led some authorities to believe that the story relating to Jesus of Nazareth was written from the chief events of a Passion Play, and this Babylonian discovery proves that the Christian story did not originate in Palestine. This discovery certainly lends added weight to this explanation of the origin of the great Christian drama, especially as there is hardly a detail of the agony, trial, crucifixion, resurrection, and ascension, as told about Jesus, that was not told about gods who preceded him, and those gods were believed to rise from the dead at the time of the year we call Easter, at the Spring Equinox, when the dead of winter has passed. They went through similar experiences before and after their deaths as are reported as happening to Jesus, and in those days of old, when only the priests could read or write, the people were kept in memory of it all by means of this Passion Drama. These passion dramas were continued by Christianity, and we find them recorded in the early days of this religion.

The special interest to us of the Babylonian account is that we have at last discovered the actual programme of the drama, which confirms the conclusion previously reached by men who have given the subject a life study, that the gospel story is just the legend of what was told in drama of other suffering saviour-gods. At each act prior to the drama being enacted the priest is believed to have either read or told the assembled throng what was about to occur and its meaning.

In the popular pre-Christian religions of Greece, Egypt, Asia, and, as we have seen of Babylon, the dramatic representation of the principal episodes in the lives of the suffering gods were regularly enacted. Herodotus tells us that this took place in Egypt, the god being Osiris. Likewise we find the same dramatic representation in connection with the gods Adonis, Attis, Mithra and Dionysos. The mythological explanation is doubtless the same, the annual death and resurrection of vegetation which was closely connected with the waxing and the waning of the sun. Thus we find these beliefs translated into annual festivals in connection with the worship of both Vegetation Gods and Sun Gods.

The various myths attributed to other gods evidently slowly came to centre round Jesus, and these were added to the early Christian writings. This also seems to have happened with the Passion Dramas connected with other gods, which also were made to have reference to Jesus. A careful reading of the gospel narratives with this in mind will perhaps make clear much that was previously difficult to understand.

Take each episode of the climax of the life of Jesus, especially as related in Matthew and Mark, and it will be realised that the narrative could easily have had as its basis this passion play centred round the god Bel. The theatrical character of the gospel story can be traced out in each event, and if anyone is sufficiently interested this whole subject will be found carefully reasoned out by Mr. John M. Robertson, who was a great authority on Shakespearean drama, in *Pagan Christs*, where much space and thought is devoted to each event recorded in the gospels. When he wrote this book the Babylonian tablet, to which I have just referred, had not been

discovered. This discovery was all that was necessary
to establish the reasonableness of Robertson's argument, taken as it was from what we know occurred
in other religions, as with the actual programme of
the Babylonian passion play now before us the
probable source has been discovered of the Christian
story.

Thus we find that a supposed event, the belief
in which has had an immeasurable influence on countless millions of lives, rests on natural phenomena,
namely the annual decrease and increase of the power
of the sun, and the consequent death and re-birth of
vegetation each year.   This was translated into the
death and resurrection of god-men.   The legends surrounding these events were dramatised in various
countries by different religions, and copied by Christians in the first or second century of our era, so as
to bring their religion up to the same level in regard
to the life, death and resurrection of its founder, as
was claimed by rival cults of that age with regard
to their saviours.

The foregoing explains why nothing was recorded in the archives of Rome about what the gospels
tell us happened to Jesus and why all the Roman
historians of the time failed to record it.   Gibbon
could never understand why men of the high intellectual level of Seneca, Pliny, Tacitus, Plutarch, Epictetus and many others could obtain no sane or sensible
statement from the Christians of the first century with
regard to their religion, and if all that the gospels
report as happening to Jesus is true, is it not extraordinary that those great thinkers and writers could
never obtain this information from the Christians of

their time? What a wonderful story it would have been, what a sensation it would have caused, and yet their writings ignore it all!

Is it not also remarkable that in spite of the marvellous works reported as being performed by Jesus, the Jews during his life considered him only a blasphemer, as one who wished to upset the beliefs of the people in the orthodox religion of his day? It is quite contrary to all reason that they should have considered him only as such if the gospel stories are true.

Even among savages one who was believed to have the power to bring the dead back to life would never have been made to suffer and to die. Surely it is more rational to accept the account of Jesus as given in the Jewish Talmud as the more probable story. *The Talmud,* containing the traditional laws of the Jews, and dating back to the second century, gives a very different story about Jesus to what is contained in the gospels. There the only reference made to him is the statement that he was arrested for blasphemy, was tried in the Jewish Court, condemned, stoned, and then hung on a tree, which, by the way, agrees with what we are told in Acts **13-29** as to how he died. This is a much more probable story than the gospel legends, filled with marvellous and miraculous occurrences, which no contemporary of Jesus considered worthy to record. Let us all, as sensible individuals, forget the mistakes of our early training, and believe that Jesus was born in a natural way, lived a natural life and died a martyr's death for his convictions. Let us relegate the miraculous in the Christian story to its right place with that of the mythologies surrounding the lives of other gods. We now know that this is where it should be placed, and that as regards the final drama, as recorded in Christian mythology, of the life of the Christian God, it is but a version in words of an earlier passion play, incorporated into Christianity, a play which, for centuries before Christianity was thought of, was enacted annually throughout the East, to satisfy the human longing for further knowledge with regard to the hereafter, which all those early religions show was just as strong then as it is to-day.

The study of Religion proves beyond the shadow of doubt that mankind in ignorance of his future, yet instinctively feeling that he persisted after death, has been immeasurably helped by the beliefs and ceremonies of religion. They have acted as a crutch to him throughout his earthly pilgrimage. True, he has been exploited by priests and religious organisations who have taken advantage of his craving for further knowledge. On the whole, however, they have helped to make life possible for him, as without their aid life would have been intolerable. Round the inherent instinct of all men and women that they have immortal souls, and that there is a greater power in the universe than themselves, have been coiled superstitions which in various ways make up the world's different religions. In ignorance man has practised cruelties in his attempt to placate what he considered was a wrathful Deity. He has imagined the necessity for a mediator between himself and God, and these mediators throughout the ages have taken different forms, and been surrounded by different ceremonies, but still the same golden thread runs through it all—the instinctive belief that humanity is destined for something more than this world has to give. In mankind's evolution, as he slowly developed in intelligence, he has suffered much through ignorance, because of this one ruling passion, this fervent desire for further knowledge of the mysteries of life and death.

The Greek thinkers of the golden age of Rome and Greece developed a philosophy for which the world was not ready. They appeared like an oasis in a desert of ignorance. Their high and pure thoughts could not be communicated to humanity, as it was not yet ready for them. Humanity still required a saviour, a god-man, forms, ceremonials and creeds, and so Christianity developed quite naturally out of other religions, and took the place it was fitted for, as the need for it was there. Mental development has continued, however, and some of us now foresee a more rational religion for humanity through the only revelation which has come to us from the other world and which proves that the after-life is a reality, and that we are undoubtedly Etheric beings.

Now that this proof positive has come so will go slowly from the minds of mankind the belief in crucified saviours, in god-men and all that appertains to them, whatever may be the cult to which they belong. The drapings only will go, but the great essentials, which are necessary to satisfy humanity, are becoming more apparent than ever. Naturally, amongst the uneducated, opposition is always apparent, as the unthinking always believe that what is must always be. The Egyptians always boasted that for ten thousand years the hand of man had never been allowed to touch one of the sacred monuments in their temples.   Orthodoxy in Egypt, just as in Great Britain, had ruled that God's revelation, as given by his authorised priests, was final and complete.   As Egypt changed so Britain will change, but we need not fear the change, as a bright and glorious dawn is succeeding the world's night of ignorance.

Just as the discoveries in Babylonia and Egypt are proving to us that Christianity is not a revealed religion but simply a new name given to the forms, ceremonies, and beliefs of the ancient world, so there is opening out before us a wealth of beauty and thought contained in the new revelation coming to mankind from the Etheric World.   Mankind finds he is not alone in his journey to some unknown destination, that he is now in contact with those who have made the change called death, and that they are now coming back to help him and guide him on his onward course.   With this increased knowledge he can throw away the crutch of orthodoxy, and step out relieved from this now unnecessary encumbrance.   To us the future is bright instead of being dark, and what was a great and awful mystery has now become clear, as the result of our increased knowledge.

In our coming freedom from the superstitions of the past we must thank not only those who have helped in opening the way for communication with the Etheric World, and thus setting our minds at rest with regard to our future.   There are others besides who have also helped, by increasing our knowledge of the past, and making us understand more clearly that what we thought was a divine revelation is but a continuation of the beliefs of earlier religions. Just as the discovery of the use of steam revolutionised our industrial life, so did the discovery of how to read the Babylonian and Egyptian languages revolutionise our religious outlook. These two latter discoveries must be looked back on as amongst the great events of the world's history, and they have been the means of making us understand the Bible in a way that we never could have done had these discoveries not been made.

Sir Henry Rawlinson was responsible for the decipherment of the old Babylonian language which was forgotten. In 1835 he took from the Behistun Rock near Babylon a copy of what turned out to be a decree of King Darius written in Babylonian, Scythian, and Persian. He made paper casts of this inscription, and it was possible, owing to the fact that the Persian was known, to translate the Babylonian and the Scythian. In consequence of this discovery, the numerous Babylonian tablets since found have been translated, and much of what is found in the Old and New Testaments can now be traced to Babylon. The stories of Adam and Eve, the Flood, the Tower of Babel, and other events, were all current in Babylonia long before a book of our Bible was written. They were copied there by the Jews when in captivity. The story of Moses being hidden in the bulrushes was obviously taken from Babylon, as we have discovered a similar story relating to Sargon, an early king of Babylon, the river in his case being the Euphrates. Sargon, by the way, was in time looked on as a God, was accredited with a virgin birth, and most of the miraculous wonders ascribed to all the great men of the past were likewise ascribed to him.

Just as we have learned much of Babylonian history from the discovery of how to read their cunei-form writing, so have we discovered much of Egyptian history through learning how to read Egyptian hieroglyphics. This came about through the discovery of what is called the Rossetta stone found at the mouth of the Nile near Rossetta, when Napoleon invaded Egypt in 1798. It contains a decree in honour of Ptolemy and is written in Hiero-glyphic, Demotic and Greek. As the Greek was known the others could be translated. These dis-coveries throw much light on the stories in the Bible, as both countries greatly influenced the political and religious history of the Jews.

Likewise both countries contributed much to the origin of Christianity. This religion was not born from one single parent but from many. Its rites, symbols, ceremonials, teachings, doctrines and legends were all derived from countries surrounding Palestine, and the religion of each helped to make Christianity what it became in the fourth century. What is called Christianity was then a reservoir into which flowed the best of all the old world religions. The reason the best was accepted, and the worst discarded, was because those who were responsible for its growth lived at a time when that part of the world, in which the religion grew up, had reached a very high state of culture. Consequently only the pure was accepted from contemporary religions, and the impure rejected. They accepted the superstitions because it was a superstitious age, but the high moral tone of Christianity is undoubtedly due to the fact that it was born at a time when the wisdom of Rome and Greece was at its height. The first century of its life was a time of greater wisdom, and then lived men of greater eminence, than the world had ever previously known.

Thus Christianity, apart from the cruel laws and impurity noticeable in Judaism, to which it is so inseparably bound, is on a higher moral and spiritual level than any of the other older religions. Its morality, its teachings, and its outlook on life are certainly higher than that of any previous religion, due to the high level of culture prevailing in that part of the world in which it took root. Both Greece and Rome had reached the highest level of thought so far attained by humanity. It was an age when much wisdom and a high morality were preached by the great pagan philosophers and thinkers. Those responsible for the preparation of the Christian documents were certainly influenced by the fact that they lived in an age of pure philosophic thought, but they were imbued also with much of the superstition of the ignorant. Consequently their writings are but poor fragments when compared with the wealth and depth of thought and wisdom expressed in the literature of the great pagan philosophers.

Christianity being born in this atmosphere, those responsible for its writings were influenced by the times in which they lived. Pagan literature is known only to the few, as our educational system ignores it, and from childhood upwards we are taught that all we have and are to-day is the result of Christianity. This is quite wrong. Cicero, Marcus Aurelius, and

Seneca, to mention only three great pagans, teach
a higher spiritual philosophy, containing higher
aspirations of virtue, toleration, and humanity, than
any other teachers of or before their time. We ignore
the source whence sprang the high level of culture of
these times, and in ignorance we attribute to Christianity what really came from Paganism.

Unfortunately when Christianity obliterated the
old religions of Rome and Greece it also submerged
their philosophy, the place of which was taken by
creeds and dogmas, so much so, that to believe in
the Trinity and other Church dogmas was the test of
a good Christian, and not his life. The teaching of
the great Pagan writers and thinkers was buried under
the dogmas of the Church, and so Europe entered
the dark ages. It emerged from them only when the
Pagan teachings were relearned in the sixteenth
century. What is called "Our Christian Civilisation" is therefore due to the great classical thinkers
who lived between 600 B.C. and 200 A.D.

Unfortunately, when Christianity triumphed
under Constantine, the civilised world received a set
back from which it did not recover for 1,300 years.
As Farrer, that thoughtful classical authority, says
in his book *Paganism and Christianity*, "There is
indeed no fact more patent in history than that with
the triumph of Christianity under Constantine the
older and finer spirit of charity died out of the world,
and gave place to an intolerance and bigotry which
were its extreme antithesis, and which only in recent
years have come to be mitigated." What a mental
and moral gulf there is between non-Christian men
such as Seneca, Plato, Marcus Aurelius, or Plutarch,

and Athanasius, Tertullian and Jerome, to mention
only three of the earlier Christian Fathers, with their
warped and narrow minds, writing always with the
object of compressing the human mind into their
narrow creeds and dogmas. What a contrast there
is between the high and noble humanitarian aspirations
expressed by the Pagans, and the creeds and dogmas
of the Christian Church!

It is utterly false to say that the idea of the
brotherhood of man originated in the teaching of
Christianity. It is one of the dominant ideas of
pagan philosophy before Christianity was thought of.
Marcus Aurelius rises from the common conception
of the political community to that of the wider community of humanity with a breadth of mind that at
no time has belonged to the Church. He and others
like him envisaged mankind in one common brotherhood, each working for the good of humanity. It
was a primary tenet of the higher pagan faith that
every man, inasmuch as he shared the spirit of God,
should consider himself as a Son of God, and that
it therefore behoved him to conduct himself in a
manner befitting such a relationship, and to regard
all his fellow men as brethren by virtue of their
belonging to the same family as himself. What a
contrast between the sublime writings and thoughts
of the Great Pagans, and the cruelties, wars, perse-
cutions, and numberless horrors, which were the
outcome of Christianity, as the result of its followers'
belief that it was the only true religion, and that all
must believe in it or everlastingly perish.

The general belief held by most people that
Christianity was responsible for raising the moral and

spiritual level of the Roman world is a pious illusion
for which there is not a particle of evidence.   By the
fifth century we find all the schools of philosophy
closed, all education and learning banned, all the
worst of paganism continuing, and the best obliterated,
and Europe in a night of intense darkness, which
lasted for more than a thousand years.   Daylight
came only when people became intelligent enough
to doubt the Christian story and the claims of the
Christian religion, and from that date the less they
have been believed the better and happier has become
the world.

   Much teaching attributed to Jesus is considered
by many to be peculiar to him and him only, and
it is supposed that he was the first to teach love,
gentleness, the love of God, and other virtues.   This
is quite wrong, though this false way of regarding his
teaching is encouraged by the Church, which claims
that he originated all these injunctions.   I cannot
count the number of sermons I have heard upholding
this falsehood.

   Long before the time of Jesus there were
teachers who taught everything that has been attributed to him, and there is nothing of value attributed
to him that was not said before his time.   "Return
good for evil and overcome anger with love," and
"he that would cherish me let him go and cherish
his sick comrade," were sayings of Buddha.
"Do unto others as you would that they should
do unto you" was said by Confucius.   "Whenever thou art in doubt as to whether an action
is good or bad abstain from it" was said by
Zoroaster a thousand years before Christ.   "One

who is injured ought not to return the injury, for on no account can it be right to do an injustice, and it is not right to return an injury or to do any evil to any man, however much we may have suffered from him" was said by Socrates 450 years before Christ. "Let us not listen to those who think that we ought to be angry with our enemies, and who believe this to be great and manly. Nothing is more praiseworthy, nothing so clearly shows a great and noble soul, as clemency and readiness to forgive" was said by Cicero 70 years before Christ. "If a man strike thee and in striking thee drop his staff, pick it up and hand it to him again" was said by Krishna centuries before Jesus was born. Similar teachings could be quoted from numerous sources in great numbers, attributed to men who lived hundreds of years before Jesus was born. The immortality of the soul was taught by the Hindus, Egyptians, Greeks and Romans, and many others. It is one of the earliest beliefs and is found in every religion.

What is termed "The Lord's Prayer" originated in Babylon about 4000 B.C., the tablet on which is written a prayer resembling it, being discovered in 1882. It is one of the oldest Jewish prayers, repeated for long by them in the Chaldaic language, they having learned it in Babylon during their captivity. The high morality and ethical teachings attributed to Jesus can all be found in many pre-Christian writings, such as the Bhagavat Gita, the sacred book of India, and in the writings of Seneca, Ovid, Aristotle, Epictetus, Plato, and many others.

As Thomas Whittaker in his able work, *The Origins of Christianity*, truly remarks, "It is a remark-

F

able fact that Christianity, said to have been revealed, has had to recur for every serious effort to find in the universe the manifestations of a rational and moral order, to thinkers who never pretended to have obtained what they might offer in this direction by anything but the exercise of their own reason.''

Those who have made a study of the origin of Christian literature are of the opinion that the various events and sayings recorded in the gospels can all be traced to earlier origins than the events to which they refer.   The four gospels are therefore the result of the collation of ancient stories and traditions prevalent in the East at the time they were written.

From a careful study of the four Gospel narratives, from the knowledge we now possess of the religious beliefs prevalent in the East 1,900 years ago, and from what we now know of the history of the Roman Empire at that time, it is possible to follow up quite a natural event right through its various developments.

I would divide these into four stages, thus :—

First Stage :   Natural birth of Jesus some years prior to 4 B.C., as Herod died in that year.   In his youth he worked with his father.   He was religiously inclined, and either joined the Essene Brotherhood or studied their beliefs, living with them probably until he was about 30 years of age.   He then went out as a teacher and healer, going from place to place over a period of less than two years.

His strong psychic power made him able to heal the sick.   He was perhaps clairvoyant and clairaudient, and so could speak with some authority of the Etheric World, which to him at times might become a reality. He attracted followers by the realistic way in which he could present his views, and his high ethical teaching made him revered by all who knew him. Maybe he was controlled at times by higher intelligences in the Etheric World and was able to impress the people by his gift of speech.

He incurred the anger of the authorities by his outspoken remarks on the orthodox Church and priests of his day. This led to his martyrdom, as it has led to the martyrdom of many reformers both before and after him. Quite possibly he was seen after his death by some of his followers. Owing to our present-day knowledge of psychic matters what seemed miraculous in those days, namely, his healing power, his other psychic gifts, and his being seen in his etheric body after death, can now be related to natural laws. What seemed unique then is to-day recognised as of more or less common occurrence.

Second Stage : Paul comes on the scene, believes he has had a vision of Jesus, also a message, and with his great personality confirms the disheartened band of Jews in the belief that Jesus was the Messiah foretold by the prophets. As it was believed that the world was about to come to an end, nothing of the doings or sayings of Jesus was put in writing, and as time went on these were handed down from father to son, with the tendency always to exaggerate and to emphasise the miraculous. Paul went about preaching this message of hope, and as the adherents of this new sect grew he wrote them letters.

The fall of Jerusalem in 70 A.D. helped to consolidate the new cult, as many in despair, as the result of the break up of Judaism, joined the new sect, being encouraged by its belief that the Messiah would soon reincarnate to restore his kingdom. The incubation period of the new sect dates most likely from this date until the end of the first century.

Either just before or just after the fall of Jerusalem began to appear, perhaps in Antioch, a narrative of this much talked of Jesus, giving a description of his simple life, sayings, and doings, and incorporating much borrowed from Essene sources. Other narratives followed, each tending to emphasise the miraculous. A diary of the Acts of the Apostles also appears relating what is claimed to be the deeds of the apostles.

The new sect is now known by the name of Christian, and Jesus to many has definitely become the Messiah, who had fulfilled all the prophecies of old. Slowly the belief changed from regarding Jesus as an earthly deliverer to that of a spiritual mediator. Thus this doctrine, attributed to Paul, took root, and the way was prepared for what was to become orthodox Christianity in the fourth century.

Third Stage : The new sect gets so strong that its leaders become ambitious, imbued by the desire to succeed to the theocratic powers of the Jewish hierarchy and found a world religion. Other sects with whom they are in contact claim their founders to be divine, as having had miraculous births, and that miraculous events had occurred at their deaths. Gradually what was attributed to other religious founders or deities was attributed to Jesus, so that by the second century after his death he was looked on by some as divine, but by others as a teacher only. Numerous writings by this time are in existence, some emphasising this divine aspect, others entirely ignoring it, and everyone differing as regards facts. It is considered by some that many of the doctrines attributed to Paul are of a much later date than his time, and that to him like Jesus was attributed sayings and doings, so as to give the authority of his name to the doctrines of the Church of the time.*

Fourth Stage : The last stage comes when this sect attracts the attention of Imperial Rome, and Constantine decrees that it is to become the State religion of the future, thus displacing Mithraism which had been the State religion of Rome for the previous 200 years. From the time of the Council of Nicaea onwards the consolidation of Christianity into an organised religion is rapid. As it had become the new State religion then it must not be inferior to its rival Mithraism which it had superseded. Four gospels in which the miraculous is emphasised are chosen out of the many, and then and later further miraculous incidents are added.

Biblical scholars can now easily trace how the early records have been added to and how what were originally simple records of a simple life became augmented with miraculous events. Thus, a life which was in every way human became embellished for the purpose of making it appear divine.

Some of the various letters which were attributed to the apostles also came to rank as divine documents along with the four gospels, but they, like the gospels, had been or were altered from time to time to suit the growing belief in the miraculous.

---

* A very interesting book on this subject has recently been published entitled *Was St. Paul right or Christ?* by Hamilton McGregor.

This sect had now become a strong organisation, and in taking the place of the old Mithraic religion it incorporated in its creed, dogmas, and doctrines the mystic beliefs and rites of the older religion, but as the gospels and epistles had been written prior to this absorption, these added beliefs and ceremonials were absent in the gospels and epistles of that time. This omission was so obvious to the Church authorities that interpolations and additions were made from time to time and these are well known to all New Testament scholars.

For instance, the only reference to the Trinity in the Bible occurs in the 1st Epistle of St. John, 5th chapter, 7th verse. This reference is not found in any Greek manuscript, as the Doctrine of the Trinity was not part of the Church's teaching until it was incorporated into Christianity at the Council of Nicaea. Consequently this verse is now omitted from the Revised Version of the Bible which was published in 1881.

In the Revised Version of the New Testament there is no reference whatever to the Trinity, and the Church has not a scrap of authority for claiming that Jesus is God and part of God, and that they together with the Holy Ghost make up one God. The intelligent leaders of the Church to-day know this, but in spite of the fact that they have not a particle of evidence to produce to justify the preaching of this doctrine, they continue Sunday after Sunday deluding the people and making them think that they have divine authority for this assertion. Never a Sunday passes but the clergy, of the Anglican and Roman Churches especially, repeat at various times through-

out the service the phrase in one form or another,
"In the Name of God the Father, God the Son,
and God the Holy Ghost." If they are in the least
intelligent they must know full well that this fundamental doctrine of Christianity, on which the whole
edifice of superstition is built, has no justification
whatever, and that the doctrine of the Trinity is an
ancient belief, which can be traced back for thousands
of years into the dim and misty past. Many other
instances could be given of what is now part of Christianity, but was quite unknown as such to the original
writers of the gospels ; but this is all that space
permits.*

As the Bible has played and still plays such a
large part in Protestant Christianity this chapter
would not be complete without some consideration of
its origin, and how it has come to us in its present
form. This being so, I shall now give a short history
of what Christians call

THE HOLY BIBLE.

I have calculated that during my life I have
listened to at least two thousand sermons, but I do
not remember hearing a parson on any occasion ever
refer to the origin of the Christian religion. Neither
can I remember ever hearing a parson tell of the origin
of the Holy Bible. Our religious teachers ignore
origins for the very obvious reason that when we

---

* Anyone wishing to pursue this subject further should read *Christianity
in the Light of Modern Knowledge*, especially the able contribution by Dr. Gilbert Murray (Professor of Greek at Oxford University), which shows clearly how Christianity developed out of the
beliefs of the superstitious and ignorant cults which abounded in
the countries surrounding Palestine 1,900 years ago, all having
their crucified Saviour-Gods and beliefs similar to what gathered
round the simple teachings of Jesus, which medley of different
beliefs came to be known as Christianity.

begin to look into the question of the origin of Christianity, or the origin of the books of the Bible, we find that the Church's claims for these have no foundation whatever. As I could therefore get no information on this subject from our official religious teachers, I have studied the subject for over thirty years and have found that the claims and assertions they make for Christianity have no basis and are quite untrue. It might here be said by some : " Why worry about an old book, or why worry about what the parson says? No intelligent person to-day takes a parson seriously." This is to some extent true, but at the same time there are many people who still look on the Bible as their sheet anchor and as their guide to another life, even as they still look on the parson as their one and only source of information as to the after-life. Besides this, there are still many people who attend Church regularly, who go through the service and accept it without question or doubt. The Church has its hold over the people of to-day solely because the average individual accepts everything that is told him and does not think for himself.

On the other hand there are a large number, and an increasing number, who are so dissatisfied with the Church and its teachings that they have ceased to attend divine service, preferring to believe nothing rather than something which outrages their reason. An increasing number are now attending Spiritualist services, which appeal more strongly to their reason and conscience.

In the old days everyone went to church regularly and accepted the words of the parson as if he were a divinely inspired authority as to how we should live in this world, and what we must do to reach the next. To-day, however, this is not so, and few intelligent people would think of making the parson their confidant with regard to their religious beliefs, for the simple reason that the average individual realises that a parson is just a cog in a wheel, that he has been taught certain theological maxims, which he has accepted without thinking, and that his business is to try to keep the old beliefs alive as long as possible, and discourage any intelligent enquiry into their foundations.

I do not wish it to be thought that I am other than on the best of terms with parsons of enlightened minds. With these I have much in common, and some of my best friends are parsons, though I regret that they do not preach from the pulpit in the same way as they speak to me out of it. There are some who believe that if the Church would honestly face the facts with which religion is concerned, it would concede that Spiritualism is the truth and must ultimately prevail.

When, however, I condemn the clergy it is to the majority that I refer, and the organisation to which they belong. I cannot but feel that the minority, if they put the truth first, would help forward the coming day, whereas they are content to do nothing but wait till their congregations are ready for the new revelation, instead of feeling that their duty is to preach the truth, and the truth only.

It is not for the pew to lead the pulpit, but the reverse, and except for the very few who make a stand for truth, the standard of intellectual honesty amongst the clergy is by no means high. They seem quite content to jog along and follow their daily routine without the consciousness that their responsibility is a great one and that their first duty is to tell the truth, no matter whether they offend the more ignorant members of their congregation or not.

I am one of the first to admire the unselfish social work of many clergy in the slums and elsewhere, but these activities are quite apart from those with which this book is concerned. Many others besides the clergy of the orthodox faith are engaged in missions to the poor, Spiritualists, Unitarians, Freethinkers, and others being amongst them. It is not the social side of the Church's work that this book attacks, but orthodox Christianity as preached from nearly every pulpit in Christendom, and it is this which affects the great majority of the people.

If I were not able to put before the people a better religion, a truer religion, and a greater religion for them to observe and follow, I would not trouble to attack what is false, as it gives a certain measure of comfort to many. Spiritualism, however, is an infinitely greater help to us in our lives and also in our deaths than the old faiths which satisfied our ancestors. My wish is not to knock down and destroy. My aim is to build a nobler edifice, but before this edifice can be built decaying rubbish about its foundations must be cleared away.

Hundreds of thousands of men and women have wasted their lives studying the Bible, trying to make all its contradictions harmonise, trying to find out what exactly was God's scheme of salvation, a subject on which so many disagreed. They have wasted their time trying to explain its cruelties, abominations and absurdities, trying to justify every crime, trying to turn a God of vengeance and injustice into a God of Love. All this time has been wasted on documents of no historical value whatever. If they had spent their time in an intelligent way trying to discover the origin of the books of the Bible, who wrote them, and when they were written, it would have been more to their advantage.

If they had spent their time studying the history of the times in which the various books were written, they would have discovered that those books as a foundation for religious faith do not deserve any serious consideration, and that it would have been much better to spend their time studying the Book of Nature, the real Bible, or the works of the great thinkers and philosophers of the past.

To very many, therefore, the Bible and the Christian Faith are a continual stumbling block to their acceptance of Spiritualism, the name given to the New Revelation. They are tied to the tradition of the past, and quote texts from some ancient Biblical book as if that settled everything. Many also believe that all that can be known of this life and the next is already known, that it has been revealed to us only in the Holy Scriptures, and that nothing beyond this revelation has ever been given to mankind. They hold the view that revelation stopped when the writer of the Book of Revelation finished the last word. They believe that God has been silent from that time onwards, and that the Holy Bible contains everything man needs to know and ought to know with regard to his life here and hereafter.

Though some will read this book who are sufficiently enlightened to realise that even to discuss the unreliability of the Holy Scriptures is a waste of time, as it is so self-evident, yet there are doubtless many who have never given the matter a thought and have always accepted what they have been told. Consequently, this attitude of mind makes them unreceptive of the new truths which are coming through to this earth from the Etheric World, to which we shall all pass in time.   Without, therefore, wishing to weary anyone by the recital of what is so obvious to many, let us consider something of the origin and history of what the clergy each Sunday refer to, either as the "Word of God" or the "Holy Scriptures." Each Christian Church has in it a Bible, and for this reason alone it is not out of place to consider something more about this book than is ever told to congregations from the pulpit.

The Bible is made up of two sections, one the Old Testament and the other the New Testament.   The origins of these two sections are very different, and it was not until the 6th century that they were brought together.   It was not until the year 405 that Jerome translated the Old Testament from the Hebrew, and the Old Testament as we know it to-day was not even then accepted among the Jews.   Since that date certain books were added and certain books were left out, but no one can say on what basis or by what authority the books in the Old Testament as we now know it were retained.   However, Jerome made a start by translating the writings now known as the

Old Testament, but it was not until the 9th century of the Christian era that we find the Bible in the shape and form approximating our present Bible, though it contained a number of books omitted at the Reformation. But let us go back to the beginning.

After two hundred years of slavery a tribe as ignorant and cruel as savages, just escaped from bondage under the rulers of Egypt, found its way into what is now called Palestine under a leader called Moses. They were poor and wretched, without any education and knowledge of the arts, but with doubtless some of the mystical knowledge derived from their time in the Land of the Nile. Their leader Moses, who we are told had been raised in the family of Pharoah, was doubtless more learned than the others, as he must have received as much education as it was possible to give anyone in those ignorant times. Moses was a great leader, and unfortunately died before his people settled in what they called the Promised Land. He was followed by Joshua, and gradually this wandering tribe conquered and took possession of what is to-day known as Palestine. After a time kings began to reign over them, but it is all a very chequered story. One after another of the kings did evil in the sight of the Lord, and the bad kings were succeeded sometimes by good and sometimes by worse. The surrounding tribes were continually pressing in on them, and wars, famines, and pestilences were frequent occurrences, but the climax came when this people was at last conquered by King Nebuchadnezzar of Babylon, in 586 B.C., who took them into captivity and subjected them to many indignities.

At last after many vicissitudes they regained their land about **74** years later, and their history is now obtained from the writings of various men who went under the name of prophets or seers. It is a very incomplete history, in which there are many gaps, and the last the Bible has to tell of them are the events that took place about the year **397** before the birth of Christ. They were conquered later by the Romans in **63** B.C. and kept in bondage, their miseries being relieved only by their belief that the Messiah, promised of old, would come on earth and become the nation's leader in driving out the hated conquerors. The New Testament recording the birth, life and death of Jesus, and the letters about him attributed to some of his followers, and a record of some of their doings after his death, complete the Bible story.

The Children of Israel made certain laws, and their seers recorded how sinful the people were from time to time, and these records were contained in what they called the Book of the Law, this book being kept in the Holy of Holies of the Temple. The time came when this temple was burned, and with it this Book of the Law. Then there arose, on the return of the Jews from captivity in Babylon, Esdras, who believed that he had instructions from God to re-write the Book of the Law. All this is told in the book of Esdras, which at the time of the writing of the text "All scripture is given by inspiration of God" was part of the Jewish scripture, so what he says should have as much weight as anything else in the Scriptures. Esdras had just returned from captivity in Babylon, and he was well aware of the Babylonian stories of Adam and Eve, of the fall of man, of the

Tower of Babel, and the Flood. He was also aware of their laws, and he set out to write a new Book of the Law on the basis of all the knowledge he had acquired in Babylonia. Thus it does not astonish us to find that the Babylonian accounts of the events mentioned, and the Biblical accounts, correspond with one another, and that many of the Jewish laws correspond with those of Babylonia.

For instance, the Sabbath, known in Babylonia as Sabatu, was the Babylonian day of rest which occurred on every seventh day, and this was incorporated into the Jewish law. The only reason the Sabbath was held sacred was because the Babylonians believed that their God ended the work of creating the earth on the seventh day, and rested on that day. Because of this Babylonian superstition, which Christian countries received through the Jews, all true Christians cease from labour, not on the Sabbath the last day of the week, but on the day following, namely on Sunday the first day of the week, considering it a holy day, and many laws were made making it an offence to live a sensible and rational life on that day. Fortunately, the miserable Sabbath which some of us remember has passed into oblivion, but it is unlikely that those who experienced it will ever forget it !

We find nothing about the Sabbath in those books of the Bible known as Judges, Joshua, Samuel, Kings, or Chronicles, nor in Job, Esther, the Song of Solomon, or Ecclesiastes, but only in the earlier books of the Bible written by Esdras after his return from Babylon, and in the Prophets. What Esdras wrote was probably written on the skins of beasts and placed in the Temple.

The Jews were then again conquered by the Romans under Titus in the year 70 A.D., the Temple was destroyed, and at the request of Josephus the Jewish Book of the Law was sent to the Emperor Vespasian at Rome and it has never been seen since.

There was, however, what was claimed as a translation of it called the Septuagint made by seventy scribes, but it was a translation of the Law only, the other books following later. These were all burned in the Bruchium library forty-seven years before the Christian era. The only other so-called copy, known as the Samaritan Roll, is considered of no value. Have we to-day a true copy of the old Book of the Law? No, it is certain we have not, and nobody knows how many variations from the original there are in our Old Testament. The oldest manuscript in Hebrew in existence was written in the 10th century of the Christian era, and the oldest Greek copy was made in the 5th century. Even if the original was inspired by God, no one knows how much has been added to or omitted from our present Old Testament and how much represents the script of the original writers. No one knows anything about the original; all that is known is that there is no basis whatever to found the belief that our Old Testament truly represents the original, and certainly there is no justification whatever to call this doubtful copy of very many copies the "Word of God" as is continually being done by our clergy, who would never do so if they set the truth before their own self-interests.

Many chapters in the Old Testament are in-complete and parts of the different books are written in practically the same words. Neither do Leviticus and Numbers agree as to facts or teaching. Nothing is said about the after-life. Wherein, then, lies the inspiration? Why attribute the Bible to God with all its falsehoods, cruelties, and crude teaching? To do so is blasphemy, and this blasphemy is uttered every Sunday from thousands of lips speaking from Christian pulpits, by those who claim to be the divinely appointed leaders of the people in all things appertaining to their souls. Spiritualists must do all they can to save the reputation of the Almighty from such an outrage.

What is termed to-day the Holy Bible is a compilation of certain of the books known as the Book of the Law with others added for some unknown reason, and to these again were added certain documents chosen at the Council of Carthage. The bringing of the Jewish Book of the Law and the Christian documents together in the 6th century of the Christian era was the beginning of what became known as the Bible, which in original Greek means the sacred book. The Jewish book became known under the name of the Old Testament, and the Christian under the name of the New Testament. This book has been looked on since the Reformation as holy, and inspired by God, as word for word true, and as man's only guide to Heaven, and only way to salvation. During the time before the Reformation it was never read by the people and only known to the priests and monks. In fact the people knew nothing about its contents. The Church and the priests only were looked on with awe and reverence by the ignorant masses.

G

Between the years 1517 and 1545 some, however, were intelligent enough to throw over the so-called Infallible Church and strike out for themselves. They went under the name of Protestants because they protested against the practices of the corrupt Church. Those who became Protestants no longer venerated a Church and instead they worshipped the Holy Bible. Claims of so fantastic a nature were made for this book that it is difficult, in these more enlightened days, to understand how ever they could have been believed.

The invention of printing helped to circulate the Bible. It came to be read more and more, and as it was the only book known by the masses it is hardly to be wondered at that the claims made for it were believed by the people of those ignorant times. Every word in it was accepted, every word in it was believed to have been given direct from God to man, and the awful crime of blasphemy was invented to prevent the authenticity of this book from being too closely enquired into. Anyone who doubted this book's authority was cast into prison and tortured.

So time went on. Gradually, as people became more and more intelligent, it came to be realised that the book contained mistakes and mis-statements, and as people became more civilised they began to realise that many of its passages must have been written by depraved and cruel men. The more the Bible has been studied in an intelligent and unbiased way, the more has it become apparent that the book is a collection of documents written at various times by different people who were just a little more intelligent than their contemporaries. No one knows who wrote any of the books of the Bible, no one knows when or how they were written, no one is reported as ever having seen or heard of anybody who has ever seen an original of any of the books of the Bible. We know, however, that the many existing copies differ greatly from one another, as the transcribers added what they thought should be put in, and left out what they thought should be omitted. The numerous inter-polations in the New Testament were put in by scribes at a time when it was not considered inspired, and thus the most outrageous liberties were taken for several hundreds of years. We are, therefore, on safe ground in saying that not one of the books of the Bible remains to-day in its original form.

From out of this welter of confusion and ignor-ance has grown the Bible, and it was not until the time when printing was invented that it began to take concrete shape and form. Since the time when the Authorised Version of James 1st of England was produced little alteration has taken place in it, as much care was exercised in preserving the text, but before that date, as I say, it is well known that every possible liberty was taken with its contents by monkish scribes.

As time went on it became evident that the Authorised Version was far from correct, so in 1881 a new Revised Version was produced, and those re-sponsible for this new version stated that they had discovered 36,191 mistakes in the old version. We now know that if a new version were published to-day the alterations which would have to be made would probably be equally striking. The revised version should have been the death blow to the Church's claim

for the infallibility of the Bible, but it still makes
this claim, and it has the support of many foolish
people who quote its texts to prove their theories.
These people read it without thinking.   When they
open their Bible they close their reason, yet if they
will consult the *Encyclopædia Biblica* they will find
that the article in it dealing with the Resurrection
points out that in the various gospel stories of this
event there are twenty-two contradictions of a most
serious character.   Why should anyone be asked to
believe in an event recorded in such a way, and why
does the Church on this evidence claim the Resurrection of Jesus to be the fundamental truth of
Christianity?

This is of necessity a very brief record of the
history of what Christians call God's chosen people,
and of the life and teaching of Jesus and his disciples.
From this mass of contradiction, born in an ignorant
past, what is called the Christian Faith has developed.
It is still claimed that we are a Christian people and
indebted to Christianity for all the progress we have
made, but there is still a vast difference of opinion
as to what Christianity really is.   This has been discussed and fought over for many centuries and many
sects have arisen owing to the many differences of
opinion.   It is difficult to find out exactly what every
different sect believes, but generally speaking they
are in agreement more or less as regards the following
tenets :—

That there is a personal God who created the
earth and the stars ; that he created man and woman
who were tempted of the devil, and in consequence
fell from the high state in which he had created them.

Mankind became more and more wicked until, God's patience having been exhausted, he drowned every living person with the exception of eight people. Afterwards he selected from their descendants Abraham, and through him the Jewish people. He gave this people laws and tried to govern them and make them good. He wrought numerous miracles, he inspired men to write the Bible, and in the fullness of time, it having been found impossible to reform mankind, God came upon the earth as a child born of the Virgin Mary. He lived in Palestine where he preached for about two years. He went from place to place teaching and preaching, occasionally raising the dead, curing the blind and the halt, and healing the diseased. Ultimately he was crucified because God had told the Jews that they were to kill anyone who claimed to be God. Consequently, God was killed as a result of his own laws, and, in crucifying Jesus, the Jews only did what God told them to do.

Christians agree, however, that as a result of God being thus crucified, he took away the sins of all who had faith in him ; that he was raised from the dead, ascending bodily into Heaven where he is now making intercession for all who believe in him ; that he will forgive the sins of believers, and that those who do not believe in him will be consigned to torment. Further, that this God is really three Gods and that Jesus is one of the three ; three Gods, yet he is only one ; and so the mystery of the Trinity has to be added to the other Christian beliefs already noted. Lastly, there are two sacraments, one of baptism for all young children, although nothing is said about this in the Old or New Testament, in which only adult baptism is taught, and that of the last supper, or what is commonly called Holy Communion, a service of commemoration of the death of Jesus.   Some hold that the bread and wine at this ceremony are turned into his body and blood, and others hold that this doctrine is blasphemy.

This is roughly a synopsis of the Christian religion, and I cannot be far wrong, as the Bishops of the Church of England only a few years ago emphasised by a resolution that Christianity was contained in the creeds and doctrines of the Church.   I have been told, however, that few to-day believe in the Adam and Eve story, and that it is accepted that we are the products of a slow and continuous evolution.   Granted that this be so it must knock away the foundation stone from the entire fabric of Christianity.   Paul, Christians believe, said quite clearly, "As in Adam all die so in Christ shall all be made alive."   If you do away with Adam you must do away with Jesus as a saviour, and so it comes about that Jesus by many is now regarded merely as an example, one to follow, though there are still some who cling to the old orthodox view, because they see that to give up Adam means the giving up of Jesus as their saviour.

What I am trying to show is that there is no basis whatever for the creeds and dogmas of the Church. They are all man-made things and must perish with other man-made things.   There is nothing divine about them, there is not a spark of divine inspiration in one single text or creed or in one single dogma of the Christian Church.   Doubtless these fictions have acted as crutches in the past to many weary souls who have found much comfort and consolation in the teachings of the Church, but against that it must be admitted that they have been the cause of numberless crimes and barbarities. The history of the Christian Church is stained with the blood of the martyrs.

I readily admit that millions have received comfort from the Christian religion. The name of Jesus has given consolation and comfort to countless multitudes, and the Bible has been a source of strength to untold numbers. Millions have entered the valley of the shadow of death with his name on their lips, to their comfort and joy. His gospel has been carried to the ends of the earth by men and women who have sacrificed much to spread his teaching. What, however, is true of Christianity is true also of other faiths, and all this in no way alters the fact that all the comfort and self-sacrifice Christianity has occasioned has no historic basis whatever, and as we grow more intelligent the comfort orthodox religion brings must decrease until it ultimately disappears altogether.

THE CONSEQUENCES OF FAITH.

The foregoing is a brief history of the foundations on which the Church has built its edifice of creeds and dogmas. We shall now consider what the consequences have been. It will now be understood that after Constantine adopted Christianity as a state religion much of the Mithraic worship of Rome was incorporated into the Church's ritual. Any one visiting St. Peter's in Rome or any other Roman Catholic Church, and taking along with him

Lord Lytton's *Last days of Pompeii*, in which
there is given a most interesting description of what
took place in pre-Christian days in a Roman Temple,
will find many similarities between the Christian ritual
and that observed by the pagans of Rome.

The Christian Church, backed by the authority
of Imperial Rome, grew and flourished. When the
Roman conquerors went out to conquer, the conquered nations were butchered into acceptance of the
new religion, until the time came when Christianity
had complete control over the greater part of Europe.
Then set in what is now known as the Dark Ages,
when in Europe nobody thought of anything but
churches, altars and relics, besides their ordinary
occupations, husbandry and fighting.

Europe, after the fall of the Roman Empire,
was submerged in a sea of barbarism, and due
acknowledgment must be given to the work of the
early monks who kept themselves apart from the tur-
bulence of the times. What civilisation there was in
those days, and it was very slight, could be found in
the monasteries throughout Europe. Monastic life
in all parts of the world had this advantage in those
days, that the monasteries were holy ground, and those
inside them were safe from devastation. The Christian Church took its idea of monastic life from Buddhism, and in the early days the copying and illumina-
ting of the Scriptures took up much of the
monks' time. The monks were just a little more
intelligent than their neighbours, and until they
became corrupt they did what healing and teaching
they could. It is difficult to imagine the ignorance of
those days, or the depth to which men's minds had

fallen from the heights reached at the zenith of the greatness of Rome and Greece. Barbarism was rife everywhere ; mentally Christendom was in the darkness of a night of dense superstition.

To relieve this monotony a ripple came over the stagnant waste with the advent of Mohammed in 622, and later in the attempt to free the Holy Land from the Turks in 1095. Europe rose as a man to free the Holy Land from the infidel. After two hundred years the Christians were driven out and nothing was achieved by this fruitless enterprise.

The history of the Crusades is the story of cruelty, treachery, and misery. Whichever side obtained the upper hand, the consequences were the same. From a Christian point of view, it is one of the blackest periods in that religion's history, and is just one record of massacre, breaking of faith and treachery from beginning to end. Crosses and hymn-singing, priests and prayers, treachery and cruelty, all combined, is the story of the Crusades in brief, and it is only one of many similar episodes in the history of the Christian Church.

Christianity for two hundred years turned Europe into a madhouse, and this insane desire to free the Holy Land from the Infidel caused untold misery, suffering and loss. Had it been confined to adults only it would have been bad enough, but the Church conceived the insane idea that failure was caused because the Crusaders were not innocent enough. Consequently it encouraged the wicked idea of sending out children to fight the infidel, and 50,000 boys and girls of tender age were gathered together and dispatched to the Holy Land. Few, if

any, survived to return.   They were captured in the
countries through which they passed, tortured,
starved, and made slaves, and so ended another of
the many tragedies of this long night of superstition.

Again stagnation followed, but in spite of the
grip the Church had, men's minds were slowly
developing and wondering, and this process culminated in what is known in history as the Reformation of the sixteenth century.   The real foundation
for this great event was laid by the break-up of the
Holy Roman Empire by the capture of Constantinople in 1453 by the Turks.   Much literature found
its way to Venice and elsewhere from Constantinople
before its capture, and in consequence the Latin and
Greek Classics which had been banned by the Church
were again studied.   It is inconceivable in these
more enlightened days, but it is true nevertheless,
that when the Church was supreme all learning,
apart from the knowledge of the Scriptures, was
looked upon as immoral and as sin.   This period of
awakening is termed Renaissance or New-birth.

If, indeed, printing had not been discovered, it
is doubtful if the Reformation would then have
occurred.   Printing was invented in 1450.   Martin
Luther was born in 1483.   Until printing was invented individual thoughts could not be passed on
from one to another, and the stagnant pool of orthodoxy remained untroubled.   The invention of printing
stuck a dagger into the heart of Christendom, and
from that day onwards Europe and the world has
gradually freed itself from the curse of priest-craft.
In the century previous to the Reformation, Wycliffe,
Huss, and others had sounded a warning note that all

was not right in the Christian Church. Then followed Luther, who took up the cause in Germany, Ziska in Hungary, and Zwingli, who espoused it in Switzerland. The adherents of the new reform movement became numerous. Much was made by the reformers of the wholesale selling of indulgences by papal agents, and when Luther attacked these iniquities he found willing followers. After much controversy the reformers boldly propounded the principles of the reformed Christian religion, and from that time onwards the struggle grew fast and furious.

Hitherto no Bible had been seen by others than the priests, the people not having been able to read or write. Following the invention of printing came the capacity to read and write, and consequently the reformers claimed that the Scriptures should become public property and not only the property of the Church. The reformers also rejected the doctrine of transubstantiation, the adoration of the Virgin and the saints, and the leadership of the Pope. Luther's excommunication naturally followed, but as the people began to read and think the Reformation spread. Ultimately the greater part of Germany, Switzerland, the Netherlands, Scandinavia, England and Scotland were won over to the new teaching.

Living as we do to-day in a more enlightened world, we do not perhaps fully realise how ignorant were our ancestors before printing was invented, and it is difficult for us to gauge how much the dawn of a new day meant to the world, after a night of intense darkness. Luther's whole religious outlook was changed when he got a copy of the

Bible and read it through. "I tormented myself to death," he said, "to make my peace with God," and there and then in his monastery he dedicated himself to the task of showing the world the errors of the Church, and what he thought was the only true way to salvation according to the Scriptures. The reformers were, however, men steeped in ignorance and superstition. Calvin advocated murder to support his religious views, and Luther denounced Galileo because he opposed the astronomy of Genesis. John Knox was only in favour of religious toleration when he was in the minority. When he gained the upper hand religious freedom was abolished.

From the discovery of printing also dates the advance of science. Prior to this event everyone took everything just as it appeared. Nothing was known of medicine, astronomy, biology or geology, and the writings and maxims of the wisdom of Greece had long been forgotten. Orthodoxy had almost completely obliterated man's reasoning powers, but as the spark of intelligence burned anew thoughtful people began to question the divine origin of the religion that had entailed such awful consequences.

The few began to compare Christianity with other religions and came to the conclusion that the difference between them was negligible. They also wondered why men had to be inspired in order to teach that God instructed his chosen people to make slaves of the people who lived amongst them, whilst Epictetus, a heathen, who was not inspired, could write—

"Will you remember that your servants are by

nature your brothers, the children of God. In saying that you have bought them you look down on the earth and into the pit. It is not the law of the Gods."

They also wondered how Cicero, a pagan, 70 years before Christ, who had never heard of the Christian scheme of salvation, could write, "They who say that we should love our fellow citizens but not foreigners, destroy the universal brotherhood of mankind, and thus benevolence and justice would perish for ever." Zeno, the founder of the Stoics, endorsed this sentiment in similar words.

A comparison of the teachings of the inspired Bible with those of the pagan writers who were not inspired brought to light the fact that the uninspired teachers were definitely superior to the inspired, which latter the Christian Church with its warped mentality still prefers. Why could Cicero uninspired write the following, "They whose minds scorn the limitations of the body, are honoured with the frequent appearance of the spirits. Their voices have been often heard, and they have appeared in forms so visible that he who doubts it must be partly bereft of reason." Yet the writer of Ecclesiastes required to be inspired by the creator of heaven and earth to write the following, "For the living know that they shall die, but the dead know not anything, neither have they any reward, for the memory of them is forgotten." Why was it necessary to inspire some-one to record that Jehovah ordered a Jewish general to make war and then gave him the following instructions. "When the Lord thy God shall deliver them before thee, thou shall smite them and utterly destroy them. Thou shalt make no covenant with them nor show mercy unto them.'' And yet Epicurus, called a heathen by Christians, could so far surpass his creator in magnanimity that he could say '' Live with thine inferiors as thou wouldst have thy superiors live with thee.''

According to Christians, God is reported in the Bible as saying '' I will heap misfortune upon them. I will spend mine arrows upon them. They shall be burned with hunger and devoured with burning heat and with bitter destruction. I will also send the teeth of beasts upon them, with the poison of serpents of the dust. The sword without and the terror within shall destroy both the young man and the virgin, the suckling also, and the man with grey hairs.'' This, according to Christians, is the morality of their God ; whereas Seneca, who was a pagan, wrote as follows, '' The wise man will not pardon every crime that should be punished, but he will accomplish in a nobler way all that is sought in pardoning. He will spare some and watch over some because of their youth, and others on account of their ignorance. His clemency will not fall short of justice, but will fulfil it perfectly.'' Again we read that the God whom Christians worship said, '' Let his children be father-less and his wife a widow, let his children be con-tinually vagabonds and beg ; let them seek their bread also out of the desolate places. Let the ex-tortioner catch all that he hath, and let the stranger spoil his labour. Let there be none to extend mercy upon him ; neither let there be any to favour his fatherless children,'' and yet Marcus Aurelius, the noblest of the pagans, who lived as he taught, and gave the world one of the finest examples of the possibilities within humanity, wrote :—'' I have formed the ideal of a state, in which there is the same law for all, and equal rights and equal liberty of speech established, an empire where nothing is honoured so much as the freedom of the citizen."

Jehovah to his servant Moses gave the command, "Thou shalt have no other Gods before me. Thou shalt not bow down to them nor serve them, for I the Lord thy God am a jealous God visiting the iniquities of the fathers upon the children unto the third and fourth generation of them that hate me." The words attributed to the God Brahma by the Hindus showed their God in a much more favourable light as, unlike Jehovah, not fearing competition, he said, "I am the same to all mankind. They who honestly serve other Gods involuntarily serve me. I am he who partaketh of all worship, and I am the reward of all worshippers."

All impartial students of the past can come to no other conclusion than that the belief in the inspiration of the Holy Bible, though it has given strength and help to millions, nevertheless has been one of the greatest hindrances to the progress of humanity. Is it not also a misnomer that this book is still called "Holy" and the "Word of God" in any civilised place of worship? We can now see why every battleship when launched receives the blessing of the Church, and is dedicated to God! Is it to be wondered at that history records that amongst professing Christians are to be found some of the greatest blackguards imaginable. How could it be otherwise when they conceived a tyrant in Heaven whom they believed issued instructions to mankind which would disgrace the most brutal savage?

However, the sayings of the great and the good

of other lands and of other faiths, men who did not worship a tyrant, brought light to Europe after a dark night of Christianity, during which the wonderful literature of Greece had been buried for centuries under the debris of orthodoxy.

It was also found that other non-Christian nations, looked upon as heathen, knew more than Christians did; that in China the astronomers, 2,449 years before Christ, had calculated eclipses, and knew something of the movements of the planets; that in Babylon, 500 years before Christ, the annual movements of the sun and moon were calculated within 10 seconds of accuracy for the entire year; whereas Christians burned and tortured their astronomers. Thinking people wondered why the writer of Kings and Chronicles had to be regarded as inspired while Gibbon uninspired could write unaided *The Decline and Fall of the Roman Empire*, and why the story in the book of Joshua about the sun standing still was inspired, when the Babylonians were not, though for 360 years they made astronomical calculations, the longest ever made by man, our Greenwich observations going back only 181 years.

Intelligent people also found that other nations had hospitals and medical services, and were in advance of Christian nations in many respects. The oldest treatise on surgery was written in Egypt 5,000 years ago, and 4,000 years ago the Egyptians were writing mathematical treatises of astonishing penetration.

People at last became tired of building cathedrals and thought the time had come to turn the huts and hovels of the people into decent dwelling houses. The

thinking people after the Reformation began to realise
that learning had almost entirely been lost, and that
if people had been educated, had known more of
the literature of Greece and Rome, had studied the
philosophy of Plato, Zeno and Epicurus, and had
heard less of the teachings of Christianity, Europe
would have been in a better, happier and more prosperous state.   During the night of Christianity,
Europe produced no literature.   For 1,400 years
the minds of men were paralysed by this superstition,
and thus after the Reformation the lamp of learning
was re-lit by the ancient literature of Greece and
Rome.   The wisdom of these two nations was
the basis on which Europe built up its literature.*
The light of Reason, which Christianity extinguished
for a time, was re-lit by the writings of men who
were not "inspired" or "called" or "saved," and
had never heard of the Christian God.   The
Mohammedans were friends of Science when Christians were burning its pioneers, and it is to the Moors
we are indebted for laying the foundations of Science.

All this which was discovered after the Reformation not only created a great change in the thoughts
of the people from a religious point of view, but also
from a scientific point of view, and we now see two
groups emerging.   One, discarding the teachings of
the orthodox Church, held to the Bible as the anchor
of their new religion, and the other comprising men
of science feeling their way by appealing to the

---

* I can recommend *Paganism and Christianity*, by Farrer, from which
the reader will discover that we are indebted to the great pagan
philosophers and teachers for our laws, our code of morals, and
our ideals, in fact for our present civilisation. Similar views are
expressed by Professor Gilbert Murray in *Christianity in the Light
of Modern Knowledge.*

H

thought and reason of mankind, by seeking evidence
resulting from intelligent inquiry, and thus leading
the thinking section of the people towards a new line
of thought and action.   The narrow way of the
Church, they argued, had led Europe into a wilder-
ness, and they advocated the broad way now being
taken, with its borders enriched by all the glories
which art, refinement, and science could give.

Those leaders of science had to suffer, and suffer
cruelly.   The early days of the Reformation had
given the old Church a cruel blow, yet it was by no
means paralysed.   We find that Copernicus felt safe
in publishing his discoveries with regard to the planetary system only on his death bed, and dedicating it
to the Pope.   Galileo, under the fear of the Inquisition, had publicly to renounce on his knees that
the earth moved round the sun, and it was not till the
beginning of the nineteenth century that the Church
of Rome admitted its error.   Spinosa was cut off by
Papal edict from all intercourse with his contemporaries, and the anathema which was placed upon
him in the name of God stated that he was execrated
and cast out of the community.   The anathema is
too long to quote, but his only crime was that he used
the sacred gift of reason, which everyone is given,
and by its exercise came to the conclusion that the
Church was wrong.

This ignorant institution did not know the shape
of the earth.   It thought that diseases were caused
by devils.   It was not the Church that demonstrated
that the earth was round, but Magellan, who left
Spain on the 10th August 1519 and kept sailing till
he reached Seville on September 7th 1522.   Bruno,

one of the greatest of men, taught the plurality of worlds, and called the Catholic Church a "triumphant beast." In those days the Church thought that this earth was the only world in the universe. In 1609 Kepler published his book "The Motions of the Planet Mars." He mathematically expressed the relation of distance, mass and motion. He was one of the greatest of our scientists, and his three laws were the foundation of the science of Astronomy. Then followed Newton, Herschell, and Laplace, and the astronomy of Joshua faded further into insignificance. Then man began to examine the rocks and strata of the earth, and found that instead of the earth being a few thousand years old it is hundreds of millions of years old. On the basis of the known rate of the disintegration of the metal uranium into lead, experts can calculate how long these two metals have been in contact, and their calculations prove that the requisite period for uranium to turn into lead is from 340 to 1,700 million years, according to the nature of the ore. The Church since the Council of Carthage had rested its supreme authority on the statements of Holy Scripture. It based all its knowledge of astronomy, biology and healing on the writings of an ignorant age, and what was the result? It plunged Europe into a night of darkest ignorance, and only when its autocratic power was overthrown by the discoveries of science, and men began to reason and think and calculate, did Europe make progress and become prosperous.

There still remained obstacles to progress, as many of the religious reformers were just as cruel and ignorant as the Church they had left, the result being that from the Reformation onwards right up to the end of the seventeenth century there is one long story of torture, slaughter and misery.   All who dared to think for themselves or thought differently from the reformed Church were imprisoned and put to torture. Though Servetus was the first to discover the circulation of the blood (not Harvey), yet because he denied the Trinity he was cruelly put to death by the Protestants.   He was the first Protestant to be burned by Protestants.

The Inquisition was not confined to what is now called the Roman Catholic Church.   The Inquisition and its accompanying tortures by thumb screws, racks, and other fiendish devices was just as formidable and just as fierce in Protestant Edinburgh and Protestant London as it was in Catholic Spain. Torture and imprisonment inflicted by one sect of so-called reformed Christians on some other sect did not cease in this country until the landing of William of Orange in 1689, when all those awaiting torture or the scaffold for their religious beliefs, were liberated from prison.

Torture and imprisonment, however, continued for many years longer in France and throughout Europe, and the most appalling cruelties are recorded. Voltaire, who is contemptuously called an atheist by some narrow-minded Protestants, abolished torture in France and helped many sufferers.   His writings, which exposed the infamies of the Church of his time, did much to break its power in France. He died an old man in 1778, after having lived a life of great vigour and usefulness.   All the ridiculous stories of his misery at his death are now proved to be lies spread by the Church.

I have described above the conditions in Europe, but the Protestants in America, whither they had gone to obtain religious freedom from the Protestants in England, were just as bigoted and cruel as their co-religionists.. Thomas Paine, for instance,. one of the founders of the United States of America, who all his life fought for freedom and liberty, and abhorred slavery, was denounced from every Christian pulpit. His crime was that he wrote *The Age of Reason.* He simply took the ground that it is a contradiction to call anything a revelation from God that does not come to us direct. The revelation must be personal, not made to someone else. He also showed that the so-called prophecies of the Old Testament had nothing whatever to do with Jesus, and that the Old Testament was too barbarous to be the work of an infinitely benevolent God. He did not think there was any evidence that Jesus was God; in other words,. he was a Unitarian. From the date of the publication of *The Age of Reason* his doom was sealed. He was denounced, deserted, ostracised, shunned, maligned and cursed. He could not safely appear in the streets, he was treated as a leper. Under the very flag of liberty he had helped to fly his rights were forfeited. He helped to give liberty to more than three million of his fellow citizens and they denied him his own. From the moment of his death Protestants started manufacturing the horrors that were alleged to have attended his death-bed, how his bedroom was filled with Devils rattling chains,. and so on. The truth is that he died in peace, but what he suffered many others suffered from the cruelty and bigotry of Protestantism, and it is as well to re-

member that all the cruelty of the past was not confined to what is now called the Roman Catholic
Church, as all Protestant children are taught.

In addition to the suffering and sorrow caused
to humanity by the intolerant Church, both Catholic
and Protestant, one other crime must be laid to its
charge, and that is one from which we are only
gradually recovering. The text in Leviticus already
referred to, " Thou shalt not suffer a witch to live,"
was responsible for the awful crime of witch burning,
and in consequence of this super-sensitive people
called Mediums were almost exterminated.

The following entry is taken from the Parish
Register of Glamis, in Scotland, dated June **1676**,
and is typical of what went on throughout Christendom for five hundred years :—" Nae preaching
here this Lord's day, the Minister being at
Gortachy burning a witch." The Church to-day
can only tell lies about Mediums and Spiritualists to congregations still steeped in ignorance of the
subject, owing to the worship of the Holy Bible. If
it had been otherwise and those gifted people had been
allowed to live, and if people had been intelligent
enough to understand them properly, how different
would have been the history of Europe ! The gross
materialism of the Church and of Science would never
have developed, and instead of science working on
purely materialistic lines it would have realised better
man's true position in the Universe. Neither
theology nor science has yet the correct knowledge
of the meaning of our existence and destiny.
Theology has searched amongst ancient documents
thinking that from them the riddle of existence could

be unravelled. Science on its part has ignored the spiritual nature of man and looked on him merely as a material creation. Both science and theology have taken appearances for reality and this has been a tremendous loss to humanity.

Since 1712, when the last witch was burned in England, mediumship has developed and revealed to us another world about and around us. It has also revealed to us man's spiritual nature and the fact that he is possessed of an Etheric Body, the exact duplicate of his Physical Body, that Mind is substance which controls the Physical Body through the Etheric Body, and that about and around us there is an Etheric World, to which we shall all pass at death, irrespective of our theological beliefs. Through mediumship Spiritualists have also learned that the material universe is not the whole universe, but only a small part of the universe. What suffering and misery would have been saved to humanity if this text about killing witches had never been written and never been believed !

The Reverend Jonathan Edwards and other Protestant divines, if the Bible had been properly understood, would never have tortured the people by such teaching as this. ''The view of the misery of the damned will double the ardour of the love and gratitude of the Saints in Heaven.'' Here is an extract from another reverend gentleman's sermon. ''The God that holds you over the pit of Hell, much in the same way that one holds a spider or some loathsome insect, abhors you and is dreadfully provoked.'' I shall only quote one more. ''The world will probably be converted into a great lake of fire in which the wicked shall be tossed to and fro.   Their vitals shall for ever be full of a glowing melting fire enough to heat the very rocks and elements for ever and ever without any end at all.''

These are a few specimens of Protestant preaching, and if they are not preached to-day it is because the Bible is taken less seriously, and owing to the more enlightened view taken by the Church in consequence of the advance in scientific knowledge and the teachings of Spiritualism.   Protestantism is as cruel a creed as Roman Catholicism.   The two who did as much as any to promote their acceptance and growth were murderers.   Constantine killed his own kith and kin, and Calvin murdered Servetus because he disagreed with him. Both the Catholic and Protestant Churches were tyrannical when they had the power, giving no mercy to anyone.   That is the consequence of an inspired Church or an inspired book.   Whenever men think that they and they only have divine authority, cruelty and intolerance follow.

Everything advocated in the Bible was considered as coming from God.   From every Christian pulpit slavery was upheld because the Bible taught it.   The pulpit was turned into a whipping post, and only as the idea of its divine authority died did England cease to support the slave trade, but the Church in its cruelty upheld it, to its lasting shame, till the 19th century.   Parsons and others held stock in slave ships and slave-trading concerns, and justified this by quoting Bible texts.   Wilberforce and Clarkeson, who dedicated their lives to the abolition of slavery, were denounced from every pulpit in the country, and on them the Christian Church poured contempt and hatred for advocating a course contrary to God.

Just as the belief in Inspiration faded so did woman rise to be equal to man. The Bible looks on woman as the slave of man and advocates nothing but humiliation for her. The Bible considers the woman as the property of the man. She is, it says, as much below her husband as he is below Christ, whatever that may mean. Nothing is to be found within its covers of a civilised home, with the wife equal to the husband. She has even to ask forgiveness for bearing children and take "a sin offering unto the door of the tabernacle, unto the Priest."

Had we been in closer touch with the Etheric World during what is called the Christian era, we should not have supported slavery by Biblical texts, or persecuted Spiritualists who, in the early days, were stoned and mobbed going to and from their meetings. Christians would not have everywhere persecuted the Jews because they had crucified Jesus, and so saved the Christians from Hell. Clergymen would never have condemned chloroform in child birth by quoting the story of the fall of man, nor would they have denounced evolution and every contribution to the advance of knowledge made by science. How different would the world have been had the Bible never been considered inspired, and how much happier the world will be when the Church, and through the Church the people, accept the principles of Spiritualism, and come to look on the Bible as they do on other books, admiring its beauties, but ignoring its mistakes and falsities. In view of past mistakes, and the crimes and atrocities it has committed in the name of its founder, the Church to-day should be humble and penitent instead of arrogant and reactionary.

I look back and see the coiled serpents of super-stition awaiting their prey. I see them seize all who try to use the sacred gift of reason. I see gorgeous temples reared amidst degradation and filth, and money spent on sacred edifices instead of on the housing of mankind. I see altars red with the blood of human beings, and the cross of Christ turned into a sword.

I look forward and I see a world freed from priest-craft, and everyone possessing the right to ex-press opinions as his reason dictates, without being condemned from the pulpit by those who think they have a divine revelation handed down to them, either through an inspired Church or through an inspired Book. I see the fear of death removed, and inter-communication between this world of ours and the Etheric World surrounding us free and untram-melled, and Mediums looked upon as sacred instru-ments and not denounced by ignorant parsons and priests as they are to-day. Just as man has developed in other directions and acquired knowledge by ex-perience, so will this knowledge come to him in time, to the great increase of his happiness and well-being.

If Jesus is God or part of God, as the Christian Church claims, and as Christians say each Sunday they believe, why did he not tell the world something new, something that had never been told before? Why did he not look into the future and say " In my name, if I do not warn you, crimes, horrors and iniquities will be committed. The hungry flames will torture millions at the stake. This must never be. That horrible text in Leviticus about burning witches must be ascribed to ignorance, and be ignored. My followers must never persecute those who differ from them, as God's holy gift of reason cannot be extinguished. No thumbscrews, racks, or scaffolds must be used in my name, and no one must be imprisoned because they will not be able to understand the Trinity, or reconcile the contradictions of the Scriptures. No one who disbelieves in the atonement will be punished in Hell, and believers in creeds and dogmas will not be the only occupants of Heaven.''

If Jesus is God he must have known of all the religious wars which would be waged in his name, and the cruelty and the misery which would follow his life on earth. Why did he not warn his followers not to shed blood, to torture and imprison in his name? Why did he leave his disciples with the idea that the world would soon come to an end? Why did he not say which books of the Old Testament were inspired and which of the New Testament would be inspired, instead of leaving it to the Westminster divines to find out, thus allowing Christendom to remain in ignorance of this vital matter for sixteen hundred years?

Why did he distinctly say that he was not God, and that there is only one God, when all the time he was one of three Gods? Why did he continually refer to himself as ''a human being,'' which is what has been translated as '' Son of Man?'' Why did he not explain that what would be translated '' Son of God '' in the original Aramaic meant nothing more than Servant of God? Why did he never mention

the Trinity, if he is one of the three Christian Gods?
Why did he give this world no details of the after-life?

Why did he not say whether Roman Catholicism,
Anglicanism, Presbyterianism or Methodism was
the way in which he preferred to be worshipped?
Why did he not say that though everything written
about him would be traced to earlier religions, yet he
was God, and that all who preceded him or followed
him, as religious teachers, were impostors, and that
Christianity was the only true religion?

If Jesus is God, the creator of the Universe,
why did he not tell his followers that this earth was
but a speck in immensity, that it was round and not
flat, and also something about Astronomy, Geology,
Medicine, and the other sciences and arts?   Why
did he not himself write what he wished us to believe,
and not leave his words to be tossed about for centuries in a sea of ignorant superstition, to be the cause
of sects and divisions in his Church?   Why did he
say nothing in favour of education, or whether Evolution or the Adam and Eve story is true?

If Jesus was God he still is God ; if God consists
of three parts, he is one of them.   Christians say,
at least once every Sunday, they believe this.   If this
be so then Jesus must have known all the past, and
the present, and the future.   To him all wisdom, all
knowledge, must have been open like a book, and
yet he went to his death without telling the world one
single fact it did not know before.

Why? Because he was a man and did not know.

Consequently, Christian doctrines, based as they
are on error, must give place to a new religion based
on truth.   Just as Christianity is the product of pre-

ceding religions which it absorbed, so in time it will be displaced by Spiritualism quite naturally, and as each year passes the resistance to the inevitable will decrease till it eventually ceases altogether.

In concluding this chapter I should like to quote from the contribution made by the Rev. James H. Baxter, Professor of Ecclesiastical History at St. Andrew's University, to that monumental work *Christianity in the Light of Modern Knowledge.* His words are as follows :—

" Upon the popular interpretation and practice of Christianity, the effect of its establishment as the State religion had been profound. If Paganism had been destroyed, it was less through annihilation than through absorption. Almost all that was pagan was carried over to survive under a Christian name. Deprived of demi-gods and heroes, men easily and half unconsciously invested a local martyr with their attributes, and labelled the local statue with his name, transferring to him the cult and mythology associated with the Pagan Deity. Before this century (Fourth) was over the martyr-cult was universal, and a beginning had been made of that interposition of a deified human being between God and man which, on the one hand, had been the consequence of Arianism, and was on the other the origin of so much that is typical of mediæval piety and practice. Pagan Festivals were adopted and re-named, and Christmas Day, the ancient festival of the sun, was transformed into the birthday of Jesus."

That Christianity was just a new name given to old religious beliefs, rites, and ceremonials there is not the least doubt. The reason people continue to believe the old dogmas and creeds is because they were taught them in childhood as true, and have never taken the trouble to investigate the subject for themselves. With mental development the light is now breaking through, and we are now finding that the new knowledge gives us infinitely greater satisfaction than the old beliefs, as it not only satisfies all human longings and desires but, more important still, it is based on truth scientifically established.

CHAPTER IV.

WHAT DID JESUS REALLY TEACH?

In the foregoing chapter I have given an account of the origin of Christianity and its sacred books, its teachings, and the consequences of these teachings. The Christian Church has no historical basis for the claims it makes with regard to Jesus. These claims are all based on tradition, on stories which passed from one to another, and no one can possibly say whether, as they are now recorded to us in print, they are in any way like the original statements.

Besides having no historic basis the claims made by Christians about Jesus are now found to have been made by other religions about their Saviours long before the Christian era. Consequently the uniqueness of Jesus has disappeared and we must all now accept the fact that, as portrayed to us, he is only one of many similar legendary crucified saviour god-men whose followers believed had died for the sins of the world.

Mr. T. R. Glover, in the introduction to his book *The Jesus of History*, states " The gospels are not properly biographies ; they consist of collections of reminiscences, memories and fragments that have survived for years, and sometimes the fragment is little more than a phrase. The gospels are almost avowedly not first hand," and yet on this flimsy basis his book advances the most extravagant and absurd claims about Jesus for which there is not a scrap of evidence. This acknowledged pro-Christian book is typical of all Christian literature, but fortunately the public is beginning to find out that it has been deceived by its Christian leaders, and that those men who have been termed "Agnostics," "Infidels," "Rationalists," and "Free-thinkers," all terms of reproach in the old days, because they viewed Christianity in a rational way, are the men who can now be trusted, as they have always put truth first and foremost, and never allowed sentiment to blind their reason. This chapter will therefore deal with facts, not with fancies ; it will keep strictly to the truth, and not try to mislead people into believing something for which there is no evidence.

If we were reading about an every-day event, an earthquake, for instance, and read that this earthquake occurred nineteen hundred years ago, and knew that the story of the earthquake had been handed down by word of mouth for forty years or so, and ultimately the story was recorded in writing, and that this writing was done by someone who was extremely ignorant of the art, also that in those days accurate thinking and writing was not considered important, and that the original had been lost, but that copies of the original had been made, and lost, but that copies of the copies existed, but that all the copies in existence differed from each other, would we be inclined to believe that the details so recorded were in any way reliable?

In this case we are not asked to believe something which we know is a common occurrence, but on this so-called "evidence" we are asked to believe that something happened that never happened before and has never happened since ; that God the creator of this immense Universe came on earth, was born in an unnatural way, raised the dead, and did other wondrous things, without the people of the time believing in them or in him ; was crucified because he was accused of claiming to be God and of having political ambitions, and that after death he appeared again in his earthly body to his disciples, ascending afterwards bodily into Heaven. If such events were reported as happening to-day no one would believe them.

We are told, further, that marvellous occurrences took place at his death—earthquakes, the day, turned into night, the dead coming out of their graves and walking about Jerusalem, and this though Pliny, who died in 79 A.D., and recorded every earthquake that happened within knowledge, never mentioned this particular event nor mentioned what the dead had to say about having come back to earth, if they were glad or sorry to be back on earth, or what the other world was like. Was no one sufficiently interested to ask them? If it had been true we should surely have heard something direct about the other world on this famous occasion. Besides that, we are told that God, thus coming to earth, took upon himself the sins of those who believed that he suffered in their place, and that these would be saved, and live for ever in a fantastic Heaven, while those who did not believe would suffer eternal torment in Hell.

That is briefly what the Churches have preached since 325 A.D., though some of the more enlightened leaders tell us to-day that this is not now the Churches' teaching. Why is this so? What has happened to make the Church change its teaching? And if the Church has changed its teaching why does it not publicly say so, and withdraw all the books and docu-

ments it has published and is still publishing supporting this teaching? Until the Church does this
publicly it must be accepted that Christian teaching
is still substantially the same to-day as it has been
since the Council of Nicaea decided what Christianity
was.

I must, therefore, accept the Nicene Creed, the
'Athanasian Creed, the Thirty-Nine Articles of the
Church of England, the Confession of Faith of the
Church of Scotland, and the Shorter and Longer
Catechisms, and all the assertions they contain, as
representing Protestant Christianity. Roman Catholicism still stands by the old creeds and never wavers,
so its position is never in doubt. If these documents
do not represent true Christianity what does ; what
is true Christianity and whence comes the authority
for modern Christianity about which everyone has a
different opinion?

Now Spiritualists, and most enlightened people
in these days, do not give a thought to these documents or assertions. They are relegated to a bygone
age. The Church to-day, they realise, has nothing
of any value on which to base its claims, and it is
supported only by people who have always accepted
what it has taught and never reasoned for themselves.
Spiritualists, therefore, know that it is only a matter
of time for the change to come, as more and more
people are now thinking for themselves, and that the
Church must ultimately adopt Spiritualism and all
Spiritualism stands for. If it does not do so all its
authority and influence will go, and it will become the
byword of the next generation.

There is very little historical evidence that Jesus

I

ever lived.*   Philo, Tacitus, Pliny, Suetonius, Epictetus and Plutarch, all first century historians of the highest standing, make no mention of him, except that three of them allude to the traditions current about him as promulgated by the Christians of their times. Celsus, the Roman philosopher of the second century, wrote a treatise to prove that there was not a historical fact to show that the claims of the Christians regarding Jesus were justified.   There is little historical reference to him anywhere except in what is now believed to be a forgery.   The only important piece of evidence we have outside Christian literature is contained in a passage by the Jewish historian Josephus, who wrote in the last decade of the first century.   This passage will be found in the 18th book of the *Antiquities* of Josephus.   It runs as follows :—

"Now about this time came Jesus, a wise man, if indeed one may call him a man, for he was a doer of wonderful works, a teacher of such men as receive what is true with pleasure, and he attracted many Jews and many of the Greeks ; this was the Christ. And when on the accusation of the principal men among us Pilate had condemned him to the cross, they did not desist who had formerly loved him (for he appeared to them on the third day alive again, the divine prophets having foretold both this and a myriad other wonderful things about him), and even now the race of those called Christians after him has not died out."

Is this passage accepted by historians and critics as genuine?   No, with very few exceptions they

---

* Historical and traditional evidence must not be confused.   The evidence on which the life of Jesus rests is almost entirely traditional.

believe that it is an interpolation. It is out of its setting, as immediately following is an indecent tale of Roman society. Origen, the early Christian father, states that Josephus did not believe Jesus to be the Christ. Origen and the early fathers, moreover, were unaware of this passage. Josephus was a Jew, not a Christian, and never became a Christian. Consequently the passage above referred to is inappropriate as coming from anyone who was not a Christian. Gibbon, the historian, distinctly states that there is no doubt that it is an interpolation added in the fourth century.

However, for the sake of argument, let us admit that it is genuine, and that Josephus did write it, and that it is a fair representation of the case. What then do we find? Nothing extraordinary, nothing certainly on which to build the creeds and dogmas of the Christian Church. He referred to Jesus as the Christ, which means the Anointed One, but this term was given to other outstanding religious teachers. He also referred to him appearing to his disciples the third day alive again, but this is not extraordinary, as apparitions were as common in those days as they are in our day. We therefore do not require to subvert our reason to accept this account of Jesus. Whether it is genuine or not is of no importance ; if it is, it is the only statement there is respecting Jesus of any value.

Let us now consider, from the unreliable evidence we have before us,* from the contradictions of the

---

* Professor Harnack (called " one of the greatest living experts in this branch of scholarship " by the Christian Evidence Society), in his book *What is Christianity?* states that he believes the gospels are only credible in their outlines.

gospel narratives, and their many obvious mistakes, what it is possible that Jesus really taught, and I think I can show from three of the gospels that what he is reported as having taught was just what we might expect from a religious teacher of his day.   In none of the four gospels does he claim to be founding a new religion.   He was born a Jew, lived a Jew, and died a Jew.

Taking, first of all, the first three gospels as a basis for this discussion, let us go through them one by one.   The gospel which is attributed to Matthew tells us that our being saved depends on how we live.   According to the gospels, Matthew was a disciple of Jesus and was constantly with him for the two years of his ministry.   Nothing is to be found here to justify the Church's creeds or doctrines. Briefly, Matthew tells us that Jesus taught that Heaven would be attained by those who were poor in spirit, merciful, pure in heart, peacemakers, per-secuted for righteousness sake, and kept the ten commandments ; also by those who forgave their enemies, who judged not, but who received righteous men and did the will of God.   According to Matthew, Jesus also taught that every man shall be rewarded according to his works, and that we must become as little children.   That we are to sell all that we have and give to the poor ; that we should forsake brethren, sisters, father, mother, wife and children for his sake ; and, lastly, that we should honour our father and mother, feed the hungry and give drink to the thirsty, shelter to the stranger, clothe the naked, comfort the sick, and visit the prisoner in prison.

Again I read in the same book, "And behold one came and said unto him, 'Good Master, what good thing shall I do that I may have eternal life?'" Now here was a chance really to find the truth. Here was an enquiry direct from man to God, so the Church says—a direct question, the answer to which everyone of us wants to know. "What good thing shall I do that I may have eternal life?" What did Jesus reply? He did not say you must believe that he is the second person in the Trinity. He did not say you must be baptised. He did not say you must believe the Bible to be the inspired word of God. He did not say you must repeat something and believe something. No! Jesus simply stated, "Thou shalt do no murder, Thou shalt not commit adultery, Thou shalt not steal, Thou shalt not bear false witness, Honour thy father and mother, and Thou shalt love thy neighbour as thyself." What right has the Church to add conditions to salvation which Jesus did not think necessary? Why add to, or take away from, this direct answer to a direct question?

I now pass on to the gospel attributed to Mark. Now Mark is considered by all students of the subject to be the most likely to be nearest the truth concerning the life and sayings of Jesus. It is the least legendary or miraculous of the gospels. Jesus is depicted as a good man, and the virgin birth and the other miraculous stories about him are noticeable by their absence.

My friend F. C. Burkitt, Professor of Divinity at Cambridge, published last year *Jesus Christ, an Historical Outline*, an attempt to form a reasonable view of Jesus, his life and teachings. It should be

read by those interested in pursuing the subject
further. He regards the gospel of Mark as the oldest
gospel, remarking, " I regard the framework of the
Gospel of Mark as based on much the same authority
as the contents, that is to say, reminiscences more or
less faithful," and again, " Matthew and Luke on
the other hand do preserve singly fragments of
genuine tradition." On this " more or less faithful "
story are built up in his opinion the gospels of
Matthew and Luke, so that is all we have to go on
in considering what is contained in the first three
gospels.

I find that in this gospel of Mark also
there are conditions stated regarding salvation
similar to those given in Matthew, with one exception, and this occurs in a passage reading
from the ninth verse to the end of the last
chapter. It does not invalidate the argument,
however, as this passage is now known to be an
interpolation. It is not in the oldest manuscripts,
and particular attention is drawn to this fact in the
revised version of the Bible. It enables one to see
how valueless the gospels are, as this is only one of
one hundred interpolations which are easily recognised, occurring as they do in later versions, and not
in the earlier versions. The words in all these interpolations are quite out of their setting and have no
reference to what is being reported. One of the best
examples of an interpolation is the remark attributed
to Jesus that Simon Barjona would henceforth be
known as " Peter, and upon this rock I will build
my Church." This simple fisherman only knew
Aramaic, the language Jesus and his contemporaries

spoke, and how could he receive a Greek name meaning a stone? This word play could only be understood by one knowing Greek, and must have been inserted centuries later when a copy was being made by some enthusiastic scribe whose enthusiasm for the Church was greater than his honesty.

Another blatant forgery is the story of the woman taken in adultery, which is a late addition and is not in the oldest known codices. This fact is clearly marked in the Revised Version, but it in itself is enough to cast discredit on the entire Bible. This and many other instances make clear that the book is just a patchwork of stories which have no veridical value, and are probably nearly all fictitious.

These interpolations and alterations to the original text started at an early date and doubtless went on till our authorised version was produced in the 17th century. To show how unreliable is the entire Bible, mention need only be made of the complaint made by Dionysius of Corinth in the year 170 A.D., who complained of the falsification of his own writings, but consoled himself with the fact that the same is done to the Scriptures of the Lord.

Passing on to the gospel of Luke, I find the same teaching, namely, good works, good thoughts, injunctions to forgive our enemies, as just as we forgive, so shall we be forgiven. In a few words, Jesus preached a gospel of love and service to our fellow-men, and love to God, our Father in Heaven.

Lastly, we come to St. John's gospel, and here we find the basis of the Church's teaching. Here we find that belief is everything, and that our reaching Heaven depends on our beliefs and not on our deeds.

This seems rather extraordinary.   Here we have
four records reputed to contain the sayings of Jesus.
In three of them we are told that Jesus taught good
works, good living, and kindness of heart, and never
a word about belief.   Why was it that Matthew,
Mark and Luke never heard anything about salvation
by faith?

How was it that they forgot to record that Jesus
said, " For God so loved the world that he gave his
only begotten son, that whosoever believeth in him
should not perish, but have everlasting life?"   If
these four records are inspired by God, why is this
and many other similar statements omitted from three
of them, and only recorded in one of them?   If
belief is essential to salvation it should at least have
been the other way about, in fact it should have been
recorded in them all.

However, reducing it to a question of mathe-
matics, we have three to one against belief, and one
to three in favour of belief, and the average good
man, when he reaches Heaven, if he is confronted
by the question on the day of judgment, will have a
very good case when he stands up to justify his claim
to be allowed to enter Heaven.   He can tell the
Judge of all the Earth that in the four gospels he
finds that three of them stated that how he lived on
earth determined his admission to Heaven, and only
one stated that it was a question of believing something he found impossible to believe.   Can you
imagine a righteous judge on earth condemning such
a man?   Certainly not, and no intelligent individual
can imagine God doing so.   We must not impute to
the Almighty a justice inferior to our own.

Now it may be asked, why is there this extraordinary difference between the gospels of St. John and the other three gospels? The reason is readily apparent to those who have studied the origin of the gospels. The gospel of St. John was not written until a later date than the first three gospels. It was written not earlier than the second century, at a time when a certain section of the Church believed that beliefs were necessary to salvation. " The contents of the gospel of John do not seem to the present writer historical at all," and " I greatly doubt whether we can distinguish often in that gospel what is derived from tradition and what is derived from imagination." This is the view expressed by Professor Burkitt in his book already referred to.

I have already shown that a large section of the early Christian Church did not believe that creeds were necessary to salvation or that Jesus was the son of God. There were two sections in the Christian Church, and the gospel of St. John represents the opinion which gradually developed, namely, that one had to believe something to be a Christian. An early Christian looked on Jesus as a teacher and doer of good deeds, whereas this opinion gradually changed until it was evenly divided, some continuing to hold the original Christian view, and others the view that belief was necessary to salvation.

Thus we find at the Council of Nicaea the two opinions were boldly expressed, and only by a narrow majority did those who held that belief was necessary win their point. From that time onwards to hold a certain belief was necessary to be a Christian, but it was certainly not the teaching of Jesus, and it was not accepted by the early Christians.

St. Paul is reputed to be the originator of the idea

that to believe something was necessary to be a Christian, that Jesus took the sins of the world, and that we are justified by faith in him. What St. Paul wrote or believed we can only surmise, as the epistles attributed to him have no historical value ; they are unsigned, and no one knows when they were written ; and the same can be said of the epistles attributed to the other disciples. Those who have carefully studied the previous chapter can quite reasonably believe that all these doctrines were later additions to the original.

None of the epistles attributed to St. Paul ever refer to or quote from the gospels, probably because they were written at an earlier date, and assuming it was St. Paul who wrote them it must be remembered that he never knew Jesus, and could not have been acquainted with his teaching as his contemporary followers were. The writers, of the epistles attributed to him, based their opinions on the Book of the Law, and were thus imbued with the idea that Jesus was the longed for Messiah mentioned therein—which, however, was only their personal opinion. As the origin of those epistles is unknown, no known person having seen the original documents, this opinion may be interesting but is of no value.

Those who have studied the question consider that the first three gospels represent the teaching of Jesus more accurately than St. John's gospel or the epistles. Nothing, it must be remembered, was put in writing for years after the death of Jesus, the reason being, as Dr. Moffatt says in his introduction to his *New Translation of the New Testament*, that there was no impulse to do so, as they were all awaiting the new age at any moment, so why should they write anything? When this did not materialise, according to Dr. J. A. McClymont in his *New Testament and its Writers*, "a considerable modification of the oral gospel would naturally take place, during the long period that elapsed before it was committed to writing."

To sum up, therefore, what is the answer to the question, What did Jesus really teach? The copies of the many previous copies of the original synoptic gospels certainly lend the greatest weight towards the belief that Jesus taught that how we lived here would determine our place in the hereafter. He taught a very simple religion : belief in the Fatherhood of God ; the Brotherhood of Man ; belief in the after-life ; that as we lived here, we should live there, and that as we were forgiving and kind here, so should we receive forgiveness and kindness there.

Putting aside all the accretions which have surrounded this simple teaching, one can believe that Jesus was in close touch with a higher order of existence, and that he saw that this life on earth was a preparation for a better and a greater life hereafter. He went about doing good, trying to heal the sick with his psychic power, teaching forgiveness, love, charitableness, and preaching against the errors of his own day. He was a reformer in his own time, a man we must respect and admire. He was murdered by the orthodox of his day, who hated his outspoken criticism of their beliefs and actions. All who have the love of humanity at heart cannot but admire this unselfish and humane man, who went about doing good ; but do not let us forget that many, both before and after him, have lived similar lives and sacrificed them for their fellow men.

His teaching was based on the basic principles which had been accepted by all the great teachers who had preceded him, and only in Spiritualism do we find those great fundamental principles emphasised and the accretions ignored. I submit that Spiritualism is the only true religion for the present and the future, just as it has been the only true religion of the past. Just as to-day it is accepted only by the few who really know the truth, so in the past has it been accepted by the few who likewise knew the truth, because they, like the Spiritualists of to-day, were in close contact and held communication with the higher intelligences of the Etheric World.

Round the basic truths of Spiritualism mankind in ignorance has coiled superstitions which in different forms have become embodied in the world's present religions. It is the duty of Spiritualists to uncoil the false from the true, and reveal the truth, which orthodoxy everywhere has hidden in a black robe of superstition and ignorance. When Spiritualists succeed in educating the world to recognise the truth, then men and women of all nations will have a common knowledge of the great facts of existence, all religious differences, now so evident, will disappear, and mankind everywhere will worship in one cathedral whose dome is the firmament inlaid with suns, and whose true and only priests are the interpreters of nature.

CHAPTER V.
ANOTHER REFORMATION NEEDED.

FOUR centuries ago what is known as the Reformation occurred in the Christian Church. This organisation had become so corrupt, and so out of touch with the times, that it was split in two, some preferring to remain within the old Church and others deciding that a new Christian Church was needed. Under the leadership of Martin Luther, what is known as Protestant Christianity carved for itself a new Christianity, discarding much that the Old Christianity thought essential, and adopting new interpretations of many of the old beliefs. Though the creeds were retained, the dogmas were changed.

The people in pre-Reformation times worshipped and adored the Church, believing it to be a divine institution, the Pope was regarded as the divine representative of God on earth, and the priests were believed to be endowed with divine authority. The priests claimed the power to forgive sin and punish wickedness, and so things went on until the Reformation. All people had to do was to go to Church regularly, repeat the Latin prayers, participate in the celebration of Mass, never giving a thought to what it all meant. They were told that if they did so they would live in bliss in the life to come, and if they did not do so they would suffer eternal damnation. This state of accepting everything the Church teaches still continues to exist amongst the ignorant people of to-day, both Catholic and Protestant.

The Protestant Church, which sprang into being at the Reformation, claimed that everyone had the right to think for himself, but that if any thought differently from what their leaders said was true, they would be damned eternally.   The Protestant leaders, now that printing and reading had come into being, took the Bible as their guide, discarding the Pope and the old orthodox teachings.   The Bible, however, was a very different book at the Reformation from what it is to-day.   It contained many books that the reformers omitted, and there were many different versions in existence.   Gradually it became realised that if the Bible was to be the standard of the new Church, a version of it must be produced which must be standardised, and so in the year **1611** what is now called the Authorised Version of the Bible was produced.

Following this, an assembly, called the Westminster Divines, met in London in **1643** and produced what is known as the Westminster Confession of Faith.   This was rejected in England but accepted in Scotland.   The Confession of Faith extends to thirty-nine chapters, ranging over the most abstruse topics of theology, and along with it are printed the Longer and Shorter Catechisms, also adopted by the Church of Scotland.   The Confession of Faith, rejected in England, meant that the Church of England still relied on the Thirty-Nine Articles, for whose production Cranmer was chiefly responsible.   It took from **1536** till **1571** to settle these Articles.   They were first ten in number, then rose to forty-two, and were finally settled at thirty-nine.   The other Protestant countries in Europe also adopted various definitions of their reformed faith, and thus we find a repetition, in the years immediately following the

Reformation, of what took place at Nicaea. The Christian religion was again recast.

The Protestant Church to-day still retains, repeats and says it believes the creed of Nicaea, formulated in 325 A.D., and the creed of Athanasius, formulated and accepted early in the ninth century. Besides this it bases its beliefs on those documents which were accepted as divinely inspired after the Reformation. The Roman Catholic Church still retains the beliefs and doctrines it has always held. There is, therefore, this feud between Roman Catholicism and Protestantism. The one is founded entirely on the findings of the Councils in the early days of Christianity, while the other is founded on the findings of these Councils, supplemented by the findings of the Councils of Divines, which met together from time to time following the Reformation.

The Church of Rome, which claims to be the expounder of true Christianity, is at variance in many vital points with Protestant Christianity, because the Roman Catholic Church still advocates and preaches the views expressed in the fourth century, whereas the Protestant Church preaches and believes the views expressed in the sixteenth and seventeenth centuries. The Protestant Church claims that it is right and bases this claim on the Holy Scriptures, and the Roman Catholic Church claims that it is right and bases its claims on the findings of the early fathers.

As education advanced, people began with increasing frequency to enquire what basis either Church had for its teachings. The intelligent person wants to know why certain doctrines are being preached, and what foundation there is for those doctrines being claimed as divinely inspired and true. They want to know why in the twentieth century, we must accept the findings of the Council of Nicaea, or the Council of Westminster, or the opinions of Cranmer. They want to know the why and wherefore of these fundamental doctrines. The more we enquire into the reason the more we find to convince us that there is no real basis whatever for these doctrines, which were promulgated by zealous churchmen with little learning but a vast amount of credulity.

We find also that the Protestant Church, basing its doctrines on the Holy Bible, has based them on sand instead of on a rock ; moreover, that this was shifting sand, and, with the collapse of its foundation, a profound change has been brought about in the outlook of all thinking people on the question of what must be considered the fundamentals of belief. The Westminster Divines pronounced the Holy Bible divinely inspired word for word, that it contained no mistakes, no contradictions, and that it was a complete and final record of God's dealing with man and of God's plan of salvation. They asserted that the Bible contained a scheme which required to be believed in, and that this scheme ensured the believer's happiness hereafter, and the unbeliever's damnation.

They believed also that God's revelation to man ended with the last word of the last chapter of the book of Revelation, and that from that time onwards God had been silent. This belief has been gradually relinquished by all intelligent Christian people, but it is still the official belief of the Protestant Church, whether it be Church of England, Presby-

terian or Methodist. Officially, the beliefs ex-
pounded in the sixteenth and seventeenth centuries
are the beliefs of our Church to-day, and consequently
the book of Common Prayer is read word for word
as it was read hundreds of years ago, and the Bible
is read word for word as it was read hundreds of years
ago. The reader commences the reading of the
Bible by saying, "Here beginneth the Word of
God," and ends his reading by again quoting God as
the author of what he has read. Every petition and
prayer is ostensibly to the same God that the Jews
worshipped, and concludes with the name of Jesus
Christ, and no petition is considered valid without
this ending. The Bible is still considered officially a
holy book, sacred and verbally true. Its stories are
preached on as if they were true, and the scheme of
salvation is still propounded as the only way of man's
salvation. No parson ever preaches from any other
book than the Bible, as the opinion of the Church
still is that it and it only has been divinely inspired.

In the English Church all these antiquated
formulæ and expressions of opinion are repeated
Sunday after Sunday, and presumably the people
who do repeat them believe them. If they do not
they are very dishonest. If they do they are extremely credulous.

Officially, the Church has never changed its
views, and still retains the same antiquated ideas
about many of the fundamental and most important
things of life. It would be easy to criticise and make
light of many of the expressions in the Prayer Book,
in connection with the baptism, marriage, and the
morning and evening services. It would be also

K

easy to criticise the funeral service, and to show how out of date are many of the expressions of opinion. How foolish, for instance, it is to believe that what the Church calls "the dead" sleep in their graves until some future time which the Church calls the Resurrection, when the bodies are fo be re-animated and rise again from the grave. It would be easy to say how unworthy it is to repeat glibly the many horrible expressions of cruelty and lust in the Psalms. It would be easy to show the cruelty and absurdity of the Athanasian creed and the stupidity of the Nicene creed. In fact it would be easy to criticise and pull to pieces the entire prayer book, but to do this would require a chapter instead of a page. Presumably, however, those who regularly attend Church believe all they say they believe, as if they do not they are committing a great sin which must react on their characters. At some future date, when they recognise more clearly the necessity for honest thinking in building up their characters, they will regret subverting their reason to common custom and usage. This criticism can also be extended to what is called the Free Churches, and the Church of Scotland, as, though the people do not repeat these absurdities, yet they listen to them being uttered by the parson.

Fortunately, however, there are people honest enough to refuse to repeat what they do not believe, and consequently they stay away from Church.

In consequence of this attitude of the Church, never to change with the changing times, the attendance at public worship is gradually getting smaller, and the pews are gradually emptying. Various devices are adopted by ingenious parsons to try to fill their churches, but they are only temporarily effective, for as the novelty passes off the church is nearly empty again. The truth of the matter is that a greater and greater number of people to-day believe that truth comes before usage and custom. They object to their reason being debased every time they enter a church. Those who feel like this are steadily increasing in number, and the progress of Spiritualism is making the decline in church attendance all the more marked.

Last century the people, rather than believe nothing, subverted their reason, thinking that in doing so they were pleasing the Almighty. To-day, however, the position is different. In every large centre there are quite a number of Spiritualist Churches, and in the smaller centres there is at least one. The Spiritualists are buying up Churches from impoverished orthodox communities, and the number of Spiritualist Churches is increasing yearly, as the people through Spiritualism are finding their longings and aspirations satisfied. They are finding in it a religion that will satisfy their reason and their conscience, a religion that helps them through life and comforts them at death, a religion that makes clearer to them their origin and their destiny.

The foregoing is a brief statement of facts and I challenge anyone to refute them. The time has come to ask seriously what are the Christian Churches going to do about it. 'Are they for ever going to remain tied to the theologians of the past? Are they never going to be able to evolve for themselves a religion which will satisfy the intellect of the average intelligent member of the community? Are they going to continue to pander to the ignorant, and when these have become educated, are they going to continue to preach the old doctrines and dogmas to empty pews? Do they think that the hand of time is standing still, and do they think that what they consider heresy to-day is not going to become the orthodoxy of to-morrow? Do they think that history is going to fail to repeat itself, as it has repeated itself in the past, for the heterodoxy of one age has always become the orthodoxy of the next. The mind of man never remains for long stationary. *Semper idem* is a very dangerous policy.

I am not prepared to prophesy what the Christian Church intends to do, as the mentality of the clergy has always puzzled me, and I would not be so bold as to try to unravel such a tangled skein. I shall, however, say this. If the Church does not move with the times and does not discard all its old dogmas and doctrines and accept Spiritualism, in another generation it will be discredited and abandoned. A new Church will have taken its place, and that Church will be guided, not by the theories and formulæ of dead theologians, but by some of the greatest minds who have survived death, and are to-day guiding the Spiritualist Church on its road to victory. No man can stem the ocean's tide, and no Church can stop the rising tide of Spiritualism, as the waves of the Etheric World are breaking with increasing force on the shores of this world of ours.

There are, therefore, two courses open to the Christian Church to follow. One is to ignore all psychic phenomena and continue to look upon them as fraud, or as the work of the devil. The other course is to accept what men and women of honour and intelligence have to say, men and women of our own time, who claim, and rightly claim, that what they affirm is not their theories but teaching which has come from those who once lived here and have been appointed by the Rulers of the Etheric World to guide the lives of those on earth. If Christians prefer to go back nineteen hundred years, and accept as true what is reported to have been said by people in those far off years, handed down in writings of more than doubtful value, then there is nothing more to be said. If they prefer to believe what someone is reported to have said that someone said about something nineteen hundred years ago, and disbelieve the hundreds of thousands of people of the present day, in our own country, who have experienced the validity of this new revelation, then again there is nothing more to be said. In Great Britain alone there are nearly 1,500 Spiritualist Churches, and at least three million Spiritualists, people of honesty and intelligence, many of whom claim to have communicated with those who have passed on, and in consequence cannot do otherwise than consider the old dogmas and doctrines to be the product of an ignorant age. The number of Spiritualists throughout the world amounts to many millions, and is increasing everywhere.

The choice is difficult for the clergy to make, as they have kept their congregations so long in ignorance, and in most cases they are as ignorant as their congregations, but the choice some day will have to be made, and that day is looming nearer and nearer.

Spiritualists have never tortured nor persecuted

those who differed from them. They have always upheld the freedom of thought and avoided doing harm to anyone. Instead, therefore, of parsons holding Spiritualists up to ridicule and scorn, calling them deluded people, the victims of the Devil and his followers, the clergy should remember the terrible history of their own institution, and the crimes it has committed in the name of religion.

Of course, all I have written with regard to the origin of Christianity and the Bible should be well known to every intelligent individual. Is it not all recorded in many standard books, whose findings have never been disproved, and also by various leading professors of Biblical history who likewise have never been proved wrong? This being so, would it not be more correct to say that the clergy and not the Spiritualists are under a delusion? It is the Spiritualists who are at pains to prove all things and whose beliefs, based on present-day evidence which is incontestable, are founded on truth, whereas the clergy rely on very doubtful tradition and ancient superstition for their beliefs and cannot bring forward any historical evidence for their assertions.

It would be well for the clergy to cease from branding Spiritualists as " The servants of the devil " when they have no authority whatever for expressing such an opinion. Just as most of the clergy in this country made fools of themselves and their congregations by denouncing evolution, so they are likewise making themselves and their congregations look ridiculous by their latest attempt to fool the people. Here are quotations taken from four recent sermons which are typical examples of many. The first is :—

" Spiritualism affords the devil and his angels the opportunity to drag men down to perdition." The next is :—

" Spiritualism is a perfectly devised instrument of the devil. A conspicuous feature of this cult is the absence of God." And this in spite of the fact that the first principle of Spiritualism is the Fatherhood of God. The third is :—

" Spiritualism breaks God's laws and is the work of the devil."

Consider the bigotry of these self-appointed interpreters of God's purpose towards men ! It is calculated that there are 100,000 séances held in Great Britain every week, and in practically every case prayer is offered to God, and protection is asked against the forces of evil. Approaching the unseen in this spirit of reverence protects us from all danger, as with minds of high purpose our Etheric friends can get into our surroundings and keep away all evil influences. This preaching against Spiritualism takes place Sunday after Sunday up and down the country, and I could fill very many pages with similar extracts, but as they all run on the same line I shall quote but one more.

" Spiritualists are a deluded people, seduced into belief in a lie, and the victims of the evil one."

I withhold the names of these four representatives of the Protestant Church as some day they will regret their folly, and I do not wish to brand them for life.

These pronouncements, however, are samples of the preaching delivered from Christian pulpits throughout the country by parsons whose job in life

is to keep the people believing the Church's doctrines
at all costs, and by throwing dust in the people's eyes,
by fair means or foul to prevent them from knowing
the truth.   They quote various Biblical texts to support their theory, but do not tell their congregations
that there is no historical foundation or basis for any
of those texts quoted, and that there is no evidence
of divine inspiration for one of them.   It is they and
their fellow-Christians who are believers in a lie, not
Spiritualists, who can adduce scientific reasons for
the beliefs they hold, and moreover, can prove to
anyone wishing to have the proof that all they assert
is true.

Unlike Spiritualist newspapers which will publish
articles and advertisements of books for and against
Spiritualism, most Church newspapers will not publish
any advertisements of books on Spiritualism and only
articles against Spiritualism.   They remind me of a
boy who has blown up a soap bubble, and who
protects it from every breath of wind in case it bursts.
If the Church doctrines were founded on a solid basis
of truth there would be no need for any fear, as truth
can always protect itself.   The clergy to-day are
either misrepresenting Spiritualism or using their
exertions in other directions to keep the people from
knowing about it.   The more they vituperate and lie
the nearer is coming the collapse of the whole edifice
of creeds, dogmas, and superstition.

The clergy add nothing to the sum of human knowledge, they produce nothing, and take the tenth
from all the produce of the land for work similar to
what is done in Spiritualist Churches voluntarily

and wholeheartedly.* The public in their ignorance pay heavily to be taught error, whereas, when they become sufficiently intelligent, truth will be revealed as they can receive it from the higher intelligences of the Etheric World. The clergy can officiate at marriages, which can be done equally well by the Registrar in a Church, sprinkle water on infants, perform before the altar, and pronounce meaningless words at the grave side, and millions of pounds are spent annually to keep this class in comfort while millions of would-be producers are in poverty. They flourish on ignorance, and where the people are most ignorant priests are most numerous. They excel in the art of devising reasons why the people should never think for themselves, and they have been the greatest obstacle to progress recorded in history. They keep the people in ignorance and then take credit for comforting them in trouble, sickness, old age, and bereavement, whereas if the people were encouraged and helped to think for themselves their ministrations would not be required.

Those of us who are known to have been in touch with the Etheric World are daily in receipt of a large correspondence from people in trouble, people in sorrow, and people who are losing all hope. Those people have lost faith and belief in the old religion and they turn to us for guidance and for comfort. Those who are paid to do this work have failed the people, and this is becoming more and more

---

* Spiritualist Churches and Sunday Schools are all run by voluntary effort, though the speaker and clairvoyant at the Church Service usually get a small fee. Funeral services are conducted voluntarily, and so also are all the social services connected with each Church. Those in trouble or sickness are helped and cared for by voluntary helpers. Most Churches have healing circles at which all help is voluntary.

generally recognised.   If the Church leaders could
see the correspondence which comes into my house
every day from people who have been kept from
suicide, who have been kept from the asylum, and
who have regained hope and received comfort, as the
result of the help, comfort and guidance Spiritualism
has been able to give them, they would realise how
lamentably the Church has neglected its opportunity,
and how disastrously it is failing in its duty.*

It would be difficult to count the number of
people who have told me of the help Spiritualism has
given them in the darkest hour of their sorrow.
This testimony is poured out on all hands.   Just the
other day a woman spoke to me after one of my
meetings and told me she had recently lost her husband.   The vicar had called, and the only consolation he could offer her was to suggest that she should
attend communion.   " How will this satisfy me that
my husband still lives?" she asked him.   To which
he answered, "We have the blessed hope of everlasting life through Jesus Christ our Lord."   She
replied, "Whatever is the good of hope?   I want help
from someone who knows, not from someone who
hopes only."   Thus he left her, and she told me that
what I had told her that night in my address was the
first real comfort she had experienced since her husband's passing.   I put her in touch with a good
Medium, and great was her delight in hearing her

---

* The following is an extract from a letter from a clergyman who is
one of the London Missionary Society's missionaries on an island
in the Pacific. He is devoting his life there to work amongst
the lepers :—" I am most happy and overjoyed with *On the Edge
of the Etheric.* This is the Gospel. All goodness is worth while
in a way I never understood before." I give this extract to show
that self-sacrifice will not cease when Spiritualism takes the place
of Christianity.

husband speak to her and prove without doubt that he still lived and that they would meet again.*

In this country alone many millions of pounds are being spent annually by the community to maintain parsons and churches for the purpose of preserving ancient and worn-out creeds and dogmas. These parsons are securely entrenched in their positions, as the majority of them are entitled to emoluments which it is very difficult for the people to divert into other channels. In the Church of England the people have no say as to who is to be their parson. He is appointed by a patron who may have no interest in the congregation, but he owns the living as an investment. These livings are bought and sold, and the people accept this system like sheep as they do everything else in connection with the Church. In Scotland this scandal was swept away ninety years ago.

Our religious leaders feel they are safe and comfortable, and they think that all they have to do is to continue as their predecessors did and repeat the same worn-out formulæ. But it will not do. Im-

---

* I arranged that this lady should go quite anonymously and no one would know who she was. She travelled 200 miles to sit with the Medium, so she was consequently a stranger to him. The following are some extracts from her long letter reporting to me the results obtained :—

"You asked me to let you know the result of my sitting. I cannot express my gratitude for all your kindness to me. It is beyond words. I had a most successful sitting. Many friends spoke to me by the direct voice. My husband spoke to me, using his pet name for me, and giving his own name correctly. It was all most convincing. I managed to arrange a second sitting and this was as good as the first. I have been truly comforted and convinced."

This is only one of many hundreds of similar letters I have received from people who have obtained conviction and comfort as the result of the contact made with the Etheric World through mediumship.

mediately prior to the Reformation the same com-
placency was exhibited by the priests of what we now
call the Church of Rome. Then men arose and led the
people into a new and different line of thought. What
happened then is happening to-day, slowly and surely,
and gradually the Church is becoming alarmed at the
number of desertions among its adherents. Those who
doubt my word have only to attend the Spiritualist
service in the Queen's Hall every Sunday and see
that vast hall packed to the roof. Spiritualists can
rightly claim that they conduct the world's largest
religious service every Sunday of the year. Where-
ever there is a Spiritualists' propaganda meeting
throughout the country the hall is packed to capacity.
The largest halls are easily filled in every town in the
land. The people are desperately anxious to find
the truth, which they cannot get in the Churches.
Everywhere the Spiritualist Churches are packed ;
the other Sunday hundreds were turned away from the
Queen's Hall. Owing, however, to the influence of
the Church, the British Broadcasting Corporation
will not broadcast a Spiritualist Service.

One by one, though only here and there, parsons
are realising that the old dogmas and creeds are dead
and that the Church must adopt Spiritualism or perish.
All honour to them for their courage and foresight,
but the great majority, had they the will and the knowledge to do so, which I doubt, fear to take the lead
and are led by the least intelligent of their congregations. There are some Spiritualists who believe that
the Church will adopt Spiritualism, lock, stock and
barrel, and discard in one fell swoop all its dogmas
and doctrines. Others think that Spiritualism will

permeate the teaching of the Churches slowly, just as the belief in evolution did. Personally I believe in the leavening process as the one likely to happen, but, however it occurs, come it will. It is only a matter of time.

Historians of the future will have the same old story to tell, namely, the Church which claims to be divinely inspired being led into the way of truth, never leading ; always reactionary, and only accepting something better when forced to do so. If truth only had been the watchword of the Church and if we had heard less of divine authority, how differently religion would be looked upon to-day ! Fortunately, at long last, the people are now differentiating between Religion and Superstition. What goes under the name of Christianity is superstition ; true Religion is something very different.

CHAPTER VI.
RECONSTRUCTION.

THE reason why I have given so much space to the consideration of the Christian religion is that so many earnest and devout people find that their belief in Christianity makes it impossible for them to accept the teachings of Spiritualism. The last thing I wish to do is to unsettle anyone's beliefs regarding the great fundamental issues of life and death. If I thought I was doing this I should be the first to regret it. Some of those who have read this book thus far may think that I have tried to destroy all that they hold most dear. If they will read to the end of the book they will understand that I have only pulled down for the purpose of building up.

History shows us that in the past the majority of the people have always been opposed to change of any kind, either in politics or in religion. Both political and religious reformers have had to suffer from the criticism and enmity of those who believed that what is, must always be. In earlier times those who wished to change the political or religious views of the people had to suffer imprisonment and often torture. However, in our day and generation all that need be expected by would-be reformers is criticism and perhaps abuse.

At the risk of repetition, I wish to make my position quite clear, so that there may be no misunderstanding. Christianity, it will be admitted by everybody, originated in an age of intense ignorance. It was born at a time when hardly anyone could write or read, and even those who could write did so in a very haphazard fashion. At that time paper was unknown, and anything that was written was written on papyrus, manufactured from reeds and rushes. Accuracy of speech or thought was hardly known. Facts had not the value then that they have now,. and greatly exaggerated stories were told and circulated about events, especially when those events were of an unusual character. Anything unusual or not understood was considered to be the direct act of God or Gods.

It is only within the last few centuries that we have come to realise that the Universe is governed by law and order, and that every event is but one incident in an unbroken chain of cause and effect. The workings of nature in years gone by were not in the least understood. Nineteen hundred years ago nothing whatever was known by the masses about Astronomy, Biology, Chemistry, Physics, the art of healing, or any of the other sciences. Only a very few could read or write. For the most part people were cruel beyond measure, and held life of little value and thought nothing of human suffering. In Palestine, at the time of the birth of Jesus, the people were more ignorant and more uncivilised than are the Arabs in North Africa to-day. They were poor, ignorant, and superstitious.

From this well of ignorance the majority in Europe and America draw all their information with regard to their religious beliefs. In the old days they drank long and deep, but as they advanced in intelligence the draughts became lighter and less frequent. What, then, is the position to-day with regard to this source of knowledge? Simply this : a large section of the Christian community still hold to the old beliefs, but in a much more feeble way than of yore, while there is a large and increasing section to whom the claims of Christianity make no appeal. Though they may be nominally Christians, they are absolutely indifferent to the whole subject. In other words, orthodox religion makes no appeal to them. They hold the view that their duty in life is to do the best they can, and if there is another life after death they will take the consequences of what they have done. A much smaller section have no religion whatever, and are strongly anti-Christian, as the result of the false claims made by Christianity, believing that all religion is superstition which should be avoided by every sensible thinking man and woman.

Lastly, we come to the increasing body of people called Spiritualists, who hold the view that the basis of all religion is the same, and that what is called religion officially is nothing more than superstition. They believe that we are destined for something better and greater than this world, but that owing to ignorance man has invented beliefs and ideas which, though originating in his religious instinct, have little to do with true religion. Religion and Superstition are two different things. Superstition is that which has accumulated round religion. Religion is a central truth in man's life, which has always been and always will be. One might say that superstitions come and go but religion goes on for ever.

Now superstition and religion are often mixed up and confused. People think, for instance, that

they are religious if they go to Church ; if they attend
Holy Communion ; if they cease from doing certain
things on Holy Days ; if they read the Bible ; if they
repeat prayers, and if they believe certain words and
certain documents to be inspired by God. Less
civilised people believe in offering up sacrifices, or
beating tom-toms, or worshipping images. Those
outward forms and ceremonies have, however,
nothing whatever to do with real religion. They are
the draperies, the superstition which surrounds it.
Real religion does not consist in believing that God,
the maker of this immense Universe, which no human
mind is capable of fathoming, came down to earth
and lived for two years wandering about Palestine.
Neither is it religion to consider a certain Book is
holy and inspired by God. It is not religion to repeat
certain words either by yourself or after a parson,
or to partake of Holy Communion, whether you consider that what you eat and drink is part of God, or
the service is only one of remembrance. These
things are only the clothes that have been put on to
religion ; religion is the something underneath the
outward drapery.

Doubtless all those acts and formulæ which have
accompanied religion were needful until the time came
when we could realise better our true position in the
Universe. We are all the product of our times, and
if our ancestors evolved a creed it was done for an
object, and if they sacrificed human beings or animals
it was also done for an object, the object being to
satisfy some human longing and desire. We have
evolved beyond human sacrifice, and as we have so
done, so shall we evolve from creeds and dogmas,

L

Holy Books and Holy Institutions.   History undoubtedly shows that everywhere creeds, dogmas,
holy books and holy churches have been abused,
though they have given great comfort and help to
many.

We have now arrived at a stage in our evolution
when intelligent people find full satisfaction for the
religious instinct in the knowledge we now possess,
without having recourse to the past.   We now know
from the definite and verifiable information we receive
from the Etheric World that we are here for a purpose, that our life on the earth is only a preparation
for a life in a better place, and that place is the Etheric
World which surrounds us and interpenetrates this
earth.   We now can converse with those who have
passed on, whom Christians call dead.   In the
Etheric World it is not those who believed in a particular creed who are the happiest, and those on earth
who think such a belief necessary are mistaken.   We
now find that as we live here so shall we live there.
If we live up to our highest ideals nothing more is
expected from us.   This constitutes true religion.
There is no necessity to attend Church, to read the
Bible, to repeat creeds or prayers, in order to reach
this other world, as it is as natural for us to pass into
the Etheric World as it is for us to enter this world.

Our birth took place with no effort on our part.
Our reaching the Etheric World will take place likewise with no effort on our part. If we prefer to live a
debased life on earth, if we prefer to be cruel rather
than kind, if we prefer to think of ourselves only and
never of others, then we shall mix with those of a
similar kind in the Etheric World.   It is all a question

of desire. If we desire something different, something better, and if we give our thoughts on this earth to the development of our characters, and try to mould our characters so that they get better instead of worse, then in the next world we shall find ourselves in the company of those who have the same ideals and aspirations in common, people of all races and religions.

It is a well-known fact that often those who make much profession lead the most selfish lives, and that those who make little profession lead the most unselfish lives. Sin is selfishness. The more unselfish we are, the less sinful we are, and the more selfish we are, the more sinful we are. I have spoken to those in the Etheric World who held strong dogmatic beliefs on earth, and I find that they are not so happy as others who have also passed on who lived good, unselfish lives on earth, ignoring entirely creeds and dogmas. Dogmas and creeds make for selfishness. The dogmatists and doctrinaires have no better a place than those who gave no thought to these matters and who lived their lives to the best of their ability, unselfishly and for the good of others. If the former continue to retain their views, they sink to a lower state of intelligence and mix with those of similar mentality.

We do not think it is necessary, on going a journey to another country, to commit ourselves to certain beliefs before we shall be allowed to enter it ; nor need we do so before starting on the journey that lies before us at death. There is nothing mysterious about it, and if we were all intelligent enough we should not require to be at the expense of keeping parsons to repeat creeds and go through various acts of devotion, in the belief that by so doing our position at death will be better than it would be otherwise.

I have never forgotten a message which came through at a séance from one speaking from the Etheric World to which he had passed at death. It was as follows :—"God never meant religion to be a mystery. It is man who has made it so. His handiwork is plain enough for all to understand, and religion was never meant to be in any way different. What should be simple has been made obscure. You have but to do your best—no one can do better, and the future will gradually unfold before you and your duty be made clear."

This is surely easy for everyone to follow, and what a gain it will be to mankind when all realise that they have been making difficulties where no difficulties exist. They have been adding to life's burdens by making themselves believe a certain Book was holy, or a certain Church was holy, or a certain act was holy, or a certain belief was holy and pleasing in the sight of God.

Intelligent people must realise that Infinite Intelligence is absolutely indifferent as to whether we believe the Bible to be inspired by God, or that God became man and dwelt with us or did not ; that Infinite Intelligence cares nothing for the repetition of creeds, or the repeating of prayers, or the counting of beads. All these man-made attempts to placate the Almighty originate in the fear of the unknown. They are the result of ignorance, and will survive only so long as man is ignorant of his true position in the Universe.

What is man's true position in this illimitable

Universe, the knowledge of which year by year seems to be more and more unfolding itself to us? As this book proceeds I hope to be able to go more deeply into this question, but first let us consider it in as simple words as possible. Why are we here and what is our destiny? These questions have been answered so differently in the past that even with our increased knowledge one hesitates to be dogmatic, and were it not for the knowledge that I have obtained from the Etheric World I should hesitate to answer it at all. Before going into the question deeply, let me tell you what was told by one who has joined the great majority and knows more than we do. His words were as follows :—

" You are just as much an Etheric Being now as you will ever be. You are just as much in the Etheric World now as you will ever be, only you do not appreciate the fact in consequence of your having a physical body attuned to physical surroundings. The Etheric World is about and around you, and at death when you discard your physical body you are in the Etheric World without having to travel any distance to get there. You became immortal at your birth, and you are just as immortal now as you will ever be. Your physical body covers your etheric body, and you cannot appreciate your etheric body because it is made up of substance at a higher rate of vibration than your physical eyes can see. When you die you will appreciate the etheric body and cease to appreciate your physical body. Your new body grows more and more refined as time passes, and you will rise to higher and higher planes of consciousness. You will see more and you will see further. You will hear more and you will hear more clearly. Any deformities you have will be corrected here. If you

have lost a leg or arm you will have it here, as it was
only the physical arm or leg you lost.   Your understanding will be enlarged, and you will be more conscious of the beauties of your surroundings than you
are in the physical body.   Your scope of usefulness will
be extended beyond the limit of your present imagination.   You will not have to trouble about money,
about earning a livelihood, about eating or about
clothes, or about a house to live in, as your mind will
be in so much greater control of your surroundings
that it will be able to mould those surroundings to
meet your desires.   There will be no more pain or
sorrow or regret, no more grieving over separation
after your loved ones from the earth have joined you.
You will cease to regret the errors of the past through
rectifying past mistakes.   You will then enter on a
life of eternal progress and everlasting blessedness.''

From the foregoing it will be seen how futile it
is on earth to give much thought to those things which
many people consider of such paramount importance,
such as titles, as you drop them when you enter the
Etheric World.

As this book proceeds our correct outlook on life
will become clearer ; but before I close this chapter
I wish to revert to the subject I discussed at the commencement, namely, the reason why I have in previous
chapters given so much consideration to the Christian
Faith.   The reason, I repeat, is that the Christian Faith is the great stumbling block to the acceptance of Spiritualism in Christian countries.   Christians quote Biblical texts to show that God does not
mean us to converse with the dead.   They quote
texts written by ignorant people in an age of ignorance,
who burned witches and perpetrated other ghastly
cruelties, while they omit to obey the instructions

given in the texts which follow and precede those texts relating to conversing with the departed.

Some people take the trouble to try to explain that those texts refer to necromancy, which has nothing whatever to do with Spiritualism ; but personally I do not think it is worth while to trouble oneself as to whether those texts do refer to necromancy or to communication with the departed. To me they are of no value whatever. They are not God-inspired, and there is no more reason why they should be taken as rules for our lives in the twentieth century than should the instructions contained in the code of Hammurabi, King of Babylon, one of the greatest and best codes of morals ever written by the ancients, and greatly superior to the teachings of the Old Testament. Hammurabi lived in the year 1550 B.C., long before a book of the Old Testament was written.

Again, people say that it cannot be right to converse with the departed, as those who speak to us say they are happy and in a better world, though many of those who do communicate are known not to have been Christian people on earth. Christians say this is a proof that it is the Devil or his angels who assume those personalities in order to deceive us and subvert our belief in Jesus as the saviour of mankind. They argue that, in this surreptitious manner, the servants of the Devil will make it all the more certain that a larger consignment of the human race will find their way to Hell than would otherwise have been the case. This is a very ingenious proposition, but I do not believe it ; neither do I believe, for the reasons previously given in this book, that

God came to earth and had any scheme of salvation through the death of Himself on the cross.

One further objection that Christians have to Spiritualism is that we are calling back the dead and that this is contrary to God's Holy Word. This can be easily answered, because it is absolutely, untrue. No one on earth calls back the dead. It is our friends on the other side who come back of their own accord, because they wish us to know that they are alive and happy, and because they wish to help to rid mankind of all the superstitions which surround religion. They realise how much we are handicapped by our ignorance, how much time we waste in forms and ceremonies, and how much we suffer through trying to believe impossible dogmas and doctrines. They want to tell us how simple a matter it all is, and that we have to believe nothing unnatural ; that all we have to do is to try to live good and upright lives. They are specially anxious to let us know that they are alive because Christianity teaches that the dead lie in their graves until some future Resurrection day. Until the advent of Spiritualism this was generally believed. I am now told that this belief is not held generally, and probably it is not, though the Church writings and hymns still convey this impression. Spiritualism has played its part in educating the people on the subject.

It is because I believe that Spiritualism is being handicapped and thwarted by orthodox Christians, through ignorance, that I have tried to show that there is no basis for the beliefs of Christianity. Christians, greatly as they err, certainly take life seriously and are the very people who should be Spiritualists, as, except Spiritualists, they are the people who more than others take the view that life on earth is more than it really seems to be. Christians, through their ignorance and through their attachment to a Holy Book which they think is divinely inspired, are obstructing the spread of a great revelation which is slowly but surely coming to enlighten the earth.

Through their ignorance they are preventing a natural development of those faculties inherent in every man and woman, which may be described as the Psychic gift. Little do they realise what pain and suffering and disappointment they are causing their friends and relatives in the Etheric World who wish to come back and communicate with them, but who rarely get a chance to let their friends on earth know where they are, and how they are, because few Christians will attend séances.

We are still very ignorant of many things, and the public Press is just a reflection of the public mind. In the old days crowds gathered from all directions to see a witch burned—anything for a change from the monotony of life. The mentality of the people to-day has only changed to a degree, and instead of paying priests to burn witches the public buys newspapers which "expose" Mediums. Of course newspapers would not do so if their readers did not approve, just as parsons would not have burned witches if they had not received the support of their congregations.

The latest style of "Witch Hunt" takes the form of "Medium Exposure." If a supply of general news runs dry something must be found to stimulate interest, so some prominent Medium is fastened on to provide a "sensation." The "stunt" takes the form of an "exposure." It is much more exciting to read about a Medium being exposed than to read that a Medium has been found genuine, and the more prominent the Medium the greater the publicity given to the "exposure."

In 1931 a *Daily Mail* reporter was present at a trance address given by a Medium named Mrs. Meurig Morris, and the reporter, who knew little about Spiritualism, wrote about her as if she were a fraud. The *Daily Mail* posters were prominently displayed everywhere announcing the "exposure." Big headlines appeared in the paper, and all who did not know Mrs. Meurig Morris, one of the most charming and delightful of ladies, naturally believed that she was a fraud.

Until recently all Mediums had to submit to these so-called Press exposures, but in this instance Mrs. Meurig Morris took the *Daily Mail* to court and retrieved her character, for although the jury found for the defendants on the plea of fair comment on a matter of public interest, their verdict concluded with the words, "we do not consider that any allegations of fraud or dishonesty have been proved."

If a woman is held to be honest it is difficult to understand how it can be fair comment to say publicly that she has been "found out." Such a verdict surely would never have been given in an ordinary case of slander ; instead heavy damages would have been obtained by the one slandered, but in this case the person slandered was a Medium. The country still contains many people who believe that no Medium can be genuine, and that all Mediums are the agents of the devil. It is only necessary for one or two members of a jury to hold to this view to prevent justice being done.

Following this "exposure" came the John Myers exposure by the *Sunday Dispatch*, of the same owner-ship as the *Daily Mail*. Myers had become famous as a Spirit photographer. In his presence, when a photograph was taken, photographs, or what are called "extras," of people who had died appeared on the plate as well as the photograph of the sitter. Many of these extras were recognised as friends or relatives of the sitters. Here was another chance for the sensational journalist. The editor employed the Marquess of Donegall, the writer of his society gossip page, who was quite ignorant of the sub-ject of Psychic photography, to arrange a sitting with Myers.

Lord Donegall, on behalf of the newspaper, offered Myers £100 for a sitting. This offer he refused, but said he would give Lord Donegall a sitting free. It was not a matter out of which he wished to make money. The first sitting under test conditions was satisfactory, and two extras were obtained. Then a request was made for another sitting, which was granted. On this occasion the *Sunday Dispatch* did not play the game, as, without the knowledge of Myers or any of his friends, the packet of plates was opened beforehand, marked, and then closed up again so cleverly that no suspicion was aroused. Besides this, a slide, which did not even fit Myers' camera, was substituted for one of his slides. Lord Donegall said afterwards that this was all done as part of the test, but as various people were concerned in the operation, how is anyone to know what really occurred? No one was present to watch the interests of Myers when the packet was secretly opened.

Now, because at the second sitting an extra appeared on a plate which had no mark on it, the *Sunday Dispatch*, on the following Sunday, announced in big head-lines on its front page that John Myers had been "exposed." If the public had only known the facts it would have decided that the *Sunday Dispatch* had exposed itself. When a test is being made it is not fair to open secretly the packet of plates beforehand, or cunningly substitute a slide, and when plates have to be marked for identification they should be marked in the presence of the Medium or one of his representatives. Otherwise who is to know whether all the plates are marked, and who is to know whether a faked extra was not put on the plate before it was taken to Myers. Myers had nothing to gain by faking an extra, but certainly if a fraudulent extra appeared it was a good story for the newspaper.

Well, at this second sitting, as I say, an extra appeared on the plate that was not marked, and so Myers was "exposed," but the attitude of the *Sunday Dispatch* was entirely one-sided. They laid great stress on the "exposure," but when challenged by *Psychic News* to explain the many and obviously weak points in their so-called test, they ignored this challenge and never replied to its well-informed criticism. I have not seen the *Sunday Dispatch* publish the fact that the "Victoria Psychic Research Society" reported, after the "exposure," that their committee of photographic experts, under the most stringent supervision, had obtained five excellent extras on specially-marked plates which made trickery impossible. Lord Donegall was challenged to a public debate by a well-known Spiritualist, but he wisely refused to accept the challenge. Neither have I seen the *Sunday Dispatch* refer to the report of *Psychic News* committee comprising the leading photographers in London. This committee was formed as the result of the " exposure," and at their second test sitting they obtained four " extras " on a specially marked plate. A copy of this report was sent to the editor, only to be ignored. Since the exposure, Myers has proved his powers over and over again by giving test sittings to professional photographers, who have been amazed by the results obtained.

This is not written as a defence of either Mrs. Meurig Morris or John Myers. I know them both ; the former is so transparently honest that this characteristic of her is obvious to anyone. Those who know Mr. Myers believe that he is incapable of deceit. He is a dentist by profession, and has his reputation to consider. That is all I need to say with regard to the Mediums involved in these two so-called " exposures."

The point I wish to emphasise is that Medium-hunting is still the sport of the public, through the Press. Every Press investigation is undertaken for the purpose of providing news, and up to the present Medium exposures have assisted the circulation of the newspaper concerned. Gradually, however, our newspapers are finding out that the public are thinking

for themselves, and realising that there is much more
than trickery and humbug in Spiritualism, and they
are finding also that Medium-hunting has not the
appeal to the public that it had a few years ago.
However, so long as the people are ignorant enough
to like this milder form of "witch burning," so long
will it be provided for them.

Can we expect the masses to be otherwise than
ignorant when they are encouraged, as they are from
nearly every pulpit in Christendom, to look on
Mediums as frauds? Every leading parson who denounces Spiritualism and Mediums is reported in the
newspapers, though within the last few years there has
been a much fairer tendency observable, and several
newspapers have given prominent announcement to
the successful results achieved in this field of investigation by men of science. After the Meurig Morris
affair the *Daily Mail*, to its credit, conducted the
fairest and most impartial investigation of Spiritualism
ever conducted by a newspaper, and its conclusions
were certainly all in favour of the view that Spiritualism had justified its claims, and was a subject
worthy to be taken seriously by everyone.

In this so-called civilised land of ours, one of our
most precious possessions, our Mediums, are the butt
of the ignorant Church and the thoughtless masses.
The first denounces them so that it can go on
deceiving the people, and the people denounce them
because they do not realise that the Church is mis-
leading them.

When a Medium is dishonest he is quickly exposed by Spiritualists themselves, not as a stunt but
as an act of discipline. Just because here and there

a pseudo-Medium has to be exposed by Spiritualists,. just as a clergyman has to be unfrocked, it does not follow that the great majority are frauds ; far from it. Up till now, however, it has benefited the Press and the Church to "expose" Mediums, and as long as it does so this will go on. It is in the hands of the public to stop it, and until they do so they will continue to get a one-sided view of Spiritualism, to their great loss. Mediumship is so new to the general public that press " exposures " have proved renumerative, but gradually, as the true meaning of Mediumship is realised, these "ex- posures " will cease, and honest Mediums will feel safe. The next step is the withdrawal from the statute book of the Witchcraft Act enacted by those who burned witches, thinking they were possessed of Devils.

Spiritualism will come into its own in time, and Spiritualists must do all in their power to illumine the darkened minds of those who guide the destinies of both Church and State. Anyone who attends the large Spiritualist meetings which are being held all over the country must be impressed by the enormous crowds who gather there. Wherever Spiritualist meetings are held, the largest halls available are packed. I have spoken in most of the great cities in Great Britain, in the largest halls, and there was seldom a vacant seat. I do this work as a duty, accepting neither fee nor travelling expenses, because the public are clamouring for the truth which only Spiritualism can give. One of the most impressive sights I have ever witnessed was that of six thousand people, in the Albert Hall, last Armistice Sunday at a Spiritualist Armistice service.   When the chairman asked that all would stand up who had had personal communication with their friends on the other side, more than three-quarters of the large audience rose to their feet.

Here is testimony enough, testimony to satisfy the enquirer without his having to rely on ancient creeds or the opinion of St. Paul or Socrates or Cicero.   All those men believed in survival, but their ideas are very crudely conveyed to us, compared with the way the evidence for survival is put forward by hundreds of thousands of responsible people in the year 1933.

The idea of immortality is not confined to a few individuals who lived long ago ; it is held in common by all the present and past religions of the world.   It has always puzzled me why the Christian religion should adopt its ideas of death and of the resurrection of the dead from the ancient Egyptians, as it has done through the teaching of St. Paul.   The ancient Egyptians embalmed their dead because they believed that the physical bodies would be re-animated by the soul on its return to earth at the end of the world, when the dead would all rise in their resuscitated physical bodies.   Paul obtained his views of the resurrection from the opinions which had prevailed in Egypt thousands of years before Christ.   The Egyptian view was accepted by the Pauline school of thought and adopted at the Council of Nicaea, as they did not know any better.   It was the best they could arrive at with their limited knowledge, but now with our greater knowledge we know that this view of death is a travesty of the truth.

Spiritualism provides the greatest support mankind has ever received to justify the religious instinct within him. It has proved that man's instinct that this life is a preparation for something better is fully justified. It is the greatest enemy of injustice. It is the greatest enemy of materialism. It is the greatest enemy of cruelty. When the world adopts Spiritualism and all that Spiritualism stands for, wars will cease and our social conditions will improve beyond recognition. Had Spiritualism been allowed to develop naturally, and had our ancestors not been so ignorant as to kill off all the Mediums, it is reasonable to believe that our social conditions to-day would have been vastly better than they are, and I do not hesitate to say that we should never have experienced the tragedy of the Great War of 1914-1918 which was caused by the material aspirations of Christian Germany. That country had no conception of any interests beyond those of this earth, and this outlook was due to the fact that more Mediums had been destoyed in Germany than in any other country in the world.

If we went back to-day to the doings of our ancestors and tried through physical means or legislation to obliterate Mediumship, the world would sink into a state of gross materialism, and humanity would be destroyed in a sea of poison gas or some other equal abomination. Only when humanity realises that life on earth is a preparation for something better than this world gives, will lust and greed end for something which we have not got, and when this happens wars will cease and so also will poverty, misery, and slumdom. Our entire social system, when this comes about, will be remodelled. Let each

M

one of us be frank with ourselves and think as rational individuals, and let each one of us realise that we have been too long harnessed to the dogmas of dead theologians, who gave to their fellow men only what they thought was the truth. Let us remember that those men were human like ourselves and, being more ignorant, were more liable to error. They knew nothing of the sciences, and they knew nothing of communication with the Etheric World.

Let us in future, when reading the Bible, read it as we would read any other book, admire its beauties, delight in its stories, realising that it is but the record of a nation's attempt to find God, but let us never attribute its follies, cruelties, and barbarous laws to the Creator of the Universe. Let us remember that they were the product of the barbarous age in which they were written, and always realise that the Bible is just a story of the past. Never let us be so wicked as to attribute its teaching to the Maker of heaven and earth, and call it the Word of God. Let us remember that the Christian Church, as it is to-day, is similar to what the Jewish Church was in the days of Jesus, and that if he were on earth to-day he would call the Christian Church a whited sepulchre, sheltering the dead bones of the past. He would direct our thoughts forward to the life to come and not to the worship of the dead past, and he would call the priests of Christendom blind leaders of the blind.

We, in the twentieth century, with our vastly increased knowledge, must not be enslaved by the theories and doctrines of the past. We must think for ourselves on the basis of modern knowledge. We must put aside all the dogmas and creeds which have been thought to be essential, and which we should now realise are quite unessential. We must not close our minds to reason when we open a Bible or enter a Church. If we follow these principles it will be possible for all of us, with open minds, to consider without prejudice the revelation which is coming through to our world, and which goes under the name of Spiritualism.

Now that I have cleared the ground I can begin to construct a new edifice. Consequently the next chapter will be a consideration of what Spiritualism is, and what it stands for.

PART II.

CHAPTER VII.

SPIRITUALISM, AND WHAT IT STANDS FOR.

SPIRITUALISM is not the faith of a sect or a cult ; it does not rest on tradition, nor on writings, ancient or modern. It has no ecclesiastical organisation claiming to interpret God's purpose towards mankind. It has no forms and ceremonies, pomp or circumstance. What Spiritualism stands for is a fact of the same nature as the fact that we exist. It is the only revelation that has ever come to man from a higher level of intelligence than exists on earth. It does not depend on the sayings or teachings of a past age, nor on inspired writings. It rests fundamentally on the fact that communication takes place between the inhabitants of this world and the inhabitants of the Etheric World. This is a scientifically established fact, and, once it is accepted, what follows is natural.

Under the required conditions, that is, in the presence of a Medium, voices quite apart from those of the sitters or the Medium speak and can be recognised. These voices are claimed to be the voices of those who once lived here on earth, who retain their earth memories, and claim relationship where it exists. They converse on subjects which concerned them and their friends while they lived on earth. They tell us that they have survived death, that death is only an incident in life, and that it results only in a change of appreciation of the conditions of life, as the

result of discarding the physical body.   They tell us
that they have an Etheric Body, the exact duplicate
of the Physical Body, and that this etheric duplicate
was the real body on earth, which acted as the frame-
work of the physical body.   They also state that
they are living in a real, tangible world, interpenetrating and surrounding our earth, composed of
substance too fine for us in our physical bodies to
sense and appreciate.

Once this fact of communication between those
who once lived on earth and ourselves is accepted,
everything that was relegated to the region of faith
emerges into the full day of knowledge.   Knowledge
takes the place of faith, and consequently errors and
conjectures are discarded.

We can converse freely with our friends in the
Etheric World and with others whom we have never
known on earth, people belonging to all religions and
races.   Though their environment is changed, the
means of communication by word of mouth is still
unaltered.   They tell us that they live under better
and happier conditions than those they knew on earth,
and none has ever expressed the wish to come back
to live on earth.   This fact at once disposes of the
creeds and dogmas of all religions, as we find that
entrance to the Etheric World does not necessitate
any passport.   Those who have passed on from this
world to the Etheric World, and who come back and
speak to us, tell us that they are living together
happily in companionship with those who had different
beliefs on earth, and even with those who had no
beliefs whatever.   When asked questions on the
subject of belief they tell us that earth beliefs count

for nothing with them, and that these are soon for-gotten, after we leave the earth. This is not sur-prising to intelligent people. Why should God wait till we die to punish us? Could He not do so here just as easily? Moreover, people of divergent opinions live happily together on earth, so why should they not in Heaven?

Our Etheric friends tell us that they can now comprehend things more clearly, and have a better understanding of the problems of existence than they had on earth. They tell us that they are instructed and guided by higher intelligences than their own, and that these greater and wiser people were once men and women like ourselves who lived on earth, but having lived so much longer and being so much more experienced than are our friends, their guidance and help are of the greatest value to all wishing to gain further knowledge and wisdom.

Here on earth we are limited in our ideas and in all that appertains to sight and hearing and the other senses. We may be likened to the Caddis worm living at the bottom of a pond, which, when the day comes for its liberation, sheds its sheath and becomes the Caddis fly, with all the expansion of faculties which such a change of condition implies. It can now sense something of the beauties of earth, which hitherto had been denied to it. So with our friends who have passed on. They have a wider vision and a greater knowledge, and they use the opportunities afforded them of conversing with us on earth to tell us something more about the Universe, something about their world, which has the effect of increasing our understanding, and making us realise more clearly the relationship of each created thing to the Universe, of which it is a part.

Just in so far as our capacity to understand increases, are we given information from those in the Etheric World, whose duty it is to guide and direct us here on earth. The ordinary individual attending a séance for the first time will doubtless get into touch with some friend or relative who will without difficulty give him ample proof that he still lives. This satisfies the great majority of enquirers, but only to those who wish to get beyond ordinary conversation is deeper knowledge imparted. A high dignitary of the Church of England recently publicly expressed the view that only trivial remarks were ever made at séances. He had never been to a séance, but this is what he thought was the case. If he had gone to one and received trivial remarks, as he called them, from friends of his on the other side who were anxious to prove their existence in another world, the reason of their being trivial would have been that his mind was entirely limited to earth conditions. I was with him once in the company of a man of eminence who had made a great study of psychic phenomena and the conditions ruling in the Etheric World. Though every opportunity was given to this churchman, he never took the trouble to avail himself of the opportunity offered. His mind was not capable of grasping the subject, and so it is with everyone save those whose minds are capable of grasping the deeper problems of life.

It is therefore only those who have kept an open mind, and have put aside prejudice and are willing to learn, who receive information surpassing that of others, however learned, who have acquired their knowledge only from what can be seen and heard outside the séance room. Spiritualists are thus guided by higher intelligences in the Etheric World, and the basic teachings of Spiritualism come from the great minds of those who, though they have passed through death, yet endeavour to guide and help mankind on earth. The basis of their teaching is very simple, so simple that the simplest of us can understand it. The basis of Spiritualism is contained in what are called the Seven Principles of Spiritualism and are accepted by Spiritualists in every part of the globe, not as an act of faith, but because the same teachings are given from the Etheric World to all who make contact with it, no matter where they be.

Those who call themselves Spiritualists believe that it can be accepted as scientifically proved that :—

(1) The universe is governed by Mind, commonly called God. That all we have sensed, do sense, or will sense, is but Mind expressing itself in some form or another.

(2) The existence and identity of the individual continues after the change called death.

(3) Communication under suitable conditions takes place between us here on earth and the inhabitants of the Etheric World, into which we shall all pass at death.

On these three fundamental principles, which Spiritualists believe are scientifically proved, the following logical deductions are naturally drawn from the information which comes to us from those who have passed on to this larger life.

(4) That our ethical conduct should be guided

by the golden rule, given first to the world by the great Confucius, ''Whatsoever you would that others would do to you, do it also unto them.''

(5) That each individual is his own Saviour, and that he cannot look to someone else to bear his sins and suffer for his mistakes.

(6) That each individual reaps as he sows, and that he makes his happiness or unhappiness just as he harmonises with his surroundings. That he gravitates naturally to the place in the Etheric World in harmony with his desires, as there desires can be gratified more easily than here on earth.

(7) And finally, that the path of progress is never closed, and that there is no known end to the advancement of the individual.

The foregoing are the Seven Principles of Spiritualism. They can be accepted by the intelligent Christian or Jew, Mohammedan or Buddhist, Hindu or Confucianist. These Seven Principles contain all that is needed by the average man or woman. They act as a guide to our conduct on earth, they give the necessary urge for improving our conduct and strengthening our character, they give us something to live for, and they give the basis for an understanding of man's origin and destiny. No one need ever fear getting old, as age is only an earth condition. Lastly, they give comfort in sorrow, especially in sorrow occasioned by parting as a result of death.

Besides this, when these principles are accepted and all the creeds and dogmas and ceremonials which surround orthodox religion everywhere have faded away, mankind will be knit together by one common belief, as would always have been the case but for ignorance. There is no darkness but ignorance. Spiritualism is filling the world with intellectual light. When mankind is bound together by the common link of Spiritualism, humanity will become as one family, and thus will be brought about the brotherhood of man, so longed for by the great minds of the past. When mankind realises his origin and his destiny and is convinced that his conduct here will determine his place hereafter, wars will cease, and our social conditions will improve beyond anything we can possibly imagine. The time wasted trying to placate the Almighty will be used for more useful purposes, and man will at last have become a rational being.

Some, doubtless, though glad to have the scientific support Spiritualism gives to their faith, still feel the need of a personal Saviour or the performing of some ceremonial. They have been imbued with this idea since childhood, and nothing will change them. They have certain fixed ideas, and nothing will alter them. This being so, their faith satisfies them and they are happy. So be it ; but the number of people holding these views is slowly dwindling, and what satisfies them does not satisfy the average thinking man and woman, especially the young. If Spiritualism had not come along to take the place of the old dying faith, our younger generation and those to come would have become atheists, denying everything outside the physical universe. With the increase of knowledge, and in the absence of any proof for the claims the Church makes for what it calls the supernatural, all belief in anything above or beyond us would have vanished. In what a different position religion would be in Russia to-day if the Orthodox Church had not kept the people in ignorance ! If there were a Spiritualist Church in every centre in Russia, as there is in Great Britain, we should never hear of Anti-God campaigns or similar propaganda.

With this brief introduction, let us now consider the Seven Principles of Spiritualism in greater detail.

THE FATHERHOOD OF GOD.

I have adopted this sub-title for convenience sake. In the past the Fatherhood of God has been taken in a very narrow sense. The Jews believed that Jehovah was their special protector, and that there was no other God but Jehovah. He was like themselves, only more powerful, but just as cruel and passionate. This peculiar and isolated view of the Deity brought them into conflict with all the surrounding nations and made them bigoted and oppressive. But their beliefs were not unique. Every other nation had its own God who was its special protector, and Christians have always believed that Jesus the Christ is their own special God, making intercession for them in Heaven. Whatever Christians have done or do, has been or is done in the name of this particular God, but besides him there are two other Gods of equal importance. Jesus, however, is the God who specially interests himself in the doings of the Christian people. To Spiritualists the doctrine of the Trinity is such an absurdity that they cannot understand how any sane and rational person can believe it. However, so it is.

Christians believe that there are three Gods, but that these three Gods are only one God. I must leave it at that and not waste time on this mathematical puzzle. The only Trinity that Spiritualists understand is the Trinity of Mind, Etheric Body and Physical Body. Here we have a three-in-one entity so long as we are on earth, but in the Etheric World it becomes two-in-one. We are a trinity, but a very different trinity from that of the theological conception of the Godhead. This, probably, is the origin of the theological idea of a three-in-one God, but only Spiritualists understand its true meaning, because Spiritualists are told from the other world that the Universe is made up of Mind, Etheric Substance, and Physical Matter.

To Spiritualists, Mind, or the directing force of the Universe, constitutes God, and the all-embracing nature of this directing Mind is covered by the words "The Fatherhood of God." We are all part of this directing and creating Mind, and through Mind we are related to the guiding Intelligence of the Universe. All members of the human race, whether here or in the Etheric World, are brothers joined together by this common link. We therefore believe that Mind, or God, has never had and never will have any particular cult on which he particularly bestows his blessing. Those who claim this special privilege do so through ignorance and conceit.

Though all the Gods of the past made in the image of man must perish, yet man made under the direction of Mind or God remains, and God in man will reign eternally.

Next to the Fatherhood of God comes

THE BROTHERHOOD OF MAN.

One follows the other naturally. If we are all part of God, we are all one family. The history of man contains much of slavery, brutality and injustice. This has all come about as the result of ignorance. Someone a little stronger, a little more clever than the rest enslaved his fellows for his own selfish ends. Man has been the sport and prey of kings and priests. Through fear of starvation he has been forced to cringe at the foot of the tyrant, and through fear of the unknown he has supported Churches and priests. He has carried on his back the officials of Church and State, who have profited by his ignorance. However, education is gradually making mankind realise that he is not here to be down-trodden by over-lords. Equal education gives all the opportunity of becoming equal, but those with finer minds will always take the lead.

Only a few years ago we found a great nation, Germany, led by a small number of officials into the most ghastly war in human history, which involved the greater part of the civilised world. Up to within a year or two ago, only the Roman Catholic Church ruled Spain, and in consequence Spain is one of the most ignorant countries in the world. Many other instances could be given from the beginning of history of how a small minority or an individual has kept a nation in ignorance and servitude, or driven it on to war. The reason of course is that an uneducated individual is like an animal. He knows enough to get a bare existence, but just as man has combined his reason with his labour has he advanced.

The ignorance amongst the masses is still pitiful,

and what it must have been some thousands of years
ago can only be imagined. Man, by developing his
mind, will free himself from his past miseries, and
raise himself in self-respect and independence.

> Then let us pray that come it may,
>   As come it will for a' that,
> That sense and worth o'er a' the earth
>   May bear the gree and a' that!
> For a' that, and a' that,
>   It's coming yet, for a' that,
> That man to man, the world o'er
>   Shall brothers be, for a' that!

Such was the wish of Robert Burns 140 years ago,
and only gradually do we see those prophetic lines
being realised. Only last century Britain freed herself from the curse of the slave trade, as also did the
United States, but still to-day there are five million
slaves in Asia and Africa, and only the combined
pressure of the civilised nations will ultimately bring
this evil to an end. Let each one of us, within the
limits of the possible, take intelligent thought for the
future. Let each one of us, where possible, rescue
the fallen and help the helpless. Let us distribute
words of kindness, cheerfulness, and encouragement.
By doing all the good we can, by binding up the
wounds of our fellow creatures, we are bringing
nearer the great day when the brotherhood of man
shall become a reality and not a platitude. To
do all the good we can is to be religious in the real
sense of the word, to do all the good we can is to
be a saint, irrespective of theological beliefs. To put
the star of hope in the midnight of despair, to help
those in need of help, and to help those who suffer,
is true holiness. This is the religion of the future.

This is what Spiritualists mean by the brotherhood of man.

Just in proportion as we cease to be the slaves of our conditions shall we advance. Just as we place a greater value on our rights does our position improve, and just as we value more highly the rights due to ourselves shall we recognise more the rights of others. Just as we come to realise that this life is the preparation for a better one, so shall we cease to try to grab all we can for ourselves and work instead for the common good. When we are prepared to give to all what we claim for ourselves, then we shall be truly civilised and the world will be fit to live in. As it is to-day, every individual to a lesser extent, and every nation to a greater extent, think only of their own needs first, and the needs of others last, whereas if all would work together for the common good of the world, poverty would fade away and the enormous sums spent in self-preservation, and promoting superstition at home and abroad, would be used to add to the wealth of the world, instead of being used in keeping the people in ignorance, or for destruction, and the preparation for the destruction of what the labour of humanity has put together. If the world could rid itself entirely of its Napoleons of war and encourage instead its inventors of instruments of cultivation, production, and distribution, and if this policy were pursued for the next fifty years, the hours of labour would be halved, our pleasures would be doubled, and the joy of living correspondingly intensified.

Only within the last two hundred years has man applied his intelligence to making the forces of nature work for him to an extensive degree, with the result that our country now supports a larger population, and every one is working shorter hours. As we get machines and the forces of nature to do our work, in like proportion will our toil lessen. In 1750 the population of the United Kingdom was about ten millions, in 1932 about forty-nine millions. To-day with the aid of machinery it is estimated that we are producing in many industries on the average one hundred times what was produced in 1750, and the consequence is that we are supporting five times the population. The working day has been reduced from sixteen to eight hours, and the standard of living is vastly higher than it was then, owing to the higher wages earned for less work. Moreover, when we can organise things better, as we shall in time, and thus absorb the unemployed into the producing and distributive trades, the daily hours of labour will come down to six, and the standard of living will go on rising. Some day, if we go on developing machinery to do our work at the rate we are doing now, it should be possible for us to get all we need for a high standard of living, by each one of us working only one hour a day ; and why should that be the end ? The problem before us is going to be how to spend our leisure, as more time becomes available for recreation and better education. Children some day will not leave school till eighteen years of age instead of fourteen to-day.

When the time comes when machinery does our work for us, a sound economic communism will naturally follow. Capital and labour will automatically cease to function apart from the State ; but

N

this is so far ahead that it is not a matter of practical politics to-day. The majority to-day, however, have luxuries denied to kings and nobles three hundred years ago. Solomon had hundreds of wives, but no carpets. His great temple was lit by rushes, if it was lit at all. To-day some of the humblest dwellings are lit by electric light. The working man in the newer houses being built for him to-day has more comforts and luxuries than had Queen Elizabeth. In her day there were no steel pins, no stoves, no cooking ranges, no baths, no carpets, no telephones, no quick travel, few books, no newspapers, no cinemas, and no wireless to entertain the people day and night with music and song. We live longer and our national health is better now than it was then.

Whom have we to thank? Inventors and discoverors first, and then all who have used intelligent thought in their work. It has all been achieved by the combination of intelligence, education, industry, and labour. Watt, Descartes, Fulton, Stephenson, Kepler, Crompton, Franklin, Kelvin, Lodge, Marconi, Edison, and numerous others such as Lister and Pasteur, are the men we should thank for all we have and are to-day, and like minds will make us what we shall be in the future.

Slowly but surely has man evolved; first the protoplasm, then the fish, then the mammal, all these branching off and forming various species, until man emerges above them all. Why? Because his brain has been the receptacle of a mind capable of more creative thought than the rest. His development in the past has been slow, but steady and sure, and each time he has advanced he has done so by giving a

little more consideration than formerly to his brother
men. Truly it is more blessed to give than to receive,
and by reason of his capacity for giving man has
advanced beyond the beast. Gradually as he advanced he became capable of understanding better the
feelings of his neighbours. Firstly, the family
gathered together, then the tribe, and then with a
further advance a nation came into being.

We have still to take the next step, when all the
nations of the world will be bound together in one
human family. This will come about naturally
through mental development. In the past man lived
at first only for himself, then for his family, then for
his tribe, and then for his country. At the beginning
of last century Thomas Paine declared that the world
was his country, and when we all come to believe that,
then will be realised the brotherhood of man and the
unity of the human race.

Spiritualism is developing in every country in
the world. Communications are coming from the
Etheric World to every country in the world. This
common link will slowly bind humanity together.
It is only a matter of time till there is an international language, one is already nearly perfected, and
then nations will understand each other better.
Wireless has already done more to unify the world
than any other invention. If we could understand
each other telepathically, as they do in the Etheric
World, there would be no need of a language, as the
mental images behind speech are the same in all cases.

It is only within the last few years that we have
really applied concentrated thought to our conditions.
For thousands of years social conditions remained

much on the same level ; mankind remained
stationary. Conditions three hundred years ago were
very similar to those three thousand years ago.
With the increase in knowledge resulting from
scientific enquiry we are now gradually getting more
and more control over the forces of nature.   We are
gradually getting more for less work, and it is not
difficult to imagine that within the next hundred years,
if the present rate of progress continues, the work of
each one of us for one hour a day will produce all our
desires and requirements.

The more we reduce the hours of labour the
greater will become the scope of our advancement in
knowledge, and I can see the time coming when mankind will have such command over his surroundings
that our whole economic system will be changed.
Our needs, in consequence of the application of
machinery to our requirements, will be met by the
minimum of effort.   We shall get the forces of nature
to work for us, under intelligent direction, and with
the expenditure of very much less manual labour.
Gradually the superiority of mind over matter is
asserting itself and becoming increasingly evident,
and some day we may be able to mould physical
matter into the shapes and conditions we require by
the minimum of exertion, thus bringing our conditions
on earth more in line with those prevailing in the
Etheric World, where creative thought can make
conditions in a way not yet understood on earth.

These thoughts may help us to understand what
our Etheric friends mean by saying that they are in
advance of the earth, and that what we now have
they have enjoyed for long.   We follow a long way

behind them, but fortunately we shall continue to
follow. We are learning to take control of our surroundings, as they have known how to do for ages.
That is why scientists and philosophers in the Etheric
World are greatly in advance of those on earth, as
many of the latter refuse to be taught by their
superiors, greatly to their loss.

I could mention many other ways in which we
are following behind the Etheric World, but I shall
only mention one more, which is that the Kingdom
of Mind on earth is receiving more respect to-day than
ever before. What one is, mentally and morally,
now receives more consideration than what was one's
social position at birth, whereas in the days of old
the reverse was the case. Slowly Mind on earth is
coming to be recognised as King, and to have all
things subservient to it.

Before I leave the subject of the brotherhood of
man, let me impress on everyone the truth that all
life continues after death. Life is indestructible, and
needless pain and suffering to any creature has been
too common in the past. As, however, we come to
realise that all creatures are endowed with mind and
can suffer like ourselves, and that all life continues
beyond death, so shall we give more serious consideration to the alleviation of needless pain and
suffering.

It is unmanly and unwomanly, to say the least
of it, to chase a fox or a stag to its death. It is a
cruel deed first to stop up all the "earths," so that
the fox can find no refuge, and then to hunt the animal
for miles, ultimately to dig it out alive when it gets
to earth, and throw it to the hounds. This is called

"sport" in Christian Britain, and never does the Church raise its voice in protest against cruelty which its founder, were he on earth to-day, would be the first to condemn. These "blood sports" are relics of barbarism, and I hope to live long enough on earth to see public opinion sufficiently enlightened to stop this needless suffering in order to give pleasure to those who always put their own feelings and selfish pleasures first, and the agony of the animal last. Such pastimes are degrading to the character of anyone who takes part in them, and just as other cruelties are passing away, as mankind develops mentally, so also will pass all forms of cruelty to the lower creatures.

As to the future. This we can read only from our knowledge of the past. In the past just as man has combined his thought with his labour, has he advanced, and improved his social conditions. So in the future, in proportion as he continues to apply his mind to his surroundings, so will his conditions improve, and just as he develops mentally, so life will become easier. To the same extent as he thinks more of others will his own happiness increase, and the greater will become the harmony of the entire human family.

CONTINUED EXISTENCE AND COMMUNICATION.

The belief in another world has existed from time immemorial, and, as has already been shown, this belief is the result of man's psychic structure. It can be traced back for thousands of years and found to be held by people of all degrees of culture right down to the savage.

If we were but mechanical creatures, and our thoughts and actions were produced only by some chemical reaction, is it imaginable that we would have devoted the trouble and the time we have to giving thought to another environment? The past, however, has relied on instinct translated into hope and faith. To-day we are in a new era ; knowledge can now take the place of faith. It is no longer a subject for hope that our friends, whom we call dead, are still living. It is easily proved that they live, by anyone who cares to take the necessary trouble. True, the number of good Mediums is very limited, and some try in vain to make contact with their friends through those who are undeveloped, because they have not the time, nor the opportunity, to get into touch through a really fully-developed Medium.

However, the next best thing to acquiring knowledge by personal experience is to learn from the experience of others. I personally, in common with most others, have never carried through the necessary scientific experiments to prove many things that I and others accept as part of our every-day knowledge. We accept them as true, because they are told us by men of repute, who have spent their lives investigating and examining the laws of nature. So the time is fast approaching when all people will accept without question what is told them by those who have experimented, and found by these experiments that survival is a fact. Up to the present we have been handicapped in accepting this fact owing to the prejudice resulting from our religious upbringing and the materialistic outlook of science.

Christians consider that they, and they only, know or can know anything about the after life, and consequently that any who believe that continued existence can be proved without the aid of Christianity are deceived, and are thus accepting a belief contrary to the will of God.   Fortunately this prejudice is passing.

All the discoveries of science are tending in the direction which Spiritualists have been led to expect from their communications with the other side. Though science has made no pronouncement on the subject, yet the number of Spiritualists amongst scientists is steadily increasing, and I could mention the names of some of our leading men of science who are attending séances regularly and gaining knowledge thereby.   One of our most outstanding physicists is attending séances regularly but does not wish the fact to be known to the public as it is not yet orthodox to do so, but his mental outlook is widening, and he is gaining new knowledge which his more orthodox brethren are still lacking.

It is all a question of mental development.   It is difficult to discover reality wrapped up as it is in appearances.   It is difficult as the result of our early scientific and religious training to believe that it is possible for another world to exist about and around us, and especially so because this knowledge is quite beyond our every-day sense perception.   Not everyone has got the objective proof that Spiritualists have received.   It is difficult to accept the fact that we have an Etheric Body which continues after death, carrying with it our mind, containing our memories and our character.   The fact of continued existence is one of the fundamentals of Spiritualism and is accepted in consequence of the communications Spiritualists receive from the other side, and also because of materialisations, apparitions, psychic photography, clairvoyance, and clairaudience.

In the past, few have believed that communication was possible until they personally experienced it. When they did experience it the belief was easy. Consider, however, the population in this country and the relatively small number of fully-developed Mediums in whose presence reliable communication takes place, and it will then be easy to see how impossible it is for everyone to get personal satisfaction. If the Mediums were multiplied a hundred times there would not be nearly sufficient of them to meet individual demands ; but meantime, till they increase in number, those who have not been privileged to hold converse with the other world should accept what is told them by those who have, just as they accept the statements of other scientific investigators. We who have been thus privileged to carry out careful experiments for years think it is our duty to make known the results of our investigations, believing that in time our results will be generally accepted.

Is it not strange that the clergy and Christian people generally will accept Biblical stories of psychic phenomena, and will not accept what present-day writers tell them on the subject? Spiritualists are shocked at the want of enquiry, the want of thoroughness in the average Christian towards his beliefs. He accepts psychic stories if they are in the Bible, never enquiring who the person is who wrote those stories, never investigating their origin, or questioning

whether they have been found to be correctly recorded.   In the earlier part of this book I try to show
how unsatisfactory is the evidence for all Biblical
records, and yet to-day Christians are bold enough
to stand up and call Spiritualists credulous people, to
jeer at them and make them out to be a deluded cult,
when all the time it is they who lay themselves open
to these charges.   Intelligent Spiritualists accept
nothing coming from the other side that has not been
absolutely proved by every possible method.

Take, for instance, the Biblical story of Samuel.
He heard a voice and reported to Eli what this voice
said.   Other instances are the story of the Transfiguration, and the story of Peter in trance.   Here
we have reports of three psychic occurrences, but
they are only three of many mentioned in the Bible,
which Christians accept as true.   There is no docu-
mentary proof that they are true, but at least this
much can be said, that events similar to those reported
in the Bible are occurring in this country every day.
They are not strange occurrences to Spiritualists, who
are quite accustomed to them.   Samuel, Spiritualists
would say, was a clairaudient Medium just as Mrs.
Annie Johnson and Mrs. Estelle Roberts are to-day,
to mention only two of quite a number.   As to the
story of the Transfiguration, Spiritualists have experienced the phenomenon referred to in this instance
on many occasions, and the most wonderful on record
are the materialisations recorded by Sir William
Crookes, one of our greatest scientists.   He published in 1874 the results of his experiments, which
lasted over many years, in a book entitled *Researches
in the Phenomena of Spiritualism.*   The story of

Peter in trance and his vision is an example of a very common occurrence with Spiritualists when in the presence of Trance Mediums ; in fact it is one of the commonest of all the phenomena of Spiritualism. There are more Trance Mediums in this country and throughout the world than any other class of Medium.

The trance descriptions of the Etheric World given by Mrs. Hadden, one of the most developed Trance and Direct Voice Mediums of our time, are far more wonderful and graphic than anything recorded in the New Testament as the result of Peter's trance. All this is happening in Edinburgh to-day and being privately recorded by a group of well-known Edinburgh journalists, while among those who regularly attend are some of the leading medical men in the city.

Most of the Edinburgh clergy know all that is going on, but with the exception of Dr. Norman Maclean and two or three others, no parson in Edinburgh has yet referred to Spiritualism except to condemn it. They must be impressed by what is taking place, as quite a number of them regularly attend this lady's séances, and at the moment there is a waiting list of clergy who will be welcomed whenever there is room available. They are given every opportunity to learn the truth, and this group gladly gives the Church every opportunity to retrieve its past mistakes, and learn what Spiritualists have known for the past eighty years.

However, when Sunday comes, these same parsons preach about Peter and his experiences, or other so-called miracles, to dwindling congregations, though those stories are thousands of years old, but they remain silent as to what is going on in their own city at the present time.   The clergy are ready to criticise Dr. Maclean and Spiritualists generally, and as he says in his lucid book, *Death Cannot Sever*, recently published, which every Christian should read, they prefer to continue to sit at the feet of seventeenth century theologians, as if those men had given the last word on everything relating to our existence and destiny.

The best that can be said about the Scottish Church, in their attitude to Psychic Phenomena, is that the leaders of the Church took some trouble ten years ago to investigate the subject, but for all the good that came of it they might as well have done nothing.   I was one of those who conducted the enquiry, and I did my best to educate the clergy who comprised the chief part of the committee.   They got marvellous evidence in my presence of the truth of the claims of Spiritualism, but it was evident throughout that they did not wish to face the truth.   It is not in their interests that the truth should be known, and they have refused ever since to open up the question again, though it has twice been raised at the General Assembly.

The attitude of the Church of England is just the same.   The present Archbishop of York, Dr. Temple, stated recently, " I am quite convinced that direct evidence of survival is not either attainable or desirable." His views on this subject are clearly set forth in the February 3rd 1933 issue of *Light*.   It is well to note carefully this remarkable sentence from a Christian Archbishop.   He considers first that direct evidence of survival is not attainable, and yet survival is one of the best proved facts of science. Next comes his opinion that evidence of survival is not desirable. This is typical of the clerical mind, and shows how superstition has rotted away the whole spiritual basis of the religion as taught by Jesus, and what is called his Church is nothing more than an organisation for the purpose of keeping alive superstitions, ceremonies, rites and practices, which have been handed down from past ages of ignorance for thousands of years.

The Church is so prejudiced, so averse to relinquish its hold over the people, and let them realise that it is not the custodian of a special revelation from God, which it has always claimed to be, that this new revelation is coming to the people through the people against the united opposition of all the Christian Churches. At my large meeting in the Usher Hall in Edinburgh last October, though all the Church of Scotland clergy in Edinburgh were asked to come on the platform, none accepted, and Dr. Norman Maclean, who acted as my Chairman, received no support from his brother clergy in his brave stand for the truth. Owing to this official opposition, only slowly will the truth permeate the Presbyterian mind. On the other hand, in England, the so-called Church of England enquiry has ended in nothing. No report has been published, doubtless because the leaders find they cannot condemn the truth, but nevertheless are afraid to admit it.

My old friend Dr. John Lamond of Greenside Parish Church, Edinburgh, always believed that Spiritualism would take root in Scottish Churches and

spread therefrom throughout the whole country.
He based his views on the fact that, narrow and rigid
as are the Scottish clergy, at least they are not tied
to a liturgy like many of their brothers in England.
Whether he was right or not, the future only can
show, but it is certainly remarkable that three of the
most prominent clergy in Edinburgh have been brave
and honest enough to declare publicly their belief in
Spiritualism, and that the old theology is dead.

I know no other city in Great Britain where
Spiritualism is more actively discussed, and where it
receives more thoughtful consideration than in the
capital of Scotland.   This is doubtless owing largely
to the fact that the leading newspapers of the city are
strongly pro-Spiritualism, in consequence of the
knowledge those who administer them have gained
at the séances just referred to with Mrs. Hadden.

All honour also to Dr. Lamond for the brave
stand he took on the side of the truth some fifteen
years ago, when he was a voice crying in the wilder-
ness !   He will go down to history as one of the
pioneers amongst the clergy, who saw where the
Church was heading, and did his utmost to divert it
from its error into the channels of truth.

Clairaudience and clairvoyance, which are so
frequently reported in the Bible, are common occurrences at the present time, and anyone who attends
a Spiritualist meeting, when good clairaudience and
clairvoyance take place, cannot doubt the fact that
some people have the gift of hearing and seeing more
than the ordinary individual, with his limited capacity
for hearing and seeing.

I have been present on many occasions when

Mrs. Estelle Roberts, Mrs. Annie Johnson or Mrs. Helen Spiers, to mention only three of our best known clairvoyantes, gave clairvoyant descriptions or clairaudient messages. From 40 to 50 correct names and messages, on each occasion, are usually given to the people in the audience, from their friends in the other world. I have often heard the most minute details of their life and appearance on earth, transferred through the Medium, the percentage of mistakes being less than two per cent. The 98 per cent correct descriptions absolutely rule chance out as an explanation, and fraud is equally impossible, as these ladies arrive at the meeting just before it commences, and on many occasions I have known them to arrive by train, half an hour or so before the meeting commenced, and go direct from the station to the meeting. They go from town to town throughout Great Britain, and I have been present at meetings when the clairvoyante had just arrived in the town on the first occasion in her life. Mrs. Estelle Roberts, for instance, who took part at the meeting I addressed in the St. Andrew's Hall in Glasgow, in May 1932, arrived in that city just before the meeting, and it was the first time she had been in Scotland in her life. She gets only a small fee of a guinea or so, together with her expenses, so it is obvious that she could not afford to pay people to make enquiries beforehand, or to have her own accomplices scattered throughout the audience. This itself would require an organisation and a considerable amount of money to maintain, so this suggestion, which is sometimes seriously made, can be ruled out as absurd. I have personal proof, however, of the genuineness of our recognised clairvoyants, as many of my own personal friends have received intimate communications through them, which have been correct to the minutest detail.

Many people have this gift. The other day a friend of mine attended a funeral. As the coffin was being lowered someone took a photograph of the mourners, and when the plate was developed the photograph of the man whose body was being buried appeared standing beside his wife. This was shown to the clergyman who officiated and he replied, "Yes, I saw him standing there just as the photograph depicts it." My friend then said, "Well, you should tell your congregation that from the pulpit." To which he replied, "I would not dare ; my Bishop would object." Yet this same parson will preach about the disciples walking to Emmaus in company with a spirit, which they saw and spoke to, but dares not say that he himself has seen one. Could anything exemplify better the present hopelessly illogical position of the Christian Church?

We have, therefore, the extraordinary position to recognise that Christian people will accept as true, occurrences recorded by tradition as happening thousands of years ago, but that they will not accept what is recorded by men and women of standing and repute at the present day. In my book, *On the Edge of the Etheric*, I refer at some length to notable men of the past fifty years who have vouched for all that Spiritualism stands for. I have recorded there some of the experiences I myself have had, but though more extensively and carefully recorded than are the experiences of most Spiritualists, they are exactly similar to the experience of hundreds of thousands of sane and sensible people who are living in our country at the present time.

It is impossible to imagine that the thousands of people who have recorded their experiences are deluded or fraudulent. Their word on other matters is accepted, so why should their word on this question also not be accepted? They have had the experience, and those who have not should accept what they say. If Christians will not accept what their contemporaries tell, they are most illogical in accepting what is in the Bible. In other words, if Spiritualism is a fraud and a delusion, so also are the stories in the Bible, the only difference being that Spiritualists affirm that their statements can be proved by anyone who likes to take the trouble to do so, whereas the Biblical stories cannot be verified by investigation.

Whether the details of the Biblical stories are correct or not, at least Spiritualists can accept them as possible without having to resort to the belief in miracles or something contrary to nature, as Christians have to do in order to believe them. Spiritualists do not believe in miracles or in the supernatural, or anything contrary to nature. They believe in law and order in the universe, and they never talk about supernatural events or miraculous occurrences. When they wish to refer to something occurring beyond our limited sense perceptions they refer to it as super-normal. No miracle or supernatural occurrence has ever taken place in the history of the Universe, so far as our knowledge extends.

In my book already referred to I have devoted

o

a great amount of space to records of conversations
I had over a period of five years with friends of mine
who have passed on to the Etheric World.   I do not
propose in this book to go into those details again.
All I would say is that I have careful records of
thirty-nine séances, and the possibility of fraud or
delusion cannot be imagined, owing to the precautions
taken.   In the reviews of my book, which number
nearly one hundred, little or no criticism was ever
made on this point, and it was generally accepted
that I had obtained genuine super-normal phenomena.

Voices quite apart from the Medium spoke to me
or to friends of mine I took with me, and many of
these voices were recognised.   I have had given to
me two hundred and eighty-two facts which I recorded
in writing at the time and afterwards verified, but
besides these I have had numerous others unrecorded.
One hundred and eighty of these I class as A1,
as it was impossible for the Medium or anybody
else to know anything whatever about the facts which
were given to me.   To ascertain what possibility
there was that these communications were guess-work
on the part of the Medium, an eminent mathematician
computed that the chances against this were thirty
billions to one.   One hundred I class as A2, as the
facts given could be traced to reference books or newspapers, though I do not believe for one moment that
the Medium resorted to this method of obtaining the
information.   One item of information given to me
I could not trace and the other was slightly inaccurate,
but if it had been given in a slightly different way it
would have been correct.

After five years' careful investigation of psychic

phenomena through the mediumship of Mr. John C. Sloan of Glasgow, I was completely convinced that the voices which spoke to me were the voices of those they claimed to be, and that neither fraud nor delusion could account for them. I have already shown in my previous book the care I took to prevent fraud or delusion, and how, slowly but surely, I was convinced against my will that I was in contact with those who once lived here on earth, who, after passing through the change called death, continued to inhabit another world around and about us.

Hundreds of different voices I have heard, of different tone and strength ; some loud enough to be heard 200 yards away, others soft, and many recognised. Of all the discoveries of man this is surely the greatest, and if it could be obtained regularly by an instrument and thus become generally known, it would be accepted as such by everyone. Unfortunately, only a comparatively small number have experienced this phenomenon, and because of its novelty only slowly are people coming to believe in its possibility.

These very careful experiments which I carried out ended eight years ago, but since then I have carefully and critically examined the experiences of hundreds of other people, and what they have told me, and what they concluded from those experiences, agrees to the minutest detail with my own experiences and the deductions I drew from them. Since I published my book *On the Edge of the Etheric*, I have been in receipt daily of an enormous correspondence from all parts of the world. I have not received a single hostile or critical letter, but many letters tell me how greatly my book has helped and comforted the writers. Others ask how they also may obtain similar experiences.

Other letters, again, are from people who have had experiences like myself, and though the letters come from all parts of the world—Brazil, the Argentine, the United States, Canada, Australia, New Zealand, South Africa, India, and most of the countries of Europe—yet they all tell of similar experiences with Direct Voice Mediums. They also confirm what has been told to me about the conditions in the other world, and show further that the explanation I received of the methods adopted for communicating with us has also been given to them. I have such a mass of information in those letters that extracts from them would make up a book somewhat similar in size to this one.

The evidence I myself have had from all parts of the world that survival and communication is a fact would be enough in itself to prove the claims of Spiritualism, even if no other proof existed. If, however, you multiply by one million my experiences, both personal and those of which my many friends have told me, you would be nowhere near the end of the sum total of evidence of survival and communication which has accumulated during the last eighty-four years. Is it conceivable that Spiritualism can be considered a fraud and a delusion when all this is carefully considered? Remember I am not the only one to bear public testimony to these facts. Others prominent in the investigation of psychic phenomena, who have written books on the subject, have likewise received numerous testimonies corroborating what they say.

I shall now only refer to three incidents to show how strong is the case for survival. The first is one of many which was given to me by Mr. Edward C. Randall, one of the leading lawyers in Buffalo, with whom I stayed when I was in America ten years ago. We still correspond with each other and interchange new information we obtain. During twenty years, he told me, he had had sittings in his own house with Mrs. Emily French, one of the world's most gifted Direct Voice Mediums, and had shorthand records taken of what took place on over seven hundred occasions. Mrs. French for some years stayed in his house so as to be under his direct supervision. In a letter received from him last February he states that the recorded sittings now number over one thousand.

Thousands of different voices spoke to him, clear and distinct, everyone different and easily recognised. The most profound problems were easily discussed, and from hostile unbelief he was led on and educated in what I might term Universal Science. Some day this will take the place of Physical Science, when our scientists are wise enough to study those great questions as students taught by Etheric World scientists. They must, however, humble themselves sufficiently to realise that their ingenuity alone cannot solve the riddle of the Universe, and that to do so they must learn many things of which they are quite ignorant, from those who inhabit the world of finer matter about and around us.

Mr. Randall and I spent many hours discussing those profound teachings we had been privileged to receive, and then we told each other some of our own personal experiences, of friends coming back and

proving their identity. I shall long remember one
of the most evidential cases of which I have ever
heard, as it rules out entirely the absurd theory held
by some that unless what you are told is unknown
to everybody, it is of no value. As this would be
impossible to verify, they say survival cannot be
proved. Those who hold this theory are very
limited in number, as well as in their knowledge of
the evidence which has come through, and what Mr.
Randall told me is a sample which excludes every
known normal explanation, and leaves only the
Spiritualistic explanation to account for it.

One morning, at ten o'clock, the Brown Building
in Buffalo, which was under repair, collapsed, and
the few people working there were all buried under
the debris. No one knew who they were, or
how many there were, and this was not known
till some days after, when the bodies were recovered and identified. On the day the building
collapsed, however, when Mr. Randall was sitting
with Mrs. French, one of those killed spoke to him
and told him that four people had been in the building
at the time of the collapse, and that he, the speaker,
was one of them. He then gave their full names as
follows :—William P. Straub, George Metz, Michael
Schurzke, a Pole, and Jennie M. Griffin, a woman.
This was proved to be correct several days later,
when the bodies were recovered.

Now when this was told to Mr. Randall no one
knew who had been killed—only the people themselves, and the people who were looking after them
in the Etheric World. No one on earth knew, so
that much-abused explanation, telepathy, will not fit

in here. I could give similar experiences of my own to prove that the Spiritualists' explanation is the only one to fit all the facts, but as I have already given some of my experiences in my previous book I shall not further deal with this question of evidence beyond giving two more very evidential cases which have occurred within recent months, the first being the experience of Lady Caillard just a few months ago.

She is the widow of Sir Vincent Caillard, who was a director of Vickers and the Southern Railway, and who died in 1930. She has published her experiences in pamphlet form, but this is briefly what she told me. She first became interested when attending a Spiritualist meeting, as then her husband was described to her by a clairvoyante as standing beside her. She then attended a séance, and her husband sent through messages by means of the Reflectograph, an earth instrument operated by the Etheric personality communicating. Her sister-in-law at the same time had a message from her husband.

The following day Lady Caillard attended another séance. She told me she heard her husband's voice, calling her by a name which only he used, and which was known only to themselves. Then he said, "I am coming to show myself to you if I can." Then he appeared standing before her and was easily recognised. He held out his hand and shook his wife's with a firm grasp. He then took her hand in his two hands and pressed it to his lips. Then conversation followed and he promised to come back again on the anniversary of his passing, which he did, and she told me, "I saw him just as he was in life." All present saw Sir Vincent, and these

numbered ten people.   " There was no doubt about
him being my husband," she told me, "and he was
seen by everyone."   He told his wife many things
which no one but he could have known.   She touched
him, stroked his hair, and kissed him.   He put his
arm round her neck and drew her head on to his
shoulder.   The Medium, I might mention, was a
woman.

I mention this case as we have here everything
one could desire, not only the voice but the bodily
form.   What more evidence could we have on earth
to satisfy our reason that we are speaking to our
earth friends ?   None.   We recognise our friends'
voices and we see their physical appearance, as Lady
Caillard heard and saw and recognised her husband.

The only difference is that our earth friends can
remain with us wherever we go, and can be seen and
heard ; but our Etheric friends can be seen and heard
only in the presence of a Medium, who gives off
ectoplasm which enables them to materialise for a
brief period.   How this all happens is fully explained
in *On the Edge of the Etheric*, and I have not the
space here to go again into the details.

Briefly, the Medium supplies a substance called
ectoplasm, which the Etherians mix with a substance
of their own, which they call psychoplasm, and the
combination of these two produces a substance called
teleplasm, with which they cover their vocal organs,
etc., and thus so slow down their vibrations that they
can vibrate our atmosphere.   It will be noted that I
use the word Etherian instead of Spirit people.   They
prefer this designation, and I hope in time it will be
used generally, and the word " Spirit " dropped, as

they are not spirits as we understand the word, but men and women like ourselves.

The last experience I shall give occurred when I was in Belfast in September last. I went there to give two addresses, one in the Ulster Hall, the largest hall in Belfast, accommodating over two thousand people. The hall was packed. My chairman was Colonel Sharman Crawford, D.L., Deputy Governor of Northern Ireland, and in his opening remarks he said, " I know that my deceased son is standing beside me." After my address, at the close of the meeting, a man from the audience came to speak to me. He described a man in Etheric life standing beside me when I spoke. He gave me a very careful description of his appearance, describing him from head to foot. Also he said the man was killed near the war period on a motor cycle, and came to-night dressed just as he was when killed, in military motor cyclist's uniform. My informant could not get his name, but said he must be a friend of mine or someone I knew. I denied all such knowledge, and he seemed disappointed. I thanked him, and told him that if I remembered who this man was I would let him know.

On my way home I told my hostess what had been told me, and she at once said, " That was Colonel Sharman Crawford's son ; I knew him quite well." This was confirmed the next day by the Colonel, and it so impressed him that he allowed it to be reported in all the Belfast newspapers. The clairvoyant, whom I learned afterwards was known for his gift, evidently saw the soldier standing between my chairman and me, and thought he was a friend of mine, whereas it just confirmed Colonel Sharman Crawford's own clairvoyance that his son was with him. Here were two independent testimonies given to me about someone I did not know, but recognised by someone else. All were honest people connected with the event, and it will be seen that no one had anything to gain by falsehood or misrepresentation.

No, Spiritualists are not a "deluded people," but very much the reverse. They are sane and practical, thorough and critical, and if a Medium is found to be fraudulent, it is Spiritualists who expose the Medium, not non-Spiritualists. It has been said, and never contradicted, that no non-Spiritualist has ever exposed a Medium. Many so-called exposures by non-Spiritualists have taken place, but it has been found afterwards that the Medium has been tricked, or that the exposure was false. I do not necessarily concur with these statements, because I have no proof to support them ; but what I wish to emphasise is this, that Spiritualists will never tolerate fraud, and if ever a Medium is proved to be fraudulent that Medium's day is past, and he sinks into oblivion. His name is published in all the Spiritualist papers, and he is discredited for the rest of his life.

I shall not deal further with this question of inter-communication between the two worlds, as I have no space to do so, and it is not the purpose of this book to give detailed consideration to the evidence Spiritualists have of survival after death. There are hundreds of books on the subject, and there are numerous standard books by men of great repute whose accuracy is undoubted. I must leave it at that ; but should the reader wish to pursue the matter

further he will find some of those books regularly
advertised in the various Psychic newspapers already
referred to.

The Fifth Principle of Spiritualism is known
under the heading of

PERSONAL RESPONSIBILITY.

It is easy to be wicked if you are not to be held
responsible for your misdeeds. It is not difficult to
defraud your neighbour if you feel that all you have
to do is to ask forgiveness and believe that Jesus took
your sins away and suffered for them two thousand
years ago. The possibility of transferring your sins
to some other person or creature is a very old delusion. Most of us know the Old Testament story
of the Paschal Lamb, which was killed as a sin
offering. The Arabs had a similar custom, and the
belief in a crucified saviour is to be found in many
of the world's religions. This belief was general
throughout the east at the time of the early Christians,
and gradually the idea developed that Jesus took the
place of the Paschal Lamb, that his crucifixion was a
punishment for the sins of the world, and made all
believers safe for eternity. This doctrine is one
of the most pernicious that has ever been preached.
It has been the cause of more crime in Christendom
than any other of the teachings of Christianity. The
idea that any individual or any God suffered for us,
and that, no matter what we do, we can solely by faith
be absolved from our sins and shortcomings, is too
ludicrous to require much consideration. It was born
in ignorance and flourished in ignorance, and those
who still preach it to-day are as ignorant as those who
preceded them.

Fortunately this belief is dying a natural death, which doubtless is being hastened by the teachings of Spiritualism. We know now from what we are told by those who have preceded us into the Etheric World that each one of us has to bear the consequences of his own sins and shortcomings, and that as we sow, so shall we reap. If we live selfish, sinful lives we shall reap our reward, not only here but hereafter, until we change. The idea of a fixed place for the unbelievers is a myth. We create our own Heaven and our own Hell. The selfish and wicked are perhaps miserable in this world, and they may be more miserable in the next, though not necessarily. The good and the unselfish in this world may be happy here and may be happier hereafter. We know now the reason and how simple it all is.

Our Mind conditions our surroundings here to a certain extent, but to a much greater extent in the Etheric World. If our Mind here is self-centred, making us selfish, if it cares nothing for the feelings of others and only for itself, it will create an isolated condition for itself in the Etheric World. Through the power of Mind we mould our surroundings to a much greater extent there than here, and as we think, so we are. It is not difficult to imagine a wicked individual here surrounding himself with equally wicked fellow beings. In the Etheric World like draws to like to an even greater extent than here, and consequently the wicked congregate together.

Just as it is with the wicked, so it is with the good ; but there is no great gulf fixed between the two, as the next world is not only a place but a condition. Those who make for themselves those evil conditions have always the power of changing them by their thoughts, of thus improving their conditions, and ultimately having harmonious relations with the good. There we get into closer harmony with our desires than we can here. Many a wicked individual on earth can cloak his wickedness by his wealth and bluff ; but not so there. Our character there is transparent, whereas here it is not so. All men and women who have passed from this world to the next have found their level. They may have been kings or queens, princes or lords, looked up to and honoured on earth because of their worldly position, but there, character only determines their position. There they live in a world of finer matter which is more easily influenced by Mind, and naturally they gravitate to the surroundings which their Minds can best influence. It would be quite impossible there, where Minds only in tune harmonise together, for the wicked and the good to live together. They naturally repel each other. It is all very similar to the conditions on earth. There, as here, "birds of a feather flock together," but as character is more transparent there than here one is summed up at once without mistake.

Each one of us is responsible for our own actions and thoughts. Our mental make-up determines our condition hereafter, and no one need be deluded by the idea that belief in some vicarious atonement is going to alter the position each Mind determines for itself.

This being so, the Sixth Principle of Spiritualism can be easily understood.

COMPENSATION AND RETRIBUTION HEREAFTER.

Each one of us will receive compensation or suffer retribution both here and hereafter for all good or evil done on earth. Each one of us will receive his reward, as effect follows cause there, just as it does here. We shall not appear before a judge at some judgment seat on some judgment day. Every day we are passing a sentence on ourselves. As we live here so shall we live there ; here on earth we are making our future conditions. It is character that counts, not beliefs. Thus it will be seen how all the inequalities of life are straightened out. Wealth and position, so highly valued here, count for nothing there ; only character. Money and working for money is unknown there, for as your thoughts are, so are your surroundings. Those who have trodden the difficult and straitened path of poverty on earth will not receive happiness in Heaven because they were poor on earth, but they will enter into conditions in accordance with the development of their minds and character here. Many of the best people on earth are the poorest in worldly goods, and some of the worst are the richest. Nature gives no thought to poverty or wealth ; nature considers only the mental calibre of each individual.

Those who have not been educated on earth will be taught and instructed in the next world, and, if their minds respond to the teaching, they will advance. All obtain this teaching who are willing to receive it, and the worst can in time become the best if the desire to do so exists ; but if the desire is not there progress does not take place. Creeds and dogmas stifle the mind. They make for selfishness, they give the believers in them a sense of superiority, and this reacts on their conditions hereafter. Many of the worst people the world has ever known were the greatest believers in creeds and dogmas. Constantine presided at the Council of Nicaea, Torquemada, the Christian Prior, presided over the Inquisition in Spain, Cortes converted Mexico and Pizarro Peru to Christianity by the slaughter of hundreds of thousands with the edge of the sword.

The knowledge that Spiritualists possess, that as we develop mentally here so shall our conditions be hereafter, is a great stimulus for everyone to live justly and unselfishly. To put it briefly, all sin can be described by the word selfishness, and the more selfish we are the more sinful we are. Selfish and unselfish people are to be found in all degrees of life, and each one of us here is making our future habitation in the Etheric World.

The last principle of Spiritualism is

ENDLESS PROGRESSION.

Every human being has a path of endless progression in front of him, and it is for him to take it or leave it. In the next world he cannot live his best by hanging about this earth and never getting away from earthly things. Loved ones on earth often keep him in close touch with earth conditions, but sooner or later everyone must lose their interest in earth and take up the new life in a natural way. We can, however, still forget about the earth and yet make no progress if we confine our thoughts solely to ourselves. If we wish to acquire knowledge for the purpose of helping others, and if we become less selfish, then the path is opened to us, and as we gain in wisdom and character we draw nearer to perfection. In the Etheric World there are seven planes extending one beyond the other from this earth's surface, and as we progress we pass from one to another. The only difference between death in the Etheric World and death in this world is that here we leave a body behind us to be buried ; but there, as we progress, we rise to higher planes and more beautiful surroundings, as our mind and body become capable of responding to the finer conditions of each plane. Progress is dependent on desire ; as the Mind develops the Etheric body responds to finer vibrations, and thus we are enabled to rise naturally to higher planes. This is a faculty possessed by the Etheric body, but not by the physical body.

Here on earth we have this condition of desire exemplified. I know a man who went out to Japan, for a holiday, and spent his time there wandering about the docks of Yokohama and watching the ships being loaded and unloaded. This he did for a fortnight and then returned home. He never saw any of the beauties of the country ; he never studied the inhabitants and the conditions of that interesting race. He consequently came home as ignorant as he was when he left this country. Mentally he was incapable of appreciating something above and beyond what was his daily occupation, that of a stevedore. So it can be understood how in the Etheric World our Mind conditions our environment, and only if we have the desire for increased knowledge and the desire for something better shall we attain it.

It does not necessarily follow that undeveloped people are wicked—far from it, but they make the conditions they are mentally fitted for. Their backward state need not last for ever ; the time comes when increased knowledge and better surroundings are desired, and when the desire comes it is gratified. For all of us, therefore, there is a path of eternal progress laid out, and we have but to follow it. If the desire is there the path will be followed ; if not, then, until the desire for progress is ours, we shall spend our existence only partially developed, and miss for a time the way which is ours as part of our inheritance.

CHAPTER VIII.

THE PHILOSOPHY OF SPIRITUALISM.
PART I.

THE foregoing chapter dealing with the Seven Principles of Spiritualism makes it clear that Spiritualism is a practical, sane and sensible religion, suitable for the sane and practical man and woman of the present day. There is no emotionalism nor sentiment about it. The intelligent Spiritualist believes in proving all things and believing only what he has proved. What he cannot prove he leaves aside till knowledge increases sufficiently to make what is doubtful more explicit. Christians, on the contrary, believe much without any evidence whatever ; they think faith such a virtue that they believe everything a Holy Book or a Holy Church prescribes, no matter how fantastic. Personally I have never in all my life seen any virtue at all in faith. Being practical by nature, I have always looked on the realm of faith as the borderland of ignorance. Fortunately we are now living in the days of the decay of faith, and entering the age of reason and knowledge.

Spiritualism is the only satisfactory religion for this new age which we are now entering. It holds that it is the duty of every man and woman to investigate questions of religion for themselves, accepting nothing without first weighing up all the evidence. No man in whose brain burns the torch of reason need fear to investigate and to think on these great problems, which in the past have been relegated to a select few to ponder over. To get some one else or some organisation to think for us is mental indolence. We must think out these deeper problems of life for ourselves.

Advanced Spiritualists, owing to the knowledge they have received from the great intelligences in the Etheric World, have now a philosophy which can harmonise all human knowledge into one complete whole. To the advanced Spiritualist religion and science are one. Scientific fact is the foundation for this knowledge, combined with the knowledge given to us from minds wiser than earth minds, about the unsensed universe around us. We cannot complete the picture until we include the study of this unsensed universe, which we can do only by making use of the contact Mediumship establishes between the sensed and unsensed. The difference between scientific Spiritualists and other scientists is that the former make use of this connecting link, and in consequence gain in knowledge ; those who ignore this link are still groping in the dark. Spiritualists by thus making use of all the knowledge available have built up a philosophy which is the most complete and therefore the most advanced existing in the world to-day ; they have a larger and a more rounded outlook of the universe, and can understand and comprehend it better in consequence.

To show, however, how greatly we are in the minority, and how few comprehend the Spiritualist philosophy, I cannot do better than include here a copy of a letter I sent to the Editor of *The Times* on 20th May last year, during a time when some of our leading orthodox scientists and philosophers were trying to explain the universe on a purely physical basis. The letter I wrote to the editor is as follows :—

The Editor,

    The Times, London.   20th May 1932.

Dear Sir,—Your columns have recently contained letters of paramount importance to scientific thought, two on the reality of psychic phenomena as witnessed at the National Laboratory for Psychical Research, and the more recent ones on the attempt to grasp space and the universe.

I believe that it is quite impossible to understand or even to get a working hypothesis of the universe from a purely physical standpoint. Those who try to do so are attempting to explain the infinite by our limited sense organs, which is quite impossible.

The material world is a transitory and passing world, and so also is the material universe, and matter as we see it is the least important thing in the universe, though to us to-day it seems to be the most important.

Psychic science, however, is opening to us a new universe, a universe of etheric substance, governed by Mind, and only when orthodox science condescends to examine this new universe revealed to us through Mediumship, can it possibly hope to get a true perspective of the universe as a whole.

A physical or material explanation of the universe is impossible because the physicist is looking at and considering only the physical universe, whereas the real universe is the etheric, and physical matter is but the result of a minute quantity of vibrations compared to those which constitute space, where the real universe exists.

Space is the real universe. We think it is empty but it is full of life and growth, a real objective world to its inhabitants.

This I have learned after fifteen years of experimenting and studying of psychic science. What I have found, others, such as Crookes, Wallace, Lodge, Barrett, Flammarion, Richet, and Lombroso, have likewise found. Orthodox science, however, will never be able to approach to a true explanation of the universe until it accepts the means nature has put before it, namely, through Mediumship. Then it will learn things now ignored and misunderstood from intelligences in the Etheric World, who look on us as children groping for something we shall never find without their aid.

Those of us who have had the privilege of being taught by intelligences greater than those of this earth find little interest in a physical explanation of the universe, as we have been taught to look on the universe as a gigantic scale of vibrations or waves of motion of which the physical represents only the equivalent of what an inch is to a mile. We are also taught that the realm of mind is the real universe, and that our individual minds are conditioned by the vibrations of our surroundings. As mind is indestructible and never dies, our appreciation of the universe changes, as mind responds to finer and finer vibrations.

How can anyone possibly explain the physical universe when we now know that after death the physical ceases to exist for us and we then appreciate the faster vibrations of etheric substance? The physical is only important to us during our earth life, but it cannot possibly represent the universe, now that we know that our earth life is only an infinitesimal part of our existence. Matter without mind is unthinkable, and thus mind must be behind everything, and only in terms of mind can the universe be explained.

Yours faithfully,

J. ARTHUR FINDLAY.

Knowing the conservative attitude of our great national newspaper, and knowing how alien the contents of my letter were to the official scientific mind and to orthodox thought, I was not surprised to have this letter returned to me with a polite intimation that the editor did not see his way to publish it. I comforted myself, however, by recalling that if *The Times* had been published in the days of Copernicus and he had sent it a communication to the effect that the earth revolved round the sun, and not the sun round the earth, he would have had his com-

munication treated by the editor of that day in a
similar way.

Spiritualism and its philosophy are so new that it
is hardly to be expected that our great national daily
paper, which almost completely ignores the subject,
would make an exception in my case. The columns
of *The Times* are reserved for official and orthodox
Christianity and orthodox Science. To these two
subjects it gives ample space, and the sayings and
doings of the official leaders of Science and Christianity get prominent notice and support in its
columns. To those who know the truth about the
history of Christianity and the basis of sand on which
it is founded, this seems extraordinary. Spiritualism
asks nothing from humanity contrary to reason. It
puts reason first as the magnetic north for each one
of us to steer by. If we try to keep to our course,
guided by reason, we may go astray, but not so far
astray as if we put something else in the place of
this God-given gift.

All the knowledge we possess, all the present
comfort and happiness of humanity, is the result of
man putting reason first, and just as he has put reason
first and faith last has he progressed and improved his
well-being. All the instruction and guidance we get
from the other world is for the purpose of helping us
to use our reason aright, but never for encouraging
us to lean on external guidance and not think for ourselves. We are here in this world for the purpose
of developing our characters, and Spiritualism is not
going to weaken them. Quite the reverse. The
primary object our friends have in communicating
with us is to let us realise that they are still alive and

happy. The second object is to let us know that we too will continue to exist with them in a similar world about and around this earth of ours. These are the two primary objects of the communication which they have opened up between the two worlds ; but in addition they are glad to avail themselves of the opportunity of guiding us and helping us, out of their added experience, to live better and more rational lives than we have lived in the past. They see the world steeped in superstition from which they are anxious to set it free.

This is as far as the average Spiritualist gets. He is quite satisfied when he has learned about his own destiny, and knows what has become of his friends. Automatically, old creeds and dogmas give place to a more rational outlook on life, and he accepts the Seven Principles of Spiritualism as a natural sequence. The average individual, whether he be Christian or Spiritualist, has no great philosophic bent. The majority have too much to do, even if they had the capacity to probe into the mysteries of existence or the riddle of the Universe. All the same there is no doubt that the average level of intelligence amongst Spiritualists is considerably higher than amongst Christians, and some have travelled far on that difficult and endless road, commonly called philosophy.

It is this side of the question I now wish to consider at some length, as the philosophy of Spiritualism is the most advanced philosophy in the world to-day. This is not to be wondered at in view of the fact that Spiritualists, whose minds run in this direction, have been greatly helped and guided by the higher Intelligences with whom they have been in touch.

After having had proof in abundance that life continues, that those who spoke were those whom they said they were, I decided that the only way to get down to the deeper problems of existence was to have private sittings, and to this proposal Mr. John C. Sloan, the Medium, kindly consented. Then it was possible to delve deeper than I could do at ordinary séances, where everyone was anxious to talk to friends and relatives. I had by then reached the stage where I wanted to get beyond those recently passed over, and make contact with much more highly-developed and experienced minds. My wish was granted, and at the first private sitting I had with Sloan, my stenographer being the only other person present, a greatly elevated mental atmosphere became quickly noticeable. No attempt was made to prove identity ; that I had already proved to my entire satisfaction. I was not particularly anxious to know who spoke to me, but I was very anxious to know about many things that I could only learn from those on the other side, who had given deep thought and consideration to them.

What follows from now onwards I put in my own words. It is the combination of my knowledge of physical science, combined with the information I have received from the Etheric World, and my own deductions from this combined knowledge. I shall make what I have to tell as simple as possible, as much of what I have to say is new. Consequently, it must be difficult for the average individual without any psychic experience to comprehend.

Though I had this privilege of having these conversations with those in the other world, of a greater knowledge than that possessed by anyone on earth, yet it took me many years before I could sort out all the information I received, and bring it within the range of my comprehension. Much I was told I could not understand and only gradually has enlightenment come to me.

In my conversations I went far beyond the knowledge of the Medium, who is a working man in Glasgow, highly respected by his employers, but not a man who has given thought to the philosophic side of life. He has suffered all his life from poor eyesight, and has told me more than once that he has seldom if ever read a book in his life. I have been in his house on many occasions and I have never once seen a book in it, and only once a newspaper. He started work at a very early age, and he has never had time to give thought to anything but his ordinary daily work. All his life he has refused to take any payment in return for his mediumistic services.

He was born a Medium and has been aware of his supernormal gifts all his life. In his presence, as I have proved on many occasions, voices speak which are the voices of intelligences quite apart from the Medium's own vocal organs and mind. They are the voices of men and women who once lived on earth speaking from the Etheric World, who have materialised their vocal organs by taking what is called ectoplasm from the Medium. I have had my ear to his mouth on many occasions when one or more voices were speaking at the same time, several yards away from the Medium, and there was not a sound

coming from it.   The Medium is in deep trance
while this takes place, and he knows nothing
of what has occurred when he comes out of the
trance at the end.of the séance.   After the séance I
have told him some of the things I have been told,
but he could not understand them, and said that they
were quite beyond his capacity to comprehend.   He
is a good workman but not a student, and his range
of knowledge is limited to what one might expect
from the environment in which he has lived.   He is
a good, upright, honest British working man, but his
being a Medium does not mean that he knows more
than his associates ; rather the contrary, as he never
hears what takes place at a séance.

   I have already accentuated the fact that
appearances in this world are very different from
reality, the outstanding example being the way we
are deceived as to the movement of the sun.   This
is one instance of many, but it is a good one.
Now I come to another deception of nature.   Matter
which appears to us to be solid is nothing of the kind.
Can anyone imagine a more real or solid thing than
a ton of iron?   If anything is solid, iron appears to
be so.   It certainly fulfils to us in every degree the
definition of the word solid.   It is heavy to lift and
it is hard to the touch.   Physicists, however, would
not call it solid.   In our every-day life the sun appears
to go round the earth, but astronomers would say
that this deception is caused by our living on a globe
which turns on its own axis, and thus gives us the
impression of the sun going round the earth.   So
with iron.   We have the appearance of solidity, but
physicists tell us that matter is an open net-work of

electrons and protons, and that the distance between these electrons and protons is immense in relation to each other.

Just as we have had to recast our views on Astronomy when using our reasoning faculties, so likewise we have had to recast our views regarding physical matter. Matter which looks so solid is, in reality, not solid at all. What then is matter made up of? Matter is made of atoms and these atoms are in turn composed of electrons and protons. The electrons condition the substance and the protons condition the weight. According to the number of protons so is the weight, and according to the number of electrons so is the substance. Thus iron, which is very heavy, has more protons than wood, which is lighter. Iron is iron because it has a certain number of electrons and protons in each atom, and wood is wood because it has a different number. In iron, for instance, there are always 26 planetary electrons in each atom, and so everything that has 26 planetary electrons appears to us as iron. The centre of each atom is known as the nucleus, and this nucleus commands the same position in the atom that the sun does in our solar system, and just as the planets revolve round the sun so the electrons and protons revolve round this centre. The distance these electrons and protons are apart from each other and the nucleus is relatively about the same distance that the planets are from each other and from the sun.

Consequently it will be easily appreciated that the protons and electrons occupy a very small space in the atom, but it is in consequence of the speed at which they revolve that we get the impression that matter is solid.   If we consider an atom as something the size of a village church, then a pin-head would represent the relative size of one of the electrons of which it is composed.   The electrons are what we see and the protons are what makes a substance feel heavy, but what they move in we cannot see.   They move in what is termed ether, which is a word scientists use for this space.   What, then, are electrons and protons?   They are electric charges, the proton being the positive and the electron being the negative.   The atom is thus composed of two charges of electricity, positive and negative.   Now we come down one step further and ask what is an electric charge?   Physicists describe   an   electric   charge   under   the   name   of "wavicle."   It is not a thing which can be pegged down, so to speak, and examined.   It is a vibration of the ether or a wave of motion ;   therefore, when we get down to the constitution of matter, we find that it is composed of certain units called atoms, which units are composed of ether vibrations.   In other words, physical matter is just ether vibrations and nothing more.

When we look at a house, what takes place to make us realise that we are seeing a house?   Now, before I can answer this question, I must give some consideration to the person looking at a house.   It will readily be granted that if no one were looking at the house, the house would not be seen by anyone. There must be two units, so to speak, to complete the picture.   You must have the house and the person looking at it.   Now, what are we?   That is the great question which, before I go any further, I shall try to solve.

The Universe, I believe, is composed of a gigantic scale of vibrations. Those which we appreciate on earth are only a small range of vibrations between two fixed points, namely, between 34,000 and 64,000 waves to the inch, or from 400 to 750 billion waves to the second. That is the section of the Universe which appeals to us, which makes up to us the physical world. Now the Physical World is only a very limited scale of vibrations compared with all the other vibrations in the Universe. We have recently discovered how to produce another range of vibrations which we are able to tune into, as the result of the various devices which go to make up our wireless set. We have learned how to make these vibrations and convert them into sound, but before we knew how to do so they had not existed, though the medium through which they reach us has always existed. Without this ether we should be blind and frozen, as it carries to us the radiation of the sun.

The Universe is just one gigantic scale of vibrations, and I cannot repeat this too often, as until that fact is assimilated thoroughly the Universe will never be understood. Official science recognises only the physical universe, and only within the last forty years has it discovered that the physical universe is made up of these etheric vibrations. That is about as far as orthodox science has reached to-day, but those of us who have taken the opportunities afforded to get into conversation with those higher intelligences in the Etheric World are able to build on this in a way that no orthodox scientist can. Science admits only what the physical senses and instruments respond to,

and nothing more ; but outside of this there is a vast
Universe made up of finer or more rapid vibrations on
the one hand, and grosser or slower vibrations on the
other.   That is what Spiritualists know and that
is why Spiritualists advise scientists not to ignore the
séance room, as until they cease doing so they will
continue to think of the Universe as a "vast pur-
poseless machine."

That other vibrations exist is well known by
scientists, but only certain ranges, one the X-rays,
which are much faster waves than those which constitute physical matter, and the slower waves called
dark heat waves and long electric waves.   These
are proved to our senses by instruments, but there are
vast spaces still unknown to physical science. There is
a big gap between the highest physical vibration and
the X-ray vibrations.   The vibrations of the Etheric
World, I am told by my informants in that world,
commence just above those of the physical world.
We have confirmation of this through the knowledge
obtained from psychic photography and clairvoyance,
and from the fact that etheric beings, called Ghosts,
have been seen from time to time through the ages.
Thus their lowest vibrations must be just about
touching our normal physical range of sight.   The
chart on page 239 makes this clear and shows how
limited are our sense perceptions.   Only the black
portion represents the physical world.   This is all
we sense of the innumerable etheric waves making up
the Universe.

We are told from the Etheric World of this vast
range of vibrations, and knowing what we do of
physical vibrations it is just one step further forward.

We have now no difficulty in relating physical matter to etheric matter. Physical matter is made up of vibrations within two fixed points. Etheric matter is made

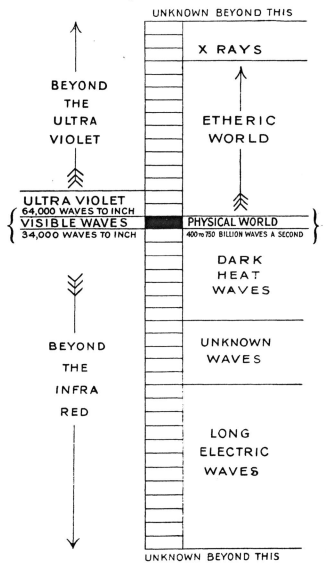

UNKNOWN BEYOND THIS

X RAYS

BEYOND
THE
ULTRA
VIOLET

ETHERIC
WORLD

ULTRA VIOLET
64,000 WAVES TO INCH

VISIBLE WAVES
34,000 WAVES TO INCH

PHYSICAL WORLD
400 to 750 BILLION WAVES A SECOND

DARK
HEAT
WAVES

BEYOND
THE
INFRA
RED

UNKNOWN
WAVES

LONG
ELECTRIC
WAVES

UNKNOWN BEYOND THIS

up of vibrations just beyond 64,000 waves to the inch.
The Etheric World is just a continuation of the vibrations beyond what our senses can perceive.   We
cannot sense above the physical range so long as we
inhabit the physical body.   Clairaudient and clairvoyant Mediums can to a limited extent, but they
are exceptional, due to their etheric ears and eyes
being less heavily coated by physical matter than
those of normal people.   How far beyond the physical
range of vibrations the Etheric World goes we do
not know.

We are, however, told that a point is reached
when the vibrations get so rapid that we reach the
range of Mind.   Mind must be termed substance, just
as physical and etheric matter go under the name of
substance, but substance is just vibration, the rate of
vibration conditioning the substance.   We must use
the word substance as meaning the effect those vibrations have on our consciousness.   Consciousness is
really the effect of substance acting on substance, or
vibrations on vibrations.

Mind is composed of such fine vibrations that it
has the faculty, when in contact with physical matter,
of being moulded into the likeness of physical things.
In the Physical World it has also the power of
moulding physical matter, through acting on it by
means of our hands and feet.   When in contact with
the finer vibrations of the Etheric World it can mould
etheric substance more easily than it can mould
physical matter on earth.   This Mind substance is
the creative power in the Universe, and is called the
Universal Mind.   Its speed of vibrations is so great
that it is highly plastic.   This plastic substance, this

Mind, makes images, as I shall explain, to which we give the name of "thought," and the more closely related these images are so is the thought more intelligent. The Universal Mind is the Thinking substance of the Universe, and it is forever seeking expression. We appreciate it on earth only when in contact with physical matter, and in the Etheric World it is appreciated when in contact with etheric substance.

What makes the electrons and protons revolve in an orderly way within the atom? Each atom must contain a minute proportion of this thinking substance. All matter contains this thinking substance, this Mind, as without it motion would cease, and without motion there would be no Universe. Mind is at the back of all physical substance, and whether it be a stone or a human being, each is controlled by Mind of a different degree. When Mind reaches a certain degree of creative strength it gathers round it etheric matter, and with this combination it can enter into contact with physical matter and promote growth. Then we appreciate life. Every cell of our body, every cell of every growing living thing is controlled by Mind in harmonious direct contact with the governing mind of that body. We are made up of this thinking substance. Life in the physical world is Mind in combination with etheric and physical substance. That combination makes what we call a living thing different from what we term a dead thing, though in reality there is nothing dead in the Universe. All is in motion, or all is motion, but only motion and growth which we appreciate receives the term "life."

Each one of us is endowed with Mind just as

Q

every living thing is, but the human being is endowed with Mind of a finer degree than any other living thing on earth.   Each one of us has our share of this Universal Mind, and its interaction with physical matter is evidently for the purpose of training it, the Mind, in mental image-making.

Mind must be something super-physical as it does not decay ; it remains permanent.   If it decayed like all physical matter, then thought would decay also.   We are continually renewing our physical covering, including our brain matter, but our thoughts and memories remain perfect right back to childhood. Mind, therefore, is something apart from the physical, working in partnership with the physical brain, only during earth life.   Death means that the partnership is severed, though we on earth see only the physical effect of this separation, in the lifeless physical body. This is just another of nature's deceptions, as reality is far different from appearance.

Mind has the peculiar faculty of forming, or moulding itself into, the images and movements of its surroundings.   These it can reproduce at will, and through the medium of physical matter cause change and movement here on earth.   In the Etheric World it has the power of moulding etheric matter in a more direct fashion, and by thought, surrounding etheric matter can be changed into the forms which the Mind imagines.   Earth, then, is the training ground for Mind which has become individualised.   Here it is trained in image-making through contact with earth's grosser surroundings, and as it develops it takes more and more control over its surroundings.   When it ceases to function through physical matter it takes greater and greater control of its surroundings in the Etheric World, until ultimately we, as represented by our Minds and our surroundings, become just as we think.

The individual Mind of each of us, our ego or our self, is therefore trained in creative thought through contact with earth, which training conditions our surroundings here and hereafter. The Mind never dies but continues developing for ever, and with its increasing command over its surroundings, both time and space become of less and less account. Ultimately they cease to exist. My Mind is "me" and your Mind is "you." It has been in existence for all eternity, though not so individualised as now. When it starts its earth experience it enters on a road which enables it to mould its surroundings more and more as it thinks. Our Minds will ultimately be in complete control of our surroundings, and as we think, so shall we be. Then I surmise the vibrations of our surroundings and of our minds will be at an equal speed—that is, in unison, and we shall be inhabitants of the Realm of Mind, our eternal home. This, I believe, is our destiny, and our first step towards reaching this control over our surroundings, over time and space, is our time on earth, and it is to achieve this end that we, individualised Minds, pass through our earth experiences. All children who die still-born or as infants are brought back to earth by etheric nurses to be trained in image-making through contact with the grosser physical vibrations.

We now can understand what we mean by saying that we see something. What happens is really this. When we look at a house we see something composed of different substances.   Each substance contains a different number of electrons and protons.   The wood has so many, the glass has so many, and the bricks have so many.   These electrons agitate the surrounding ether in accordance with their speed. The substance that has one agitates the ether in a different way from the substance that has a hundred. This affects our Mind by the following process. Light, comprising the entire range of the vibrations of physical matter, strikes the house, and its vibrations are thrown back to us in accordance with the vibrations of each substance.   These we term colour. These vibrations agitate the atoms composing our physical eye and, by means of our nerves, they are transformed into vibrations of our physical brain and thence to our etheric brain, which is an exact duplicate of our physical brain.   Through the etheric brain they mould our Mind, that plastic substance with which we are all endowed.

The Mind in consequence builds itself into the image of a house, and what we say we see and appreciate, is our Mind-image of the house.   The Mind is never at rest, always in action, always building itself into images, always creating new images, and as these images are, so are we.   Our existence is made up of the images which the Mind constructs. Likewise our Mind gets the impression of solidity through our nerves by the same means.   When we stand up or sit or lie down, we are continually being bombarded upwards and supported by a great multitude of vibrations delivered by the atoms making up the substances on which we rest.

It is, however, incorrect to say that here or the

hereafter is an illusion. That word gives an entirely wrong impression of life. Life is real here and hereafter. Our surroundings here and hereafter are real because all matter substance acts on Mind substance, and without substance there would be neither Mind nor matter. This world is consequently real and so will the next world be, because reality is this Mind image-making, and wherever you have this you have reality. It is impossible to imagine Mind without something to act on, or this something acted on without Mind to image it or appreciate it and fashion it.

Hence, wherever Mind is individualised, it will image and then create, fashion and mould its surroundings, and so in the Etheric World, its inhabitants create houses, clothes and everything else that the Mind creates on earth. So also the Mind that forms the images of trees, flowers and grass on earth, through physical matter, likewise forms them there through etheric eyes alone, as the vibrations of etheric trees, etc., appeal to Mind there, just as here. All, and much more, that exists on earth exists also on the various planes of the Etheric World. Thus life there to its inhabitants is very similar to life here, but to those capable of appreciating its beauty it is more beautiful than the earth, in consequence of the finer vibrations of the Etheric World.

Mind has initiative of its own and can build up images for itself without influence from without. Once it has learned to make an image it can make it again, and here we have the constructive capacity of Mind, as Mind, working always through the etheric on to the physical brain, can build physical matter as it conceives. All our bodily parts are built up as.

conceived by our Mind.   Every bodily movement, sensed or unsensed, is first imaged by the Mind. The Mind first thinks every heart beat and every movement of the body, and when the physical body cannot respond, then follows the separation called death, as if mind cannot function it leaves its physical instrument, taking with it the etheric body.   Thus we see how Mind is the most potent influence in every living thing, in the world and in the Universe ; in fact, it is the only reality, all else being its servant.

CHAPTER IX.

THE PHILOSOPHY OF SPIRITUALISM.

PART II.

I WISH now to go back to the beginning of all life, and trace its action and interaction with physical matter from the humble protoplasm, through the worm stage on to the fish stage, through the reptiles and the marsupials to the apes, and then on to man. I wish to trace briefly the evolution of Mind in its association with physical matter.

Evolution is but a word to comprise the long, long story of Mind expressing itself through physical matter. Mind can act on physical matter only through etheric substance. The vibrations of Mind are too rapid for it to be able to obtain direct contact with physical matter. Mind therefore works always by first building up an etheric counterpart, and as this etheric counterpart grows it attaches to itself physical matter. If we go back to the humblest protoplasm we find Mind in the humblest form acting on physical matter. Protoplasm is the physical basis for life, and in its humblest form such as the protozoa, it propagates by dividing itself into two perfect cells. If we think carefully of this marvellous act, we come to the logical conclusion that life is propagated by part of the original trinity coming away and forming a new individual unit. As the original unit must have been guided by Mind, it is evident that part of the Mind which guided the original must have distributed itself between the two. Here we have a simple illustration of the propagation of the species. In humble life

sub-division causes propagation, but as life develops
it requires the sub-division of male and female to produce offspring, but the method is the same.

At some time far back in history, when this world
of ours cooled sufficiently to enable Mind through
etheric matter to contact with physical matter, a
humble speck of physical matter was gathered round
a humble speck of etheric matter. This humble
speck of etheric matter was governed by Mind substance, and this trinity originated life on earth in the
earliest forms by sub-division. Life was propagated
until the waters of the world, before the Palæozoic
age, swarmed with protozoas. Once contact was
made with physical matter Mind became better able
to express itself, and it conceived all sorts of forms
and shapes. Just as it conceived them, so it built
them up. Physical matter seems to be like a garden
in which Mind is capable of growing and developing.

Propagation gradually assumed more complicated
methods, but still the principle was the same, the
parents passing down to the offspring a part of their
own trinity—Mind, etheric body and physical body ;
and again and again the old story was repeated of
life, growth, propagation and then decay through
Mind and etheric substance parting from the physical.
Mind could only remain in contact with the physical
for a limited time. It was not a permanent habitation. The etheric duplicate could only retain the
physical around it for a short time, as physical matter
is always in a state of decomposition, and evidently
the etheric body could renew and build up this material
for only a limited time. Our physical body is completely renewed every seven years, but the etheric

structure is of a permanent character. Consequently it survives the physical body. The time comes when this renewal of the physical body cannot be continued, and what we call death then follows. Death, how-ever, is death only to the physical which has been temporarily animated by Mind capable of creative thought. The life-giving Mind still persists, con-trolling the etheric duplicate.

How long this combination of Mind and the etheric counterpart continued apart from physical matter in the days of primitive life, no one can say; but this we know, that a time came when the combination did continue, when Mind was strong enough to retain its individuality and persist in the Etheric World as an individual unit. Before this time, doubtless, the individual Mind unit was not sufficiently strong to stand alone and it merged into the mass Mind of the Universe, to manifest itself again at some later period in some other physical form. Mind is only recognised by us through the physical, and had we not the guidance and knowledge obtained through Spiritualism we should be at a loss to under-stand what life really is, and what it means.

The time came, after a long period of evolu-tionary effort, when man arrived on the scene, a thinking being; but had we not the evidence of Spirit-ualism we could not account for his existence or know his destiny. Except for the evidence of Spiritualism there is little to make us believe other than that he is a thinking being through some chemical reaction taking place within his brain, and that when death comes the reaction ceases and his consciousness be-comes extinguished. The fact that this is not so

accounts for the religious instinct in man, and we
know through the evidence obtained from Spiritualism that this instinct has a real meaning behind it.

Just as the original protoplasm was not merely a
physical creation, so likewise are we not a physical
creation.   We are a mental creation.   We belong to
a higher substance than physical matter, and physical
matter is just like a diver's suit.   It is very useful
for the diver when on the bed of the ocean, just as
our physical body is very useful to us when in contact
with the grosser vibrations of the earth.   Just as the
diver is not at home on the sea bottom, so are we not
at home on the earth's surface.   Otherwise we should
not spend so much of our time in giving thought to
what follows death.   It is because instinctively we
know that we are only temporary inhabitants here that
we have reached out to obtain knowledge of our
hereafter.

Animals have not this instinctive feeling because
their minds are not sufficiently developed to retain
their individuality permanently as man does.   They
retain their individuality for a time only on the animal
plane in the Etheric World, and then with memories
dissipating like a dream, their minds return to the
mass Mind of the Universe.   They have not the
power to continue image-making.   'Animals, therefore, have only a temporary individuality which
persists for a short time in the Etheric World, but
affection on the part of an etheric being for an animal
can retain that animal's individuality for a longer
period than is possible if no human affection exists.
This affection seems to stimulate the mind of the
animal, but it is only a temporary stimulation, as ulti-

mately the animal mind must return to the mass Mind. To put it briefly, creatures guided by instinct only, retain their individuality after death for a period, but with man, guided by intelligent thought, the personality persists.

Human beings persist, though the lower types of human mind, more akin to the animal mind than the human, doubtless follow the line prescribed for animal life. Only the mind capable of continuing this image-making retains its memories of the past and its individuality. When we reached this stage who can tell, but the time did come far back in history when the individual persisted after death and did not return to the mass Mind.

It is Mind that makes us what we are. It seems to remember all experiences it has had in the previous forms of life, as prior to birth each one of us goes through all the different shapes and forms of more primitive lives. In the first four weeks after conception, there is little appreciable difference between the embryos of a man, of a dog, and of a tortoise. The ultimate difference is due to the fact that we went on developing before birth to the man stage. A still-born child continues its development in the Etheric World and develops into a man or woman.

Mind is the constructive thinking substance of the Universe. It fashions all the flora and the fauna, and in the most advanced of us it seems to be so refined that it has become more closely related to the directive power of the Universe, and is thus attracted to it like a magnet. We can thus understand what it means when we are told, by our friends on the other

side, that as our Mind develops we reach finer and
finer planes of consciousness, where the Mind has
more and more direct bearing on its surroundings,
and can mould and be moulded by its surroundings
in a way unimaginable here. Our destiny seems to
be that we ultimately become as we think, when Mind
has such complete control of its surroundings that to
think is to be—always, however, retaining our individuality. Just as the sea is composed of individual
atoms, so our individuality and personality persist
when we reach the ocean of full control and understanding, which is to become in full affinity with the
Divinity, the all-directing power of the Universe.

The Universe is only limited by the limitations
of Mind, but, as it is impossible to imagine a region
where Mind cannot penetrate, the logical conclusion
is that the Universe is without limit. Limit is related
to physical distance and time. In the region where
Mind is supreme and in complete control, nothing is
limited, and there the Universe will be compre-
hensible. The Universe, as I have previously
said, is just one gigantic scale of vibrations.
The finer ranges I term Mind, which has the
capacity of directing the other vibrations into
the ways and shapes it conceives. This substance
that Mind acts on I term matter. Mind is the
positive, matter the negative, and these two substances, Mind and Matter, make up the Universe.
Matter without Mind is impossible to imagine, just as
it is impossible to imagine Mind without matter.
Mind and matter are co-related ; they are always
found together. Mind cannot be acted on by
nothing, and without Mind it is impossible to imagine
matter.

Mind and matter are the two substances of which the Universe is composed. Mind is that subtle substance which directs matter, and which is the cause of matter, as all matter has Mind behind it, causing the vibrations which we call matter. They are twin brothers, inseparable. Mind directs the moving protons and electrons, but it is crude Mind and cannot be compared with the Mind which appreciates that such things exist. Mind is present in a tree ; it is also present in the animal, but it is mind of a different degree. In the former it directs the growth of the tree and what nourishment it is to absorb and what it is to reject. In the latter it does all this and more ; it appreciates the tree as well. The tree cannot appreciate the animal, but the animal can appreciate the tree. Plant life, therefore, does not make mental images as animals do, and thus does not survive death. Only mental image-makers do. Mind in the animal appreciates the tree according to its development ; the appreciation of a dog is different from that of the bird. To the savage the tree means less than to the botanist.

Mind is of two degrees, one directing growth and the other capable of appreciation and intelligent thought. The first is called the sub-conscious and the other the conscious Mind. Mind in a stone directs the whirling electrons and protons. Mind in an architect fashions the stone to its own design. The mind of the architect has therefore two qualities, the sub-conscious sustaining the functions of his body, and the conscious capable of creative thought. Mind can therefore be divided into four categories on earth —the lowest as found in a stone ; then the mind of plant life ; next the mind of animal life ; lastly the mind of man capable of creative thought, and thus all things are subservient to him.

Mind in different degrees, therefore, controls the Universe. It is the cause of the vibrations of the Universe, and matter is the effect. In its higher degrees it can control and fashion matter, its less intelligent brother, and as it reaches states of finer and finer matter so does its control increase.

Matter is the effect of Mind. Mind, this all-powerful cause energising the Universe, causes motion and that motion is matter. Matter, therefore, can be termed Mind in motion, and the effect on us of this motion is what we term matter. Mind, therefore, is the Universe, and all that we see and sense is Mind acting on Mind, one rate of motion on another rate of motion. We are therefore part of a Universe of motion or vibration, the entire Universe being motion and only motion. The slower motion, namely matter, inter-acts with the faster motion, namely Mind ; but all is Mind varying in degrees of motion.

What we call physical matter, as I have previously explained, is just this motion at a certain fixed rate of vibration. Mind in contact with the physical can only appreciate a certain fixed scale of motion. Etheric matter which we do not sense is matter at another fixed rate of vibration, and as this rate of motion varies so etheric matter varies in its relation to Mind. The mind, as it travels onwards through death from plane to plane, appreciates finer and finer rates of vibration just as the sheath that covers it becomes more refined. At death, the heaviest sheath is cast aside, and Mind appreciates a finer range of vibrations which constitutes the first stage of its journey in the Etheric World ; but as our etheric body gets more and more refined it becomes fitted for a finer environment, and so it rises into realms of finer matter which surround this world, the only difference being that on earth we leave a body behind us.   In the Etheric World our etheric body gets more and more refined in itself, and thus it becomes fitted for a finer environment.

Everywhere throughout the Universe we find these two states of motion existing, and as the variation of motion is, so is the thought.   Thought is the effect of these two motions.   Their combination constitutes our consciousness, and consciousness consists of the mental images, which are constantly being formed by our mind, as the result of the continual bombardment of minute vibrations through our sense organs and brain on to the Mind.

Therefore it follows that the different combinations of thought make up the individual's existence. Here in the physical world, Mind plus physical matter makes us what we are, and is the explanation of our existence.   In a further stage Mind plus etheric matter makes us what we are, and in a stage still further on, when the combination changes again, so shall we be as the combination is, and so on till we reach the stage when surrounding matter is so refined that it can be moulded into whatever shapes the Mind conceives.

Then, and then only, shall we be able to comprehend the Universe.   Boundaries and limits, which to us here on earth are such an insuperable difficulty in our arriving at an understanding of the Universe, will by then have disappeared, as limits are associated

with matter but not with Mind. Our present difficulties in grasping the Universe arise through our
mind being in association with physical matter, which
is limited in its vibrations, and through attempting to
explain the Universe from a physical or limited angle.
When we reach the region of Mind, which is the
Universe, the all and in all, our difficulties will disappear. All we need to do now is to accept the fact
of Infinite Mind, and that the Universe must be
viewed from that angle and not from our finite or
physical angle. Then the rest is easy.

In some far off stage of our career, if we have
the desire, we can become one with Infinity or
Divinity, but until that stage is reached the Universe
will always remain a problem. The way to make it
cease being a problem is in imagination to enter this
region of pure thought and look on the Universe now
as we shall look on it then. Only when Mind is fully
developed can it comprehend all, but in imagination
some of us can envisage a timeless, spaceless, limit-
less Universe where Mind is all and in all.

Beyond this we cannot go even in imagination.
We have now reached the stage of pure thought and
have become as Gods, with our surroundings at our
complete control. We need not dwell too long in
this region, as the illimitable time and distance between
us and it is so great. What is more important is
what practical conclusions we can draw from this
better understanding of Mind.

As the Universe is motion and the planets and
stars which we sense here on earth are just motion
at the same fixed rate of speed as our physical world,
it is likewise conceivable that the sun and each planet

has surrounding it an etheric world also, and that the
etheric sun gives light to the various etheric worlds.
'Are the belts round Saturn not an etheric world in
process of formation, and was our world at one time
not like it, far back in history? The sun is the centre
of our planet system and round it are moving spheres.
The sun itself is moving round another centre, and
that centre may be moving round another, and so on.
Where lies the fixed centre, if there be one, no one
knows. There is doubtless an explanation of this
seeming infinity of physical matter, but always remember that all physical appearances are different
from reality, and so the explanation may be simple
enough to understand when we are sufficiently
developed mentally to realise the reality behind the
appearance.

To take our own earth to begin with, by a slowing
down of vibrations it has reached a stage to which we
give the name physical, but that is not our entire
world. To physical people, yes ; but theirs is a very
limited outlook. In the slowing down of vibrations
and the forming of the earth, can we not imagine how
it all happened? Imagine a world at one time vastly
larger than our globe as we know it. Imagine this
whirling mass of fine substance, let us say ten
thousand times the size of our earth. As it cooled
the centre vibrated more slowly than the outer cir-
cumference, and so the cooling process went on, a
hard material centre forming which we now call the
Earth, and all round it various degrees of substances
which we cannot sense, but still they exist and are as
much a part of our world as we are. The earth is the
centre of the world, but the greater part of the world

R

extends far out into space and it is quite unsensed by us
physical beings.   Heaven is no fantastic realm as it
has been painted to us in the legends of the past.
It is an astronomical locality, and this being so, I
would suggest that in future it receives the name
ETHERIA, instead of the name Spirit World or
Etheric World, which has been used in the past to
denote the super-physical world.   It is not in some
far-off region in space, but is part of our world and
goes round the sun along with this earth.   Just as our
earth turns on its axis, so the Etheric World turns
along with us.   It is all part of one whole.   The
earth is like the stone in a peach and the Etheric
World is like the fruit surrounding it.   Just like the
stone, so the earth is the life-giving seed to the
Etheric World.   Another good simile is that of an
onion, which, made up of different skins, mak ; one
connected whole.

The complete world, then, is made up of a fixed
scale of vibrations, and only a small range of these
affect our senses.   As time goes on we shall go up the
rungs of the ladder, leaving the physical for the first
plane beyond the earth, and so on, always appreciating
the surroundings in tune with our etheric body ; but
though we shall appreciate only one range of vibrations normally, yet by thought we shall be able to
lower our vibrations and come back and appreciate
the lower ranges through which we have passed.

To begin with, far back in history, Mind could
only enter into contact with physical matter in a crude
state ; but gradually the physical was able to accom-
modate Mind of higher and higher quality, or in other
words, of finer and finer vibration.   It is logical to
believe that we shall return to the range of vibrations

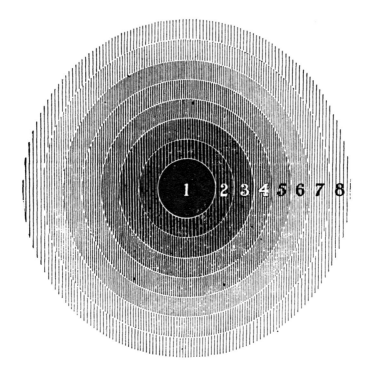

The above diagram I have prepared for the purpose of representing as clearly as possible the real world. No. 1 represents the Earth, and from Nos. 2 to 8 the various etheric worlds, each of which has a surface. They interpenetrate each other, but the distance of each surface from the other, which is represented in the above chart as being equal, must not be taken so literally, as the distances vary between the respective surfaces. It must also be understood that the Etheric worlds extend to great distances into space, and that their relation in size to the earth is proportionately much greater than is here shown.

However, this is the best representation that can be made, and the reader must imagine each of the eight worlds interpenetrating each other and yet forming one complete whole. This can be more easily imagined when it is kept in mind that each sphere is made up of atoms vibrating at different speeds. There is nothing known to physics to prevent waves of different frequencies being simultaneously present in the ether.

The earth is vibrating between 34,000 and 64,000 waves to the inch, which range represents the limit of vibrations we physical beings can appreciate. Each sphere has a range of vibrations of its own, which can be appreciated only by those attuned to its vibrations, and each range follows the other in speed. Thus the highest earth vibrations just touch the lowest vibrations of No. 2, and so on.

I cannot find anything in science to contradict in any way the above conception of this greater world; in fact I would go further and say that the latest theories of physical science leave a place open for the etheric world, and I believe that it is only a matter of time before it is accorded its proper place by orthodox science.

from which the Mind originally came, just as the beings below us will reach the range from which their mind came.   It seems as if part of the Universal Mind reached down to the physical and in each individual is returning whence it came, like to like. Thus can be understood the saying, " We are all the sons of God, we come from God and we return to God."   So also can be understood the reason for all the rites, ceremonies and symbols of all religions.

So the action and reaction goes on, Mind embedding itself for a time in the physical and then leaving it, taking with it the etheric body, which it has shaped and which has been encased by a physical garment.   This latter returns to the physical earth, to become at some later date the habitation of another mind.   Thus can be seen the true meaning of the resurrection of the dead.   The physical bodies as we know them, in the shape and form in which Mind constructed them, are not re-animated at some future date by the return of Mind to its former habitation. The particles, however, which composed the body, in one form or another will be re-animated by another Mind, and again give physical form to a living creature.   This comes about through plants which give food to animal life.   This food replaces the wastage of the physical bodies of all animal life, and so what was once an animated physical body dies to return to form a part of other physical bodies.   In this, and this way only, can we accept the physical resurrection of the dead body.   The frame-work, the etheric body, which held the physical together, however, passes from it at death, never to return.

This action and reaction goes on day by day, and

each one of us is awaiting our turn to go through the same metamorphosis as has been gone through by all that lived on earth before us. This interplay of the two states of motion, to which we give the names Mind and Matter, has taken place on earth since the first protoplasm developed in some stagnant pool. It has gone on by slow degrees till the mind became sufficiently developed to act independently apart from the physical, and through the etheric become at death an etheric human being with a seemingly endless career before him. With this etheric body the individual is able to develop in a methodical way, though the body may change in shape and form as it reaches higher stages of development. Mind and the etheric body are inseparable ; to imagine Mind without a body is unthinkable. Immediately after death it reaches the level of vibrations to which the mind can respond through the etheric brain. It reaches its plane of thought, which is just as real and tangible to it in this new state as it was in the physical.

Doubtless this individualisation of mind came slowly and it was long before the individuality could be maintained ; but the time came when it could, and then it was that the Etheric World was man's real home. Then step by step as the mind became more and more developed, so the Etheric World became inhabited, and we are now told of seven distinct planes of habitation, real and tangible. Each succeeding plane is more beautiful and each in turn is inhabited by minds more and more advanced in proportion as the surrounding matter is more refined.

The place we reach immediately following the earth plane is of finer matter than physical matter but

of grosser matter than the plane above it, and so on,
each plane being composed of finer and finer substance.   As the mind develops so it automatically
rises to the place to which it becomes attuned.   Our
mind must reach a state of harmony with its surroundings or otherwise there is no happiness, and,
as in the Etheric World we can harmonise ourselves
with our surroundings more easily than on earth, so
we reach the plane of our desire quite naturally.
Consequently the Etheric World, to all of a happy
and contented disposition, can be a happier and more
contented world to live in than is the Physical World.
As the mind is, so is our happiness or unhappiness.

Mind always responds to the vibrations to which
it is fitted, from the physical to the etheric and from
the etheric to the super-etheric.   We are told that
there are eight known planes comprising this world
if we include this earth's surface, but that there
is a region beyond that quite apart from this
world which we shall eventually enter.   Then this
world will cease to be for us, and we shall cease to
move with it.   However, when we get thus far, all
earth memories will have faded, and so there are none
to return to tell us.   Wherever life is, all is natural,
and so life on the next plane of thought is a natural
and rational one, as our mind reaches the conditions
to which it is attuned.   Just as it is attuned to certain
conditions on earth, so it will reach similar conditions
in the etheric.   It is the same mind and it attunes
itself to the vibrations to which it responds.   Nature
makes all changes slowly, and death is no exception.
It is little noticed by some.   Many pass on and
hardly realise at first that a change has occurred, as

the mind at once attunes itself to the new conditions, and these conditions, to begin with, are very like those to which we are accustomed in our earth surroundings. Many, however, cannot get away from earth conditions, as their minds are so conservative, and in such cases, as they were on earth so they are there. Do we not know many people who never want to change, and are always satisfied with their present conditions? Only the mind that is prompted by the urge for something new and something better advances to higher realms. All the same I am told that to all, sooner or later, comes this urge or impulse, and with it the desire for something better, and then progress commences.

CHAPTER X.
THE PHILOSOPHY OF SPIRITUALISM.
PART III.

I HAVE been at some trouble to find out the different experiences which different types of mind have had after the change called Death. Immediately surrounding the earth there is the lowest etheric plane of all, where life continues for a time for those of fixed earth ideas. Those with crude religious beliefs, definitely fixed, attend the religious services on earth to which their minds have been accustomed. Those of low morals attend the low places of the earth. Those with drunken habits frequent our public houses. Conditions are decided by desire. The man absorbed in business or politics maintains for a time after death his interest in these, attending at the office, or the factory, or political meetings, and showing no desire to rise above the earth plane. I have come across those who for years have been wandering about the earth's surface, interested only in earth's affairs and some quite unaware that they had left the earth for ever. They could not understand how it was that they could go from room to room in their own houses, see everything that was going on, and yet could not be heard or appreciated.

These persons are sometimes seen and heard, and are the cause of hauntings or ghosts ; but they are exceptional. They are bound to earth by very definite ties of memory, such as a murder, or on account of something forgotten which affects their friends on earth, or some deed which is regretted.

Those with something on their conscience may hang about this earth for many years, but to them time is very different, and what to us seems a long time to them is not necessarily so. Gradually the earth memory fades and they rise to higher planes of consciousness and mix with others who, though they may have earth memories and may return to earth from time to time, yet realise the change that has taken place, and live a natural life in the new world to which they have become accustomed.

It is not those people who haunt the earth who come to séances, but they are at times brought to séances for the purpose of awakening them to a realisation of their new surroundings. Such séances are called "rescue circles," and are being held all over the civilised world. They are for the purpose of awakening an urge or desire for something better in those people who have never been able to untie their minds from earth, and reach the surface of their new abode. The old term Hades doubtless was meant for this Interland between the two surfaces, where roam undeveloped souls. Etheric missionaries, however, are always at work trying to enlighten them, and raise them by thought to their proper place, and with the desire for something better they leave our earth's surface and reach the one above quite naturally. These helpers often find this impossible to do and make use of us on earth to help them, as we are able to influence those backward people in a way they cannot do.

At the ordinary séances we meet again those who have passed on to their proper plane, and come back to tell their friends that they still live and are happy.

The majority find their new level and take up the new life quite naturally. They realise the change that has taken place without much delay.

The mind plays a much larger part in the Etheric World than it does here, and so it can attune itself to the surroundings for which it is fitted in a way it cannot do on earth. We all know people who are out of harmony with their surroundings on earth. That does not happen there. Here on earth we are all living on the same surface. We are meeting the good and the bad, the intelligent and the ignorant, though we may have nothing in common with those we meet. There, those of the same type of thought meet and live together. There the power of Mind is so much more in evidence that like draws to like in a far greater degree than here. Here our work and every-day occupations bring us into contact with minds of all types, but there minds of like development congregate together, and the higher the development the higher is the surface or plane they live on. Harmony of thought is the magnet which draws like to like, so that, though, within limits of development, all kinds live on the same surface there as here, communities having similar ideas and ideals live together. The only earth example I think of is a university or public school, where all live together with a common interest.

Recently I obtained some further valuable information, by means of the Direct Voice, with reference to the exact situations of the various planes surrounding the earth, and the conditions in each. The replies I obtained to my questions are in complete agreement with the replies I received eight years ago when John C. Sloan was the Medium. The Medium in this instance was a London lady of independent means and gives her services only to a few friends. She prefers that her name should not be mentioned. However, the same phenomena occurred as occurred through Sloan's mediumship. I was anxious to have further information on this subject of location, and the replies I received will now be read as an important addition to the many replies to my various questions which I gave in *On the Edge of the Etheric.*

1. *Question.*—Do the planes on which you tell us you live, exist above the surface of the earth?

Reply.—These planes move with the earth and form part of its orbit. The first plane is a kind of Clearing Station where the different nations live together. Family Life is most important, and the members await relatives of their generation to go on together to the next plane. So far as the first plane is concerned, it does exist above the surface of the earth, but it also is in connection with the earth plane.

2. *Question.*—What is the distance of the first plane from the earth's surface, and the distance of the other planes which extend out into space?

Reply.—The first plane is quite close to the earth. There is a distance between each plane, but distance does not mean quite the same thing on this side as it does to you on earth.

3. *Question.*—If you live on a surface beyond the earth's surface, how do you get back to earth?

Reply.—By mental effort. It is easy for those in a higher plane to go to the lower, but those in the lower cannot go to those in the higher. Those coming from higher planes bring their atmospheric or rather etheric vibrations with them.

4. *Question.*—Do all people who die on earth live on the same surface just as we live together on the surface of the earth?

Reply.—The general answer is "Yes"; but it must be remembered that there are earth-bound souls who do not arrive at the first plane without assistance, and in some cases for a very considerable time, so far as time is reckoned on the earth. There are special places for children to be brought up in, as well as healing stations for those who come over, and other healing stations for those living on the first plane. But the word "place" does not quite signify the same thing as is meant by it on the earth plane.

5. *Question.*—Does our surface appear to you as the bed of the ocean appears to us? Namely, you are above us and can get down to us?

Reply.—It is true that the etheric planes are above and around the earth, but the first plane is close to the earth. The reference to the bed of the ocean can only be accepted as a simile. We have nothing quite corresponding to your earth vision of the ocean bed which we can give as an illustration of what your surface looks like when you are coming to us from earth.

6. *Question.*—Has what is equivalent to our earth's surface in your world, got trees and houses?

Reply.—Trees, houses, hills and vales exist on every plane from the physical plane upwards. When we have lowered our vibrations down to the physical plane we experience what exists on your earth's surface. The flowers and trees are brighter on our hills than they are in the vales; it is a matter of light.

7. *Question.*—Are your vibrations similar to ours but faster? Are they of the same nature, but just above our capacity to sense?

Reply.—The vibrations are faster and finer. This applies to each plane; that is, the higher the plane the faster and finer the vibrations.

These replies should be read in conjunction with the replies given in my previous book. It is evident that the Etheric World is part of our world, that it extends out into space, that each sphere has a surface which is somewhat similar to our surface. Each surface and sphere can be penetrated by what they term lowering their vibrations by thought, which explains how it is they can get back to earth, just as it explains how those who die reach the surface of the plane which is to be their home. Further, etheric substance of which it is composed is as free to its inhabitants as our air is to us, and as it can be moulded by thought into the shapes required without manual work as here, so life is easier, and there are no such things as working for money, or master and servant, all being free to live just as they choose.

The Etheric World is different to every type of mind. To those of high and noble thoughts it appears different than to those of low intelligence. All in the same plane can sense the same things, but these appear different according to the mental development. To the good and high-minded these are beautiful, to others the reverse. Everything is natural and responds to the vibrations of the various types of mind.

We hear of some having brighter clothes than others, the reason being that they are living in surroundings of finer matter, and consequently their garments affect the clairvoyant as being of a different quality from that of those living in grosser surroundings. The effect the finer surroundings have on the clairvoyant causes the clairvoyant to appreciate them as radiant light, whereas those living in low surroundings impress the clairvoyant as being of a darker nature. It is all a question of vibration. Dark objects vibrate more slowly than bright objects.

These various planes are actual localities surrounding this world, but it is difficult for those in the Etheric World to convey any definite ideas of distance. In that world to think oneself from place to place is to accomplish the journey almost at the speed of thought.   Consequently what would be called distance to us becomes no distance, to speak of, to them.   However, these localities extend far above the earth's surface, and we are told that Etheria is made up of seven spheres interpenetrating each other, and if we include the earth there are eight spheres.   Each sphere has a surface, called a plane, and above the surface of the first sphere is the surface of the second sphere.   Those on the surfaces of the spheres below can look through the surfaces above them, just as we on earth are looking through all those surfaces and do not know it.

Each succeeding sphere is composed of finer substance, and consequently the surface that is of finer substance than the one be!   cannot be seen by those on the lower surface.   development proceeds, those who progress be   more and more attuned to the finer substance bey nd and above them, and so parting takes place there as here.   Call it death if you like ; but there is no body to bury, and those who pass to a higher plane can come back to their friends at will.   By lowering the vibrations of their etheric bodies by thought, they come through their own surface from plane to plane right back to earth, but they cannot rise above the surface to which they are mentally and bodily fitted.   Those inhabiting the Etheric World are in advance of us here on earth, as this inter-travel between the various planes is a common occurrence and part of their lives.   Here on earth, gradually and slowly, the return of our friends from Etheria is assuming greater and greater pro- portions.   In time it is reasonable to assume that, as we develop psychically, our appreciation of the presence of those called dead will become a more frequent occurrence.

Instead of being ignored on their return to earth, our friends will come back to be greeted by all, and then death will have lost its sting. Remember always that this earth of ours is a very small part of our real world, of which we are the inhabitants. Our earth, composed of matter called physical, is only a very small proportion of the matter which goes to make up our world. If we consider the whole world as composed of matter at different rates of vibration, and imagine the sum total of all these as a hundred, then we might say that twelve per cent of this matter has slowed down sufficiently to become physical. The remaining eighty-eight per cent still forms part of the world revolving with us, but it is unsensed by us physical beings.

Did the physical first give life to the eighty-eight per cent, or did the eighty-eight per cent give life to the twelve per cent? Did the physical propagate life in the etheric or the etheric life in the physical? Life is something apart from the physical, as the physical alone would be devoid of life. A dead tree has lost something a live tree possesses. When Mind reaches a stage to cause movement which can be appreciated, we call the object capable of movement animated, or living, and the cause of this we term Life. The word includes mind the motive, and the etheric counterpart the mechanism. This then is Life, and as life includes mind and the etheric structure, it pertains to the etheric and must have come from the etheric. Life can exist in the etheric apart from the physical, but not in the physical apart from the etheric. The physical, therefore, has been impregnated and is still being impregnated by this invisible inter-action with the etheric.

From the etheric has all life come and to it will it return. The physical, however, gives individuality to life, but what constitutes life must have been in existence before the physical ever was. We think of life only in conjunction with the physical, but in this we are wrong. Life may have existed before the physical was formed, but of its nature we can only guess. What we believe is that the physical gives to life the individuality it has to-day and had in the past, and life after passing through the physical retains individuality for a length of time according to the mental development. Other types of life exist in Etheria which differ from those of this world, and presumably they came into being through interaction between the planes on which they exist and the planes above them. But all physical life came from the etheric just as all etheric life has come from a higher source. The planes nearer the earth, therefore, are more like this earth than those further away, as their vibratory conditions more closely resemble earth conditions.

And now in conclusion. From the information I have been given from the Etheric World, we now realise that the earth is but a small part of the real world, and that the real world is composed of various spheres at different rates of vibration. We also now realise that Mind is the governing power in the Universe, but only when it is in conjunction with the physical can we appreciate it. Mind, however, never acts directly on the physical but through the etheric counterpart on to the physical. The etheric duplicate is first conceived by the mind, and just as it grows it attaches to it physical matter.

The time comes to every individualised life when physical matter cannot be retained, and the etheric counterpart, governed by Mind, returns to the etheric environment. We subconsciously will our own death. This interaction of Mind with the physical has been proceeding on earth since the first protoplasm moved on its own initiative. Up through the various stages of evolution on earth, finer and finer mind substance was able to manifest through the physical, and so has all life developed. It has propagated itself through part of this trinity, mind, etheric matter and physical matter, detaching itself and forming offspring.

Mind has developed itself through coming into contact with the physical. For a time it was not strong enough to retain its individuality and its memories sufficiently long to become an etheric being, and consequently Mind returned to the Mass Mind to again enter the physical, each time becoming stronger and more individualised. Then the time came when the first individual unit was able to retain his memory and identity, as his mind images were sufficiently strong to last in the etheric. Thus man became an etheric being, but not immortal. Only as Mind developed did the stage come when his mind remained indefinitely individualised in the etheric. Then the etheric was his real home and the physical only the starting point in his career.

If we now follow man in the stages onwards, we

s

find that this individualised mind harmonises with its
surroundings and consequently reaches conditions to
which it is attuned.   Mind is capable of development
and so it can rise to finer and finer surroundings, and
it does so, owing to its obtaining greater and greater
power over its etheric body, which it can attune to
its surroundings by the power of thought.   As Mind
gets into finer surroundings it can act with greater
ease on surrounding substance, because that finer substance is more akin to Mind.   The Mind behind it
is more easily reached, as all substance is animated
and guided by Mind.   Just as each of us can influence other minds on earth, so the time will come
when we can likewise influence our surroundings.

Gradually the individual rises to finer and finer
surroundings, and as he rises he gets more and more
control of his surroundings, until ultimately his
thoughts so condition his surroundings that he
is as he thinks, and thus he reaches the region
of pure thought.   That is man's destiny as far as I
can tell ; call it reality if you will, but all is reality to
us in every stage upwards.   The reality of one stage
ceases to be so at the next, which in turn becomes
real, and so we go on from one reality to another,
looking back on the previous stage as but an inferior
expression of the one reached.   No finite being at
our stage of consciousness can comprehend more than
this state of pure thought.   A picture that is going
to take eternity to paint cannot be grasped when
the preliminary sketches are first being pencilled in.

After we have reached this stage of pure thought,
will each individualised mind not reincarnate?   So
some think, but to me it is inconceivable that Mind

when it reaches that stage will ever think of returning to earth. It has reached a stage of strength and virility, its earth memories are forgotten, it becomes separated from this whirling mass of physical and etheric matter, and it is in a state of reality, all other stages having been passed and forgotten. To return would be retrogression, and we have no evidence that this is Nature's plan. It sounds simple and believable to those who have never thought out how we obtain our individual minds and become individual beings. These come from our parents as already explained. There is no mystery about it, so the one who believes that he or she is the re-incarnation of some individual who once lived on earth must explain how this separate individual mind took the place of the combined minds of his or her parents at conception. It is caused by a misunderstanding of the facts, and sprang from minds which could conceive the virgin birth, an old belief with no scientific authority behind it. To me, the re-incarnation of a strong individualised mind is impossible to imagine, though the weaker undeveloped minds may possibly return to the mass Mind just as do the minds of animals, but I have nothing to support even this suggestion. These views, I may say, receive the support of my informants in the Etheric World, who say that they know of no one who has incarnated again on earth. They have with them those who lived on earth thousands of years ago, and those not with them have gone on to higher planes.

It is reasonable to imagine the Universe as a whole, as one great developing thought or a series of myriad small thoughts connected into one harmonious whole.   As we know by experience that developing thought never goes back but only changes, so we must assume that thought is continually evolving to higher heights of expression.   There seems no end to Mind so there is no end to thought, and no end to life.   What we know is occurring in this world of ours we can assume is likewise occurring in different degrees in the other worlds in the Universe.

To try to explain the Universe from a physical standpoint, therefore, becomes obviously ridiculous. To us some day the physical will be the least important thing in our lives, and if this is to be so, why try to explain the Universe from a physical point of view, as some of our noted scientists are still trying to do? When they realise that the Universe is Mind and that the physical is but an expression of this mind, our science will be revolutionised, our healing will be revolutionised, and our social conditions will be revolutionised.   We shall come to realise that our time on earth is for the purpose of developing creative thought, and so the development of mind and character will be the object before every intelligent individual.

> " Two men looked out through prison bars—
>   One saw mud, the other stars."

Could two lines better express the power of Mind over our surroundings?   As it is here, so will it be hereafter.   Some minds are only sufficiently developed to see mud, but others to comprehend something of the majesty of the Universe.

CHAPTER XI.

WEIGHED IN THE BALANCE.

ABOUT 2,500 years ago a Chaldean King gave a great feast to a thousand of his lords, so we are told in an ancient record. This king, Belshazzar by name, commanded that the golden and silver vessels, taken from the temple at Jerusalem, be brought and used at the feast. In the same hour came the fingers of a man's hand and wrote on the wall, much to the discomfiture of the king, his princes, his wives, and his concubines. They saw the writing but they could not understand its meaning, so Daniel was called that he might interpret it, which he did.

And this is the writing that was written :—
MENE MENE TEKEL UPHARSIN, which he translated into meaning :

"God has numbered thy kingdom and finished it. Thou art weighed in the balance and found wanting. Thy kingdom is divided and given to the Medes and Persians."

That night the king was slain and Darius the Median took his kingdom. This is an old, old story, but its lesson is as evident to-day as it was of yore. Nature never stands still. Progress is the law of Nature. Kingdoms and beliefs come and go, and nothing remains permanent in the Universe. "Change and decay in all around" is as true to-day as it will be to-morrow and as it was yesterday.

An individual or a community of individuals, be they a nation or a church, if they do not progress, are bound by immutable law to perish. Each one of us, each community, is constantly being weighed in Nature's balance, and our record taken. If we are found wanting, our Kingdom is finished. Life pursuing life and in turn pursued by life, the fittest only surviving. Thus we are to-day what we are. This mental urge has raised the humble protoplasm and made of it thinking men and women.

Those who say that "the religion of my father is good enough for me" will be found wanting when each individual mind takes account of its past and weighs up all the opportunities missed. It is so much easier just to accept and not to think for oneself—just to slide down life's stream, to be a drifter and not a thinker. Some day, either here or hereafter, a rock will be struck, and the drifter will have to take stock of his surroundings and decide if drifting is to be forever his means of navigation, or if he is to take command of himself, use his reason as his compass, and learn to steer for himself. Otherwise when he reaches the sea he will be either a helpless piece of wreckage, tossed to and fro with nothing to guide him, or on the other hand a capable navigator able and willing to use the gift of reason implanted in each one of us.

Humanity is made up of drifters and thinkers, the drifters scoffing at the thinkers and the thinkers pitying the drifters. If there were no drifters and only thinkers in this country, this book would never have been written. Neither would it have been written if there had been no thinkers. The information given within these pages has not been assembled by a drifter, but by a thinker. History will repeat itself, and the conclusions here reached will be criticised and derided by the drifters, who have never given an hour's thought to any of the subjects discussed.

From the time I was at the University I have given much thought and time to the study of Comparative Religion, to the origin of the Biblical records, and the origin of Christianity, and for over thirty years I have been interested in this subject. I have been familiar all these years with the questions with which it deals, and until I became a Spiritualist I was, as the result of my investigations, an agnostic, one who believed that nothing could be known of God, or the after life, by our limited powers of comprehension. Those were questions I could not solve. I did not deny their importance, but left them aside till my knowledge increased.

I feel no bitterness towards any Church, although when I was younger my patience was severely tested. So far as I personally am concerned, it does not matter what the Church preaches or what the people believe ; in these days everyone tolerates the opinions of others and recognises the right of each individual to think for himself.

Why, therefore, should I trouble to write a book? Certainly it is not for profit. How can one explain the desire to share with others the knowledge possessed by a few but not by the majority? Why have some of us this desire to pass on the knowledge, knowing that criticism will follow and nothing material will ever be gained? Why did Bruno not recant and tell the Church and the priests of his time that he would believe anything if they would only leave him alone? Personally I would have done that rather than be tortured. I would have told them that rather than suffer torture and misery I would be silent for ever and they could remain ignorant if they wanted to ; but I am not the stuff that martyrs are made of. At least, I think so now ; but had I lived in those days of ignorance my attitude might have been different. The minds of our ancestors were different from ours. There was little toleration on either side. Intolerance bred intolerance. They were not so refined in mind in those days, otherwise they could not have inflicted pain as they did, and they could not have endured pain as they did. Their minds were coarser and likewise their feelings.

However, in this land of the free, everyone is at liberty to express his honest and dishonest thoughts, and as I shall not be burned by the Church I have taken the trouble to pass on what I honestly believe is the truth. It is because I see indifference on the one hand through the folly of the Church, and ignorance on the other through the people accepting the Church's teaching, that I feel compelled to put my thoughts once more on paper. Besides that, it is only right that the general public should know the truth about Christianity and Spiritualism. The clergy frequently scoff at and ridicule Spiritualism and Spiritualists ; but this book will show that they should put their own house in order before interfering with honest, intelligent people, in the unmannerly way they do. Their folly, I trust, I have made clear to everyone.

It is because the indifferent are losing so much, and the ignorant are losing so much, that I trust this book will still further open the minds of

those who are coming to believe that there is truth
in Spiritualism, but cannot accept it because it is contrary to the Church's teaching or the Bible. To help
them I have told them what I believe to be the truth
about all three, and if they still prefer to cling to a
decaying institution or an ancient book and ignore
the testimony of men and women of repute of the
present day, on the facts relating to survival, then
no more can be done.

Let me give the latest opinion of the Church
as to its belief in Survival after death. This is contained in the January 1933 issue of *Life and Work*,
the official publication of the Church of Scotland,
in an article by the Very Reverend Professor W. P.
Paterson, D.D., LL.D., Professor of Divinity at
Edinburgh University, whose opinion carries great
weight in the Protestant Church. In this article he
criticises Dr. Maclean's book *Death Cannot Sever*,
and while not denying some of the claims of Spiritualism, advises Christians to keep to what he calls the
"Christian certainties." Let me quote from this
article of nearly four pages *the only* reason he can
give for Christians believing in Survival :—

" The fundamental Christian certainty is that we
shall survive death. This has been believed
from of old, and many arguments were given in
support of it, but the event which gave our race
confidence truly to believe it was the rising of
Christ from the dead."

This is a good example of clerical logic. He
gives two reasons, the first being because our ancestors have believed in survival. So have all races and
creeds. If this is an argument we should believe
that the earth is flat and that diseases are caused by

devils. According to Dr. Paterson, something that has been believed in of old is a certainty.

The second reason given is the rising of Christ from the dead, but the Church has always insisted that this was a miracle, and if it was it is illogical to say that because a miracle occurred 1,900 years ago, we survive death. Moreover, he does not explain the connection between what he calls the second member of the Trinity overcoming death, which power is surely an attribute of God, and a humble member of the human family likewise surviving death. God having done so, according to Christian teaching, is certainly no argument that humanity will do likewise. Besides this, Dr. Paterson knows, just as other intelligent people know, that the so-called evidence of Christ's resurrection is based on nothing but doubtful tradition, a very flimsy basis, and as the story was copied from earlier religions, there is no basis whatever for the belief in the physical resurrection as reported in the gospels. It was the physical body of Jesus, we are told in the gospels, that rose from the grave reanimated, and after a short time on earth ascended into Heaven. Whatever has this miraculous event to do with our own death and survival? Dr. Paterson is on surer grounds when he concludes his article as follows :—

" Revelation was restricted in scope, and we have been left in ignorance of many things that we should have expected to know and that we desire to know."

When, however, Spiritualists tell of their experiences, and how they are certain that they have been in communication with those who lived on earth but have died, their testimony is ignored by the institution to which Dr. Paterson belongs, and which he admits is in ignorance of many things its adherents desire to know. Instead of accepting our trustworthy evidence, it puts forward as a "certainty" of survival a non-historical event, which it says occurred 1,900 years ago, and which has no relation to the individual, as it occurred, so it asserts, to God.

Why this ignoring and denouncing of the claims of Spiritualism on the one hand, and on the other, this doping of the people with falsehood, combined now with an admission of ignorance? Is it not that the clergy cannot now ignore the fact that the people are finding out the truth for themselves, but are still rigidly jealous of their rights? Since the adoption of Christianity as the State religion of Rome, Christian clergy have been looked on as holding a privileged position, being considered as endowed with a special authority from God to interpret what they claim as his message to humanity. They will not relinquish this privileged position without a struggle, and the comfort Spiritualism brings is a secondary matter to them when their own prestige, and that of their organisation, is concerned.

Dr. Paterson's ignorance of the after-life agrees with what a high dignitary of the Church of England said to me a few months ago :—

" We do not know whether we survive death or not, and we have no means of knowing. Personally I do not believe that we do, but if you could prove it to me, I should be for ever grateful to you."

This man was honest to me. He is the natural product of the institution to which he belongs, which never has believed in investigation, but only in faith, which so often fails, as those who rely on this easiest of all methods never give thought to the necessity for evidence on which real belief rests. He did not repeat to me worn-out phrases which mean nothing to the thinking man and woman. He told the truth as he understood it, and did not make claims for his religion which have no basis in fact. So long, however, as the public will accept what is told them by those whose interest it is to keep alive an ancient superstition, then so long will this deluding of the people continue. The way the public accept everything that takes place and is said in Church is pitiful. The Christian funeral service should revolt the reason of every thinking individual, and yet it is conducted hundreds of times, day after day, with never a protest.

Recently I attended a funeral service at one of our parish churches. The man who had passed on was rich, so there were four parsons to bury his body. The service was a long one. If he had been poor it would have been short, and one parson would have been sufficient. However, their combined efforts consigned the "soul to rest till the great resurrection day," when "through the mediation of Jesus Christ he would be accounted worthy to live forever with the blessed." The various orthodox phrases were repeated from which the following extracts are taken :

" Only through Jesus Christ shall he see life eternal."

" We leave him in God's hands till the great resurrection day, when body and soul will be reunited."

" He that believeth in me though he were dead yet shall he live, and whosoever believeth in me shall never die."

" For since by man came death, by man also came the resurrection of the dead."

" For as in Adam all die, so in Christ shall all be made alive."

" We shall not sleep, but we shall all be changed in a moment, in the twinkling of an eye, at the last trump, for the trumpet shall sound and the dead shall be raised incorruptible, and we shall all be changed."

" The sting of death is sin, and the strength of sin is the law."

" O Lord most mighty, O holy and most merciful Saviour, deliver us not into the bitter pains of eternal death."

" Spare us, Lord most holy, O God most mighty, O holy and merciful Saviour, the most worthy judge eternal, suffer us not at our last hour for any pains of death to fall from thee."

" In the sure and certain hope of the Resurrection to eternal life through our Lord Jesus Christ, who shall change our vile body, that it may be like unto His glorious body according to the mighty working whereby He is able to subdue all things to Himself."

" They rest from their labours."

" Lord have mercy upon us, Christ have mercy upon us, Lord have mercy upon us."

" That we with all those that are departed in the true faith of Thy holy name may have our perfect consummation and bliss."

" O merciful God, the Father of our Lord Jesus Christ who is the resurrection and the life, in whom whosoever believeth shall live though he die, and whosoever liveth and believeth in Him shall not die eternally."

" For them that sleep in Him."

" That we may rest in Him."

" And that at the general resurrection in the last day we may be found acceptable in Thy sight, and receive the blessing which Thy well beloved Son shall then pronounce to all that love and fear Thee saying, Come, ye blessed children of My Father, receive the kingdom prepared for you from the beginning of the world."

" Grant this, we beseech thee O merciful Father, through Jesus Christ our Mediator and Redeemer."

All this is contrary to what Spiritualists know to be

true, and the Church has not a scrap of evidence to support any of these extraordinary statements.

The words "Jesus Christ," or "through Jesus Christ," were repeated twenty-nine times at this service. God was asked not to lead us into temptation, which is something we should attribute to the Devil, and not to Infinite Wisdom. God was also told many things he was to do and not to do. The following are extracts taken from the hymns sung :—

> "Day of wrath! O day of mourning!"
>
> "When our final doom is near."
>
> "Leave we now thy servant sleeping."
>
> "He who died for their release."
>
> "Leaving him to sleep in trust
> Till the Resurrection day."
>
> "On the Resurrection morning
> Soul and body meet again."
>
> "Here awhile they must be parted
> And the flesh its sabbath keep."
>
> "For a while the tired body
> Lies, its feet towards the morn."

All this again is quite contrary to what Spiritualists know to be true. Christianity looks on death as a curse which was removed, for believing Christians only, by Christ's death. Spiritualists say this is an ancient superstition having no relation to present-day thought. Death is not a curse but a blessing, a step further on in our life of progress towards some far-off goal. It is but a change of appreciation and comes to all for our good. The belief in Christ does not affect our destination in the least, and for Christians to go on concurring in these antiquated opinions shows mental indolence and a low conception of the Almighty, the giver to all mankind of a natural death as of a natural birth. This is twentieth century Christianity. The Protestant Church, like the Roman Catholic, has not varied a jot in its fundamental beliefs since 325 A.D., when its creeds were manufactured by an assembly of ignorant men presided over by Constantine, a murderer.* Moreover, it never will make any advance till the people cease to accept what it offers them as the truth, and think for themselves.

This entire funeral service is a travesty of the truth. What the Church believes was St. Paul's opinion is always given at length, but no mention is made of the great fact of survival contained in thousands of Spiritualist books and records written during the past eighty years by men and women of our own time, some of whom were men and women of eminence. These testify to the return of the departed and to their being able to communicate with us. This testimony is so overwhelming in its power that it should compel the attention of any who have any regard for facts. The facts it presents are among the best attested of those which constitute our present-day knowledge.

Let it be stated once more without any equivo-

---

*Those who doubt this statement have only to read *What it means to be a Christian,* just published by Dr. Headlam, the present Bishop of Gloucester, to find all the old superstitions reiterated with emphasis. Not a particle of evidence is given in support of the tremendous assertions he makes, such as " Jesus was God," " Jesus was truly God," and " Jesus was perfect God." If Jesus was God it follows that God, the creator of the seemingly infinite Universe, was Jesus. This degrading of the Infinite to the level of Humanity is blasphemy, and moreover the past tense should not be applied to Infinite Intelligence. The Infinite must always be, but never was. According to present-day Christianity God is therefore Jesus, just as Jesus was God to the ignorant framers of the various Christian creeds. Christian people unfortunately use words so loosely and seldom think what they mean. Dr. Headlam admits the unreliability of the gospel narratives and relies on Church tradition and the creeds to support his assertions.

cation that those the Church calls "dead" come
back and say they are very much alive and active, and
further that, in their world, no one believes that any
of them will come back to take up their old bodies,
even if they could find them. They also testify that
Jesus Christ has nothing to do with the question of
life and death, and they know nothing about the
"Mediation of Our Saviour Jesus Christ."

In answer to this testimony, Christians say it is
Devils who come back to beguile us and delude us ;
but, as I have shown, Christians have nothing whatever wherewith to support their beliefs. These are
unscientific and unhistorical, and Christians are
too ignorant, too stupid, or too lazy to change with
the changing times. So long as the Church continues to propound and preach flagrant lies about
those who pass on, it deserves the contempt of all
intelligent and honest people. I am sure there must
be many enlightened parsons who will welcome the
truth being told, though they may fear to tell it themselves.

What a difference between the service just
referred to and the service at the burial of the body
of a Spiritualist ! There it is all brightness—knowledge instead of hope, praise that the etheric
body is liberated into a fuller life. Clairvoyants
present see many friends on the other side who have
come back, often bringing with them the one whose
physical body is being buried. The knowledge of
what death really is, is accepted as a matter of course,
and the expectation is expressed that the departed
will be back again soon through some Medium to
report his safe arrival on the further shore. There

is no mourning, no black, as all is understood. Death is known to be but a step round a bend in the road of life, so there are no vain repetitions from ancient documents which mean nothing, and which are of only slight comfort to the ignorant, and of none to the intelligent.

Such is a Spiritualist's funeral. Spiritualists are guided by those who have made the change, Christians by ignorant speculation thousands of years old. Which of the two affords the greater comfort, the true or the false? I shall leave it for each reader to judge. While Christians have been drifting, Spiritualists have been thinking.

The following is one of the most vivid pen pictures of what really happens at death and of humanity's failure to grasp its true meaning. Who wrote it I know not, but I give it as I found it :—

As the faint dawn crept upwards, grey and dim,
He saw her move across the past to him—
Her eyes as they had looked in long-gone years,
Tender with love, and soft with thoughts of tears,
Her hands, outstretched as if in wonderment,
Nestled in his, and rested there, content.

" Dear wife," he whispered, " what glad dream is this?
I feel your clasp—your long remembered kiss
Touches my lips, as when you used to creep
Into my heart; and yet, this is not sleep—
Is it some vision, that with night will fly? "

" Nay, dear," she answered; " it is really I."

" Dear heart, it is you I know,
But I knew not the dead could meet us so.
Bodied as we are,—see, how like we stand! "

" Like," she replied, " in form, and face, and hand."

Silent awhile, he held her to his breast,
As if afraid to try the further test—

T

Then speaking quickly, " Must you go away? "
" Husband," she murmured, " neither night nor day ! "
Close to her then she drew his head,
Trembling, " I do not understand," he said.
" I thought the spirit world was far apart . . ."
" Nay," she replied, " it is not now, dear heart!
Quick, hold fast my hand, lean on me . . . so . . .
Cling to me, dear, 'tis but a step to go ! "

———

The white-faced watchers rose beside the bed;
" Shut out the day," they sighed, " our friend is dead."

Such is a description in poetic words of what is happening thousands of times every day.   Is it not time
that everyone should wake up and try to grasp the
true meaning of death so that it can be looked upon
as a friend and not as an enemy?   Only Spiritualists
can teach the lesson.   Only Spiritualism can save
the world from blank materialism.

Only Spiritualism will unite mankind in one
religion, a religion that can be accepted by the Hindu
or the Mohammedan, by the Buddhist and the Christian.   Spiritualism will make the world one great
family, will make all men brothers, will make all men
free. Some day all such labels as Christian, Moslem,
Hindu and Buddhist will disappear, and then there
will be no need for the label Spiritualist, as all will
merge into one, the great religion of humanity.   On
the platforms at my meetings throughout the country
I have had supporting me men and women of all
creeds and sects, namely Mohammedans, Hindus,
Jews, and all the sects of Christianity, who, now that
they know the truth, realise the futility of the creeds
and dogmas of the religions into which they were
born.   Only through Spiritualism will war cease, and

only through Spiritualism shall we reach a new and juster social system.

Spiritualists do not believe in sending missionaries to try to convert those belonging to the leading eastern religions. It is futile to replace one superstition by another, and yet millions of money have been, and still are, spent in trying to convert the "heathen Chinese," the "heathen Buddhists," and others whose ancestors all had a part in laying the foundations of Christianity. This is like taking coals to Newcastle! Spiritualism will succeed, however, when other efforts have failed, as its principles lie at the back of all religions.

Meantime Spiritualist organisations grow and flourish. In every large city there are many Spiritualist Churches, and at least one in the smaller towns, where those who wish to get into touch with their friends and relatives on the other side should go, as connected with them are the reliable Mediums of the district. These Churches hold services every Sunday and lectures and discussion classes during the week. The Sunday Schools, which go under the name of Lyceums, are well-organised and cared for. These Churches advertise their meetings in the weekly Spiritualist papers already referred to. In those papers will also be found advertised those organisations which make a special point of helping the enquirer. They are becoming large and influential, and for a small annual subscription the subscriber has the privilege of attending their lectures without further charge, enjoys the use of the library, and can have sittings with the best Mediums at the minimum of expense. To help the enquirer I give the names and addresses of the leading institutions in this country.

Marylebone Spiritualist Association,
   Marylebone House, 42 Russell Square, London, W.C.1.

London Spiritualist Alliance,
   16 Queensberry Place, Kensington, London, S.W.7.

British College of Psychic Science,
   15 Queensgate, London, S.W.7.

W. T. Stead Library and Bureau,
   5 Smith Square, Westminster, London, S.W.1.

The Britten Memorial,
   64A Bridge Street, Deansgate, Manchester.

The Edinburgh Psychic College and Library,
   30 Herriot Row, Edinburgh.

A new society has recently been formed for the purpose of helping to educate the clergy in all matters pertaining to Spiritualism.   Several progressive parsons are behind this, as it was thought that the clergy should have a society all to themselves, owing to the fact that they dislike being seen with laymen at séances, lectures, etc.   This new society is called the Psychic Evidence Society, and further particulars of it can be obtained from the Stead Bureau whose address has just been given.   The intelligent clergy see that they have to become as little children and learn anew just as we all have done.   Naturally they are anxious to make going to school again as little conspicuous as possible, seeing that they are the ones who should have been leading the world on the subject, and not the Spiritualists.

I can only briefly refer to one aspect of Spiritualism which is of growing importance, namely, that of Psychic Healing, through healing Mediums.   This is not what is termed faith healing, as faith no more enters into it than it does when we consult and are treated by medical science.

The patient attends the centre where the healing Medium works in trance, and with the help of assistants with psychic power, but not in trance, healing takes place through the touch and massage by the Medium or the assistants. The diagnosis of the disease is remarkable for its accuracy. In serious cases the patient has been put to sleep by the Etheric Doctor working through the Medium, and thus no pain is felt. Thousands are being cured by means of psychic rays working on the Etheric Body of the patient, as it is through the Etheric that the cure of the Physical body is effected.

One of the best healing Mediums in this country at the present time is F. J. Jones, who works under the direction of a doctor in the Etheric World, giving himself the name of "Medicine Man." He claims to treat over 20,000 cases a year, and to have treated over 60,000 during the last three years. The Etheric Doctor just makes use of Jones to pass the psychic healing force through him. Mr. Jones has said that he makes nothing out of this except his out-of-pocket expenses, and all the assistants give their services free. No charge is made for the healing, each patient only giving something, if able. This wonderful Medium who has accomplished so many cures through his Spirit doctor "control" is only one of quite a number in the country to-day, and their great work is slowly being appreciated. Mr. Jones attends regularly at the Marylebone Spiritualist 'Association, which is becoming one of the largest healing institutions in the country. Mrs. Estelle Roberts also works there as a healing Medium.*

All in need of help of this kind should apply to any of the institutions already named, as they have healing Mediums under their direction, or to their local Spiritualist Church which will know of the nearest healing Medium. I have made special mention of the work of Mr. Jones as I have made a personal study of his methods and have followed up many of his cases.

One word of caution. Psychic healing is not yet sufficiently advanced, owing to lack of the necessary development in mediumship, to make it wise to employ it for life-and-death cases. Still there are many ailments for which it is well worth trying Psychic healing. In other cases, where earth doctors can do nothing further, this method should be tried. I know of more than one cure having been effected in cases which earth doctors have given up as hopeless. Take your doctor's opinion if he is broadminded, as many doctors believe in Psychic healing and send patients to healing Mediums. I personally know a dozen doctors who do so, and their number is increasing.

Psychic healing is still in its infancy, but now that Mediums are safe, it is rapidly developing, and I

---

* Mrs. Estelle Roberts is not only a remarkable healing Medium but the world's greatest clairvoyante. Besides this she is one of the best direct voice Mediums in this country. Her séances, given once a fortnight, free of charge, to a group of leading Spiritualists and their friends, are reported regularly in *Psychic News* by the editor, Maurice Barbanell, who is always present, along with a stenographer, who takes careful notes of everything said. Mr. Barbanell has just published a book entitled *The Trumpet shall Sound*, giving a record of a series of these séances, and it should be read by all who desire conviction that voice communication has been definitely established between the two worlds. I, personally, can vouch for the honesty and accuracy of all concerned.

believe will become one of the greatest blessings to mankind in the years to come. From what I am told by Etheric Doctors I am hopeful that, by means of a ray with which they are experimenting, a cure for cancer will be discovered. The various rays used are quite perceptible by the assistants, who experience a sharp pain if their hands intercept them. Judging from cases that have come to my notice, Psychic surgery is just in its infancy. In time I believe surgical operations will not be impossible by Etheric doctors, who will dematerialise the part to be removed and thus no cutting will be necessary. This forecast is no dream on my part, as I have facts to go on which indicate the possibility of such developments. Is it to be wondered at that I should feel it a matter of the greatest importance that we do everything possible to develop mediumship in every way, seeing how immensely humanity will benefit as a result? Mediums are our most precious possessions ; they should be state-protected, state-aided and state-developed, until the ecclesiastical and medical professions come to realise that it is their duty to look after them as trustees for the nation. In time there will be a Chair of Psychic Science at both Oxford and Cambridge Universities, and thus the greatest of all the sciences will receive its proper recognition, and receive the attention it deserves from trained investigators.

The study of the power of the Mind over the body is another subject which will get more attention as the years go on. As yet healing by this method is little understood, but no one can read Mr. Alexander Erskine's testimony given in his book, *A Hypno-*

tist's Case Book, without realising to what an extent
the mind dominates the body.

Spiritualists do not pretend to have solved all the
problems of mankind.   We do not think that we can
comprehend the Universe.   We do not believe that
we have reached the bottom of the well of knowledge,
but we do most emphatically believe that Spiritualism,
combined with Science, will solve many problems
thought to be beyond the wit of man.   Spiritualism
is opening up for mankind a grand panorama, and
only as man increases in intelligence will he be able
to grasp its full extent.   Spiritualism is founded on
the sure rock of reason and experience, and on this
foundation the next generation will build their religion,
and thus make this world a place worth living in.
Meantime, we believe it is better to work for the
brotherhood of man and his advancement than to
repeat meaningless creeds.   It is better to love our
fellow man than to fear a God created in man's own
image.   It is braver and nobler to think and investigate for yourself than to let some institution think
for you.   We do not expect to accomplish our work
in a few years ; the prevailing opposition is too strong
to enable us to do that, but we do want to do all the
good we can in the holy cause of human progress.

We are not laying the foundations of a new
sect, but of a noble temple in which all humanity
can gather together, having the same knowledge,
animated by the same great ideals, believing
that duty to man is the first principle in all true
religion.   We believe that it is more important to
serve our brother man, whom we can help, than to
waste our time trying to placate an imaginary wrathful

Deity, who expects us to believe the impossible before we can enter Heaven. We are doing what we can to hasten the great day when Reason will be robed, crowned and enthroned, and when those who do all the good they can will be the saints in the truest and noblest sense. We are doing all we can to relieve suffering, to comfort those who mourn, and to place the star of hope in the midnight of despair. This we consider is true holiness. We pity those who attribute to the Almighty deeds and words which would debase a savage, and we look forward to the day when all who do so will be considered blasphemers and not looked up to, honoured, and given positions of wealth and importance, as they are to-day in the Christian Church.

This is the ethical side of the religion of Spiritualism. The old creeds are too narrow ; they are not for our world of to-day. The old dogmas lack breadth and kindness ; they are too cruel, too savage, too merciless. We are growing more humane in spite of them. The many who repeat them would not themselves, if they were God, enforce them.

There is only one acceptable creed, and that great creed contains all the truths that man has uttered. There is only one litany needed by mankind, and that contains all the aspirations, all the noble thoughts, all the ecstasies of the soul, all dreams for nobler life, all hopes, all joy.

The real Church is built on all that man has discovered, the real edifice is adorned and beautified by all the arts, by all the beauties of nature ever depicted by colour on canvas. The real choir contains all the beautiful music of the world, and the true worshippers are all who have made the world a better and a happier place to live in. Its Priests are the true interpreters of nature. Its Bible is all the ennobling literature of the world, and its Mediator betwixt earth and heaven is that gifted class of people called Mediums, who can bring heaven to earth and unite the two worlds in one.

When Christians are intelligent enough to organise their worship and their Churches on these lines, then will gather in them all the good and true, the learned and the simple. All together will hold communication with the great and the good, the true and the noble who have passed on, and who now come back willing and anxious to help us in our search for the truth and the real meaning of existence.

This is what Spiritualism is working for, and as the knowledge of it increases as the number of Mediums increases, so will its principles become more and more widely accepted and the new religion grow and bear more fruit. But never will Spiritualists hand over their precious knowledge to the orthodox Churches to be compressed into creeds and dogmas, or to be embellished by ritual, pomp and circumstance. The Church which should have been the protector of those gifted persons, our Mediums, has so long persecuted and ill-treated them, that it cannot now be trusted with their care and protection. The Church which has mistaken the blundering guesses of ignorant men for the wisdom of Infinite Intelligence must purge itself thoroughly of its folly before it will be trusted with the teaching of Spiritualism.

The Christian Church has been weighed too

,often in the balance and found wanting, the ecclesiastical mind is too narrow, too closely related to that of the theologians of the past, for Spiritualists to wish to see a fusion of Spiritualism with Christianity. The time will come when the Christian Church will absorb all the teachings of Spiritualism and agree to bury and forget its creeds, its dogmas, its holy documents and holy relics, but it is not yet. Spiritualism has no need of a fusion of the past with the present. It need not go back to the days of ignorance for its beliefs. It is a religion based on the facts of to-day.

Meantime we work and wait, we watch the flow and ebb of life and death. We contemplate with greater knowledge what those who are ignorant call the mystery of Death. Ignorance still holds the stage, and players act their part and disappear. The orthodox and the stupid play their part and disappear without the slightest knowledge of the significance of their part or the purpose of life's drama. The scene shifts, some new actors come, and disappear. The scene shifts again. To them all is mystery, mystery everywhere. They try to explain and the explanation of one mystery contradicts another. To them, behind each veil is just another. Life is an enigma. The Church claims it has had a revelation from Infinite Intelligence, and yet this revelation tells us nothing. Everything of value in life man has discovered for himself. This revelation has never explained the wonder of growth, production and decay, the reason for our existence, or our destiny.

All things are of equal wonder. One drop of water is as full of wonder as all the oceans, one speck of dust as all the worlds, one butterfly with painted wings as all the things that fly, one egg as wonderful as the thinking breathing creature that emerges from its shell. The smallest seed is as wonderful as a mighty oak, a stone as all the whirling stars. If we now know something more of our wondrous Universe than those who lived before us, it is because some have thought and reasoned for themselves and have not been content to rely on so-called holy records as their guide.

An institution relying solely on such sources as these need not look for help to Spiritualists, who have suffered too long from the abuse of the ignorant to wish to amalgamate with them. Spiritualists will work and wait till the Church discards all the old garments of ignorance. Till it does so Spiritualists will uphold the torch of truth alone. They know the strength of their position and the weakness of that of their opponents. They know that their religion is built on the rock of truth, on experience, on reason, and they are content to wait till the edifice built on sand crumbles and disappears. It is only a matter of time. Truth always wins through in the end.

Meantime, we work for the great day when mankind will be mentally free, and when the truth and the truth only will be preached and believed.

CHAPTER XII.

LIFE'S CERTAINTIES.

AMID the confusion of beliefs in this age of the decay of faith, what then have we to rely on? So much that we were taught as certainties we find in these days of greater knowledge must be discarded as error. What now remains?

Everything there is of value remains. It is only the chaff that we must throw away. All the aspirations of the soul can now be satisfied, not by faith and hope, but by knowledge. We have seen how our ancestors, realising that here on earth both life and death are equal kings, took from natural phenomena their beliefs, arguing that as the sun sets to rise again, and as vegetation dies to come again to life, so would humanity likewise follow the course of nature, and that death was but the threshold of another life.

Around this universal instinctive belief that death is not the end of life, there developed in many crude and often cruel ways a ritual which, in course of time, became a religion. From observing the forces of nature our ancestors argued that there was a force, an intelligence, in nature outside themselves, and so in a simple way there developed the belief that various separate intelligences governed the world. Their gods then became like men, only stronger and braver, but just as cruel as their creators. To them were given attributes drawn from natural phenomena. Later still were given to outstanding men after their death the attributes of the gods, and thus there was

wound round their lives the fables and myths told
about the gods.

So we come to the present time, when still by
far the majority believe the truth of these stories told
of these god-men.   Some, however, have found by
research the basis of the world's beliefs, and so have
come to realise that what so many believe in as
religious certainties are but ancient fables spun to
please a childish world.   Most people are still the
slaves of habit, the followers of custom, believers
only in the wisdom of the past.   Custom is like a
prison locked and barred by those of long ago, the
keys of which have followed them to their graves.
Old beliefs thus die slowly and very few can see the
light.   The multitude still kneels at the shrine of
antiquity and worships what it believes are the sacred
products of the past.

The educated, the thoughtful, the really intelligent person now thinks for himself, pities the
mistakes and follies of the people, and tries to enlighten their minds and conscience by pointing to the
future and not to the past.   The thinking man and
woman are the ones who help to carry forward the
light of truth, and thus bring nearer the glad day when
the world will be filled with intellectual light.

With all the fabled treasure of the past gone
beyond belief, what have we still?   Are we now
without a lamp for our feet and a light for our path?
Assuredly no, for have we not the knowledge now,
instead of the hope which caused our ancestors to
weave legend and myth, and develop ritual, much of
which has come down to us in the garb of sacred
and holy beliefs and rites?

What then are our certainties?   Firstly, so far

as the great mysteries of life and death are concerned, knowledge has taken the place of faith and hope. With knowledge fades away all creeds and cere-monials. During the past hundred years the mystery which has kept mankind in fear and bondage, the mystery which has kept and still keeps in being a mighty organisation throughout the world has been explained and unravelled. The Sphinx has spoken. From over the seemingly wide unending sea have come floating on its waves, twigs and branches, to show that life exists beyond the horizon, and that the seemingly cruel sea is just a bridge, a span from life to life. Where the dead have gone reason now can go, and from the further shore the revelation has come. No need to feel now that life is but a narrow vale betwixt two bleak eternities. No longer need we strive in vain to look beyond the heights, nor cry aloud and hear only the echo of our wailing cry. No longer need we say that from the lips of the unreplying dead there comes no word to calm our fears.

Life we now know is a greater, a grander, and a nobler thing than ever our forefathers imagined. Life we now know is a great privilege. The creative Intelligence that made it possible has wisely planned our future, and it is the duty of each one of us to live worthy of its thought and design. Nothing in nature is lost, and as we think here so shall we be hereafter. Our thoughts will be with us eternally to be our judge. As our thoughts are but ourselves, we shall judge ourselves justly, and the place we reach will be the place for which we have fitted our-selves here.

The invisible Universe which will be our eternal

home is beyond imagination, as there to think is to receive ; as we think so we are.   We must therefore give serious thought to our future, as we are building here what will be our future home.   We have a great future planned out for us, but here with our limited physical senses we can barely imagine the wonderful civilisation which we shall join some day, to be either its good or its bad citizens, to be one of the honoured and respected, or one of the degraded, of that vast community living unsensed by us around this earth of ours.

All wish for happiness beyond this life.   Immortality is a word that hope has whispered throughout the ages.   In the democracy of death the rag of wretchedness and the purple robe lose distinction and only character counts.   Our thoughts there condition our environment in a way they cannot do here. There is therefore nothing wiser, nothing grander than for each one of us to sow seeds of noble thoughts and virtuous deeds, to endeavour in every possible way to help to liberate the minds of our fellow men. A noble thought, just as a noble life, enriches all the world and hastens the harvest of universal good.   It climbs the heights and leaves all superstitions far below.   Those who have worked for the advancement of mankind are the leaders of the human race, and had it not been for such outstanding men and women of the past, who have led humanity upwards, we never should have risen beyond the beasts.

In every land and every clime, in every age, there have been the orthodox, the stupid, and the backward on the one hand, and on the other the thinker, the investigator, and the inventor.   The former have always tried to frustrate the latter ; there has been a continual warfare between them, and fortunately for humanity the thinker in the end has always won. The battle still continues between the two, and the thinkers are now fighting the greatest battle of all, which when won will liberate mankind from the fear of death, and make clear to all what has always been a mystery.

When our day here is over, nature returns the worn-out body to earth, and releases the psychic structure which, during earth-life, has been limited by our physical limitations. We cannot hear the words of welcome which greet the released individual, but we know that they are said. We cannot follow yet those who leave us, but we can leave them in the tender care of the friends who have gathered to give them welcome. What causes sorrow here gives joy and gladness there.

Nothing is more touching than the death of the young and the strong, but when we realise that to them it is not loss but gain, we need not sorrow unduly. Death comes, however, to the aged like a benediction. When the duties of life have been nobly done, when the sun touches the horizon, when memory becomes dim, nature bends and smiles and relieves the weary traveller of his burden. The day has been long, the road weary, and the tired wayfarer lies down to rest, to reawaken refreshed and gladdened by the change called death.

On making this change, a world beyond imagination for its delights will be the home of all who have lived here aright. The flowers, the colouring, the scenery, the beauties, the absence of

U

care, of pain, and of fatigue, will at once become apparent, and none will ever wish to return to live again on earth.

All physical deformities will become right, as the physical was the cause, and Mind there controls the etheric body in a way it cannot control the physical. Pain and suffering here are the result of our mind being out of harmony with its physical vehicle, but in Etheria the vibrations of mind and the etheric body are more akin. Consequently pain and suffering are almost unknown, as mind by thought can conquer pain. The next life would be naught unless we know and love again those we once loved here, and this reunion will be an added pleasure, though the grief at parting from those on earth will last till this reunion is complete. Grief in Etheria, however, is not so acute as it is with those on earth, as our friends there can still hear us and see us, and to them it is just a brief span between the parting and the meeting.

The Divine Intelligence which has planned it all has decreed that for the present we on earth cannot appreciate all that life holds out for each. We are limited for the present to our earth condition, but we can gather information now from those who have made the change, and faith and hope have changed to knowledge. The more we learn the more we realise the importance of right living and right thinking, as retribution to the evil is relentless and sure ; but the very thoroughness of it all in time raises the mind to thoughts of higher things.

Everything that man has made or done was first a mental creation, first pictured in the mind, then translated into its physical representation. All the wondrous creations of mankind were first mental creations, produced mentally, and only thus was it possible for them to take shape. The physical can be changed primarily only by thought, and then by touch, and so we realise that Mind is behind the physical wherever there is change. However, in the world of finer matter about us, though unsensed, mind is much more apparent, as there it can change its surroundings by thought without the necessity of touch. As we sow here we reap hereafter, because there we create our surroundings by our thoughts.

Our mind is always recording our deeds and thoughts, and like a moving film they are passing, some think into oblivion, but this is not so. No mental creation is necessarily forgotten, and all our good and noble thoughts will be our companions for ever, and so will be our evil thoughts till they become obliterated by the good. If evil persists over good we sink lower and lower till sheer misery will make us change.

Back of everything is Mind, which can only find expression for ages to come in lower vibrations than its own. Out of these it constructs our conditions just as we have trained it. If we keep to pure and noble thoughts, and self-denying deeds, face facts and accept only what is true, our future habitation will be in harmony with our thoughts, and our companions will be likewise. Honesty is the oak round which all the other virtues cling. Without character, without integrity, there is only poverty, an abyss. We never finish our education, we never cease to learn, though some learn folly, and some learn wisdom. Those who have thought wisely in the past have scattered the priceless seeds of knowledge, and we are now reaping the golden grain.   Consequently our surroundings here on earth are better and happier than ever before, as on earth just as in Etheria our thoughts make our surroundings, but not so easily.

Not so many years ago the investigators, the thinkers, the unorthodox, were looked upon with horror, and cruel laws were made against them. Antiquity those thinkers said added nothing to probability, the lapse of time could never take the place of evidence, and dust can never gather fast enough upon mistakes to make them equal with the truth. They believed that the unbroken and eternal march of cause and effect had never been arrested.   They were denounced and traduced, persecuted, tortured and martyred by the mob which never thinks.   After their deaths the same mob returned to worship at their graves, and embellished their names as saints and heroes.

In their day they were told that God never gave us a mind to question or to doubt and that everything we could know of life and death had already been revealed.   They were told that great was the mystery of Godliness ; great was the mystery of the Trinity ; great was the mystery of the Godhead ; great was the mystery of Life and Death and the Hereafter.

Fortunately all the opposition of a powerful organisation was unable to prevent the mystery being explored, and the more it was explored the clearer did it appear that what had been preached as a special revelation from God was no revelation at all, and that what was thought to be a Divine revelation was nothing but the blundering guesses of superstitious

men. Humanity is only just beginning to appreciate
that this discovery has released it from a mighty
thraldom. Knowledge begins where faith ends, and
faith no longer satisfies the hunger of the intelligent
mind. To those with knowledge the warp and woof
of the fabric of the mystery of death has been rent
and through it we find a more beautiful world, a
grander civilisation, than was ever dreamed of by the
seers of old. In this newly discovered country we
find a wondrous race who look on us in pity for our
ignorance, as so many here still rest on crutches,
which they could so easily discard, and walk erect.

In the next state there is no gold, no money,
and all we gain there is mental wealth, but no one
can wish for more, as the mind gives us all we wish
to have. To increase our possessions we must
develop our mind, and this can best be done by
helping others less fortunately placed than ourselves,
as there we cannot live for ourselves alone. Thus
and thus only is our happiness increased, just to the
extent to which we impart happiness to and increase
the knowledge of others. We need not wait ; let us
learn to do it here and now, and let those who know
the truth tell all they can. Let those with experience
and knowledge proclaim that there is no death, that
what seems so is transition, a change of appreciation
only. When this becomes known the happiness of
the world will be increased a hundredfold. Mankind will be knit together in the common knowledge
of a common destiny. The brotherhood of man will
then be understood in its true meaning and war will
be no more.

Let us therefore cease from giving thought

to ancient beliefs, developed when the world was young, and instead give thought to the development of our characters, as character alone counts, not belief in creeds.　Thus we are commencing here the refining process which will lead us to the life in the higher spheres beyond.　Let us try to loose the shackles of those still bound by creeds and dogmas, who think that by believing the impossible they are pleasing their Creator.

Unfortunately we have still many of the ignorant, the uneducated and the superstitious amongst us, and so long as we have these so long shall we have priests and prelates, who benefit by their ignorance.　Just as oil and water cannot mix, neither can priest-craft and intelligence.　Spiritualists are doing all they can to spread the great news that mankind's greatest enemy, Death, is conquered, while the clergy, led by the Archbishop of York, stand within the pulpit's narrow curve and decry them for their efforts.　It is not desirable, say our religious leaders, for the public to know.　To the leaders, public ignorance of this vital matter is better than knowledge, as so long as the mystery lasts the organisation is maintained.　It is not desirable, they say, for man to have his greatest longing satisfied !

Just so long as ignorance flourishes will money be wasted keeping up an expensive organisation for the set purpose of keeping humanity ignorant.　The ignorant cannot see that it is in the interests of the priests and clergy to continue keeping them ignorant, as when knowledge comes their influence ceases. Let all, therefore, who have the good of humanity at heart oppose these purveyors of superstition, help the helpless, put the star of knowledge in the midnight of despair, and show the ignorant that all who live aright here have a bright and happy future before them.

We are not exiles here from God, which the mystery of life and death made our ancestors imagine we were, and thus made them create Saviours and holy records. The belief in these they thought adjusted the difference, but now we know from those who have made the change that all this was wrong, and that what the ancients felt they needed they created out of their own imagination. Let us therefore not look back, but forward, and remember that every stream, no matter how it wanders, turns and curves amid the hills and rocks of life, however long it lingers in the lakes and pools, will sometime reach the sea, and every one of us in time will reach the sea of full understanding.

These views enlarge the soul and make us tolerant with wrong-doing, though ever anxious that the stagnant pool be cleared and mental indolence not last too long. Let us adopt the serene philosophy which relegates the creeds and the needless ritual to a bygone age. They are but phases in the development of man. Remember that Infinite Intelligence planned our birth, our life, that we are part of this Divine purpose, and as such must always be, and never can we cease to think.

Let us therefore spread the doctrine of the Brotherhood of Man, and that we are all part of the Divine, and that having a common heritage and destiny, to kill each other in war is such a crime that those responsible will suffer terribly. Spread this news far and wide, until the rulers of the world, in fear of what their own fate will be, will never dare to rush their people into war. Then and then only will the League of Nations function smoothly. As no one should allow an organisation to think for him, so no one should allow a government to force anyone to kill his brother man. If all will only think aright, war will cease, and all disputes be justly settled, as the result of harmony between the minds of those whose duty it is to settle international differences. Let us not be either tyrants or slaves but thinking men and women, and let us help to make the whole world free. Everyone of us has the power to be equal with the greatest, irrespective of birth or wealth. It is mental wealth that really matters, and each can reach the mental level of the greatest if the desire exists. In the democracy of the Mind the peasant can be equal to the king. In the intellectual hospitality of the Mind all can be equal. The domain of the Mind is unbounded and in it all are kings.

Next best to finding the truth is to search for it, and to do so all should question and reason, as these are the guide posts scattered on the winding road that leads to truth. Truth loves discussion and the doubting questioning mind of the investigator, which results in intelligence, candour, honesty, sympathy, and charity for all. Truth is the enemy of ignorance, prejudice, egotism, bigotry, and hypocrisy. The one lives by day, the others by night. Let us each, therefore, be a torch bearer of the truth and always strive for light, more light.

We now realise that all past mistakes just taught mankind to reach the road of truth. We pity the follies of the past but understand them. We admire the achievements of the past and should try to emulate them. All the past errors and mistakes of man, with their consequent sufferings and cruelties, were caused by the stones of ignorance, on the road that leads to perfection, over which he stumbled. As a result his next steps were taken with greater thought.

Let us strive to follow the Religion of Duty and forget the Religion of Mystery. Let us follow the Religion of Reason which will result in the civilisation and mental development of humanity. Let us preach the gospel of humanity and that each should be noble enough to live for all. Let us teach the religion of Knowledge and of Truth. Let us preach the religion of Humanity which destroys prejudice and superstition, ennobles and lengthens life, which drives from every home the wolf of want and from every heart the fiends of selfishness and fear. Pure thoughts, brave words, and generous deeds will never die. A noble self-denying life increases the mental wealth of the Universe, and a life well spent runs like a vine for all to see, and every pure unselfish act is like a perfumed flower.

I have had impressed upon me, by those who have spoken to me from Etheria, the necessity of right thinking, as those who teach error here must after death stand on the threshhold of the after-life and meet again all those misled. What is shrouded here will be clear there, and error will unfold itself with relentless certainty. Those, therefore, relying on ancient tradition must divest themselves of prejudice and learn anew. Think straight and true and put truth always first and foremost. Never say something is true and must be believed because it is found in an old Book, unless you yourself have proved it true by definite evidence, and never attribute to God something for which you have no evidence.

Around an open grave the clergy should speak of the life beyond as something real, as something greater and grander than the one here, of the meeting again with those loved here, and proclaim that what to us is loss is gain to them. Clergymen, tell your congregations that the next world is a real world, and that in it live real men and women, with the bodies they lived in here, but were unseen because of the physical covering. Tell the mourners of the great institutions in our various cities where contact between the two worlds is made. Do not add conditions and reservations for which you have no authority. Do not talk about salvation as if some are saved and some are damned. Try to be rational, thinking individuals, and do not make God appear irrational. If you do not know about the after-life, as very few of you do, then learn from those who do. Read and if possible experience for yourself. Your duty principally lies in ministering to the ignorant, and if you are as ignorant as they are you cannot help them much. Remember you will meet every one of your congregation again, and when the meeting comes about you will have to explain to each the reason for your preaching the creeds, dogmas, and traditions of the past. Your future happiness and unhappiness will rest on the amount of truth and of error you have preached. The more this great revelation increases the greater is your responsibility if you neglect it and let pass opportunities of telling the people the truth.

Open your pulpits to those who really know, and cease from thinking that you are a select body apart from the rest of mankind, as all thinking people now realise that you know no more and are no better than the rest of humanity.

My message to all who live is this. From the world which some day will be our home come messengers bearing words of good cheer to all who live on earth. They tell us we need do but our best, think straight, and apply ourselves to the uplifting of humanity. We must cease from wasting our time on that which is unnecessary. We are not born to live only upon this narrow strip of substance called the Earth. A great and glorious country awaits us after death. Mind knows no limitation, and each one of us is Mind and nothing more.

When the end of earth life comes let us not think that we have reached the twilight, or that for the last time the golden sky is fading in the west. Let us not think that night has come, but that a grander sunrise awaits us beyond the grave. We must meet death as we meet sleep, knowing that the morning follows night. Thus should we enter the dawn called death.

No one has ever seen the structure behind the man or woman, flower or tree. All we see is the outer garment that life wears and functions in during a short physical life. The real man and woman is something far beyond what the physical senses can appreciate. We all have a duplicate permanent body governed by a mind which none can see nor touch. We can see but the physical expression of this Mind. No physical matter has sensation and all our feelings come from our etheric body. No one has seen the seed that gives life to earth, but only the physical garment which is warmed and wooed by sun and rain, and from a tiny speck of dust-like stuff a violet or a rose springs forth.   It was not the physical that gave the life, but the Mind within, and when we realise that Mind is all and all is Mind then we shall begin to understand the Universe.

We know now that death is better than life, as death is but the name given to the door through which we enter, to reach another phase of our existence, in a world which is better, happier, and easier to live in.   Death is only a change in our appreciation of the vibrations which make up the Universe.   We now know that life on earth with its gleams and shadows, its thrills and its pangs, its ecstasy and its tears, its wreaths and its crowns, its thorns and its roses, its glories and its Golgothas, is but a preparation, a school, which all must pass through, and learn life's lesson, a lesson which does not end on earth, but is for ever being taught.

Slowly we are learning to appreciate that wondrous stream of life, with its cataracts and pools, that rises in the world unseen, and flows through earth back to that Etheric World from which it once emerged.   What seems a struggling ray of light, twixt gloom and gloom, that lightens for a time this strip with verdure clad, between two great unseens, is never dimmed.   What appears a dream between the shores of birth and death is a great reality, and though we seem to stand upon the verge of crumbling time, to love, to hope and disappear, yet it is the greatest of life's many certainties that each individual life will never die, because each one of us is part of the Divine Mind, which never dies.

EPILOGUE.

Last year, when in Edinburgh, I stood in that wonderful Cathedral, built on the pinnacle of the Castle Rock to the memory of the sons of Scotland who had passed on to a fuller life, so that freedom and truth might take the place of greed and brutal strength.

As I stood within this magnificent shrine I thought of the meaning of it all. Scotland had expressed her soul in the grandest war memorial in the world.

And just as the minds of the people of Scotland have expressed themselves, so is the Universal Mind, of which they are part, forever seeking expression throughout its boundless domain.

Just as the graceful lines of this beautiful building denote a perfect thought in stone, so is Mind forever seeking, everywhere, to reach in everything a fuller and more perfect expression.

What an advance from the Pictish dug-out I had seen in Aberdeenshire the previous day, to this noble thought in stone !

How Mind had developed in its capacity for expression ! What a chasm of time between the past and the present ! What a contrast was presented between the mind of the primitive savage living like an animal in the ground, and that of his descendants of to-day !

Mind, I realised, must be a developing, expanding, growing substance, when it is capable of such an advance as was here illustrated. It must be something apart from the physical body through which it works. The chemical ingredients of the physical are still the same. Mind has advanced and in doing so has been able to express itself better with the material at its disposal.

What a distance between the Savage and the Savant, between the primitive coracle and our ocean palaces, between the crooked stick and the motor plough! Man has developed just as he has applied his mind to his surroundings, just as he has mingled his thoughts with his labour.

I thought of the countless multitude who had passed through the portal of death, and of the gathering hosts which for ages have been populating the world beyond, and I wondered at the magnitude of it all. I thought of the myriad minds out there in space, waiting for improved communication to pour out to us on earth their wisdom and experience accumulated through countless years.

At the altar of rugged rock within this great monument to self-sacrifice, I wondered at the great unceasing purpose of the Divine Will; I realised how Mind in man had advanced to happiness and perfection just in so far as each one had put himself last and another first. I realised how his happiness had increased when he found it was better to love than be loved, and to serve than be served.

I realised how self-sacrifice is not the individual's loss but his gain; how what seemed unjust and cruel was in the end both generous and kind; how Infinite Intelligence counts not our years on earth, when time to us is infinite. I realised also that when our work here is done it is but continued elsewhere; that death is but a bend in the road leading to the Infinite; that each one is part of one great whole, which never loses strength or power, and that what seems loss to us is never so to that which always was, is now, and ever shall be.

I thought of that unceasing Divine Mind of which we are each and all a part or an expression— always developing, always expanding, always creating.

It then seemed to me how feeble are our efforts to define it all in rigid words. How can the part define the whole? How can we, in face of our obvious limitations, hope to express in words what none on earth can ever comprehend?

How careful all should be to prove all things true, to accept only what is so, to entertain nothing that our reason assures us is contrary to the truth!

To speculate on what is yet to come without a basis to build upon is mere folly and unworthy of our intelligence. Better to say we know not than to hazard guesses without knowledge; better to be candid and honest than pretend to a knowledge we do not possess.

Our ignorant ancestors, believing that all had been revealed to them, recorded their beliefs in words, on stone, on skins and parchments. Thus they produced the entire story of our origin and our destiny, and to this day their faithful followers in our midst strive in every way to justify it all.

To leave the past aside, to live in the present, and to contemplate the future from the standpoint of our present knowledge, is surely wiser. To the historians let us leave the past to be placed in its proper setting and perspective; they are the best judges as to what is true and what is false.

For us it is better far to assimilate the knowledge of the present than the ignorance of the past ; better far to show our gratitude to the past by profiting by its mistakes and by avoiding their repetition.

To those of the past who by intelligent thought have laid the foundations of our present knowledge, let all praise be given, but never let us exalt the past at the expense of our present knowledge, or attribute to Infinite Intelligence the barbaric cruelties and false claims of the past.

Let each one of us remember that our destiny lies not in the past but in the future, and that as we lay the foundations of our characters now, so shall we erect the structures that will be ours for ever.

Let each one of us make the most of the present, learning all it has to teach, as Nature's revelation is greater and grander to-day than ever before.   All the knowledge of the ancients is as nothing compared with the knowledge of the present.

We should not let the past think for us ; rather should we make full use of the treasures of Nature's store-house, and avail ourselves of all it has to offer us now.

Those who do not think for themselves, who fail to use the holy gift of reason, who employ some others to think for them, are slaves to tradition.

All we have of value has been accomplished by man himself. In his upward struggles against the forces of nature, he has burdened himself too long with those who professed that they, and they only, could understand the deeper things of life and death.

Just as our countrymen fought and conquered the forces of reaction during the Great War, so will all thoughtful people in time defeat the purveyors of superstition everywhere, and thus help to carry forward the light of truth and bring nearer the glad day when the world shall be filled with intellectual light.

When this time comes, sects and divisions will disappear, and the world's religions will be united into one. Religion and science will join together for the common good of all mankind, and war will be no more.

That this book may make clear to all the fundamental certainties of life, and also help Christian people, and through them those of other creeds, to extricate themselves from the quicksands of superstition and to reach the rock of truth, is the author's earnest hope and desire.

PRINTED BY LAIDLAW & MACKENZIE, 95-97 HOLM STREET, GLASGOW.

ON THE EDGE OF THE ETHERIC

OR

Survival after Death scientifically explained.

BY

J. ARTHUR FINDLAY.

The book that makes the Spirit World understandable, and is steadily revolutionising the scientific and religious thought of the world.

It is now accepted that this book scientifically located the Etheric World, and put it on the map of the Universe.

The following is an extract from a recent letter to the author, from a reader personally unknown to him, but one well qualified to express an opinion :—

"I consider your book the most convincing, satisfying, and consoling that has ever been published, and the coping stone to the work of communication with the real world. It has done more to give consolation to the bereaved than all the parsons of the Church of England. Indeed you have done a great work which you might well be proud of to the end of your days."

Translated into various European languages, Japanese, and also into Braille for the blind.
Published in all English-speaking countries.

Publishers:
DAVID McKAY COMPANY,
Washington Square, Philadelphia.

CPSIA information can be obtained at www.ICGtesting.com
Printed in the USA
BVOW011200120612

292427BV00011B/207/P